*What people from different walks of life
are saying about* Becoming Good—

"*Becoming Good: Building Moral Character* is a must-read
and a must-make-part-of-your-life book for Christians working in the new
economy. This book helps to lay the foundation and moral
compass that can help us walk the path laid out by our Lord Jesus,
instead of being lured by money and power into the tidal wave
and rip tide of the new economy. This book is especially useful
because it is written by a man who has a heart for serving God and has
spent many years getting to know God instead of only studying God."
CHARLES H. KWON
business executive and entrepreneur

"David Gill has drawn on insight from Jesus' teachings in the Beatitudes to
provide a practical framework for character in the 21st century. The
anchors of Scripture come alive in this book as they have in his teaching."
ALBERT M. ERISMAN
research director in information technology and mathematics

"*Becoming Good* is a clearly written, biblically rooted,
systematic and down-to-earth introduction to ethics—
a perfect text for an adult education class or study group. It bridges the gap
between formal theological education and the random
moral exhortation Christians generally receive from the pulpit."
LAUREL GASQUE
art historian

"When all harbors appear open and every direction arbitrary, one's ability
to steer his or her moral ship in our contemporary culture seems futile. But
guidance is not so far off. Gill dusts off time-honored classical and biblical
moral principles and applies them to our real lives in the real world."
CAMERON ANDERSON
campus minister

"Whoever thinks ethics is a dry, theoretical subject
has a pleasant surprise in store in David Gill's book, which is peppered
with wonderful examples, stories and illustrations.
Here we find dinner invitations as a form of peacekeeping and the Ten
Commandments transformed into a restaurant menu."

JOYCE MAIN HANKS
French professor

"With *Becoming Good*, David Gill has issued a profound call
for ethical renewal—a must-read for biblical people in a society
that has lost its moorings."

SHARON GALLAGHER
magazine editor

"David Gill presents a persuasive case for grounding Christian ethics
in the theological and practical exhortations of
Jesus' Sermon on the Mount. If even a small number of
Christian attorneys and litigants would allow their character to be formed
by the Beatitudes in the manner that Gill proposes, the impact on the
American legal community and the courts would be significant."

KEN MORRIS
attorney

"David Gill's style is at once readable and challenging.
Becoming Good is a modern call to the practical living
out of our Christian beliefs."

DENIS BROWNE
business executive

"*Becoming Good* is a powerful plea for the formation of Christian character
with the gospel as the ruling criterion."

DONALD G. BLOESCH
theologian

"David Gill, in *Becoming Good: Building Moral Character,* provides us
with insight and information about the formation and building
of good moral character based on sound biblical principles.
The book is easy to read and understand for a layman like me. This book
will be a valuable resource as I build a team and seek to do God's will."

MIKE HOLMGREN
pro football coach

Other Books by David W. Gill

BECOMING
GOOD

*Building
Moral Character*

DAVID W. GILL

InterVarsity Press
Downers Grove, Illinois

InterVarsity Press
P.O. Box 1400, Downers Grove, IL 60515
World Wide Web: www.ivpress.com
E-mail: mail@ivpress.com

*InterVarsity Press® is the book-publishing division of InterVarsity Christian Fellowship/USA®,
a student movement active on campus at hundreds of universities, colleges and schools of
nursing in the United States of America, and a member movement of the International
Fellowship of Evangelical Students. For information about local and regional activities, write
Public Relations Dept., InterVarsity Christian Fellowship/USA, 6400 Schroeder Rd., P.O. Box
7895, Madison, WI 53707-7895.*

All Scripture quotations, unless otherwise indicated, are taken from the New Revised Standard
Version of the Bible, *copyright 1989 by the Division of Christian Education of the National
Council of the Churches of Christ in the USA. Used by permission. All rights reserved.*

Cover photograph: © Hideki Kuwajima/Photonica

ISBN 0-8308-2272-0

Printed in the United States of America ∞

Library of Congress Cataloging-in-Publication Data

Gill, David W., 1946-
    Becoming good: building moral character/David W. Gill.
       p. cm.
    Includes bibliographical references and index.
    ISBN 0-8308-2272-0 (pbk.: alk. paper)
    1. Christian ethics. 2. Character. 3. Virtues. 4. Conduct of life. I. Title.
BJ1241.G55 2000
241—dc21
                                    00-033509

18	17	16	15	14	13	12	11	10	9	8	7	6	5	4	3	2

14	13	12	11	10	09	08	07	06	05	04

For my friends at
Berkeley Covenant Church
and University Covenant Church
with gratitude

Contents

Preface

Becoming Good is a study of what is called virtue or character ethics. This subject has been getting renewed attention in recent years. Alasdair MacIntyre (in moral philosophy) and Stanley Hauerwas (in moral theology) have done great and influential work in this direction, persuading many to take character and virtue seriously. In politics, questions have been raised about the personal character of Bill Clinton, Oliver North, Newt Gingrich and others among our leaders. In business, Max De Pree, James Collins and Robert Solomon are leading a new emphasis on the character of corporations and of executive management. In their writings about education, Christina Hoff Sommers, Peter Kreeft and William Bennett have argued for character education, not just values clarification. All of this is pressing us to ask not just what the moral rules are, but what kind of people we are.

What kind of people are these violent predators on the weak we read about every day? Or these terrorists who would kill the innocent and run off to their cowardly hideouts? Or these garbage-dumping destroyers of our environment? Where did all this selfish greed that corrupts our public officials come from? What kind of people are we who can close our eyes to the poor, the unemployed and the homeless around us? We could go on.

It's the character issue—and not just the personal character of individuals but the character of our communities and institutions. What kind of a business, school, church, neighborhood, city or nation do we have and want? Are we welcoming to the stranger, comforting to the hurting and empowering to the weak? Are we an inexhaustible source of good news and redemption to the lost? Are our institutions and practices just and fair?

Becoming Good is "*a* Christian ethic." It does not pretend to be "*the* Christian ethic." As "Christian" ethics for the whole church, not just some segment, it intends to stay close to the biblical text that we share as our common guide. We want to understand the Bible's great classic texts, grand themes and general contours concerning character. The term "building" in the title emphasizes that we are looking at a lifelong process, not a fixed-state accomplishment. At the beginning of this new century the pace of change and the scope of the challenge to human life will make a Christian ethic founded on good character more important than ever before.

Becoming Good is the foundation for and companion to *Doing Right*. In *Doing Right* we will look more precisely at our doing, at the principles and practices God might term "right" and how we can apply these to the hard cases of our time. But to "do the right thing" we need not only principles and rules to guide us, we need the capacity and inclination to understand and carry out such directives. Of course, there are no guarantees: good people sometimes do the wrong thing—and bad people sometimes do the right thing. But those are the exceptions; the rule is that we need to shape good people if we want to see the right thing done more often. Without making progress on what and who we *are,* it will be impossible to know and *do* what is right.

> There are no guarantees: good people sometimes do the wrong thing—and bad people sometimes do the right thing. But those are the exceptions; the rule is that we need to shape good people if we want to see the right thing done more often.

Becoming Good has two major parts. In "Prepare" (part one), the stage is set for building good character by looking more closely at

ethics today, character formation, God's goodness and our community realities. In "Build" (part two), we look in some detail at the
content of a good character. My account of this content is drawn
mainly from St. Paul's virtues of faith, hope and love, and from
Jesus' Beatitudes. The biblical material on character is massive; I
have attempted to draw it together in a five-part synthesis that will
ring true in relation to the whole and the parts. This study closes
with "Test" (part three), a brief consideration of how our character
gets tested and tried, and then either crushed or strengthened.

This is not a heavy, pedantic, scholarly study written for professional philosophers. I would like, of course, to think that my work
on ethics might be of interest to some of my colleagues. Nevertheless, my primary interest is among the people outside the scholarly
guild. What I hope, above all, is that the Christian laity will be
helped by my work. My primary audience is thoughtful Christians
who live and work as engineers, managers, bus drivers, youth soccer coaches, restaurant workers, PTA
members, attorneys, gardeners, physi-
cians, nurses, teachers, journalists, parents, neighborhood volunteers . . . These
are the sort of people (with their pastors
and teachers) for whom I write.

For those wishing to probe my argument and Christian virtue ethics in
greater depth, the footnotes provide guidance to further reading.
My text is full of quotations of, and allusions to, the Bible. There is
no other way to arrive at a satisfying, persuasive ethics for biblical
people.

> The biblical material on character is massive; I have attempted to draw it together in a five-part synthesis that will ring true in relation to the whole and the parts.

I have highlighted many of my arguments in the text in what I
think of as "billboards." If you must drive yourself quickly through
my text (and not pore over each elegantly crafted phrase or snicker
at each humorous aside), I want you at least to glance at these billboards and get the big picture as you are speeding along.

There are many analogies and illustrations along the way, but it
is also important to consider some concrete examples of the good
character traits we will study in part two. We need personal exam-

ples and models who show that the virtues of good character can be lived out in our place and time, but only God is in a position finally to approve somebody's "humility" or "integrity." I might be wrong in my judgments, and even when I am right, these people will be embarrassed! The course I have chosen is to encourage you to think about whom you have seen exemplify one trait or another (or a corresponding vice!). Maybe this can be safely shared in a small discussion group context.

Each chapter concludes with some questions for reflection or discussion. It is my hope that these will make *Becoming Good* of greater help not only to individual readers, but to classes and study groups of various kinds.

David W. Gill

Acknowledgments

For the development of my ideas on ethics, I am indebted to many teachers and authors—and to many students and audiences. Some contributed their insights and creative ideas to me; others gave critical responses to my own developing views. Among the teachers, Jacques Ellul has been the most influential. His impact on my approach to Christian ethics and social analysis will be obvious, although, in general, he was not much impressed with the virtue ethics he had studied. His flashes of insight into the meaning of faith, hope, holiness, freedom, modern culture and so many other subjects still leave me in awe. I never knew anyone else with his genius, who knew so much, with such profound insight, about so many things. At the same time, I found him to be a gentle, humble, wise, patient friend and mentor, with a good sense of humor. His death in May 1994 was a huge loss for the world, for the church and for me personally. He would have liked a lot of what I have written here—and pushed me to the wall with his criticisms of other parts of it![1]

Alasdair MacIntyre is the contemporary moral philosopher most influential on my approach to ethics. I also very much appreciate

---

[1]More information on Jacques Ellul, including some biography and bibliography, is available at <www.ellul.org>

Plato and (still more, on most topics) Aristotle, whose *Nicomachean Ethics* is the greatest book ever written on moral philosophy. I have come to appreciate Thomas Aquinas's comprehensive, integrative approach to moral philosophy and theology, although temperamentally I feel more at home with Søren Kierkegaard's railing against the system. Stanley Hauerwas's moral theology has been a major force in helping me understand and appreciate character and community in Christian ethics. I love Peter Kreeft's insights into various specific virtues, as well as his overall approach. John Howard Yoder left a few valuable and permanent contributions to my thinking about biblical and Christian ethics. Karl Barth and Donald Bloesch are the systematic theologians who have helped and inspired me most in trying to understand Christian theology and its ethics. On the Beatitudes in particular: from the ancient church I have found John Chrysostom the most insightful; in our era, the writings of Alphonse Maillot of France and John Stott of England have been especially helpful. On faith, hope and love: Ellul is the best, but Jonathan Wilson's recent *Gospel Virtues* is also a wonderful study.

So my teachers are an eclectic bunch. I have learned so much from all of them and countless others. And yet, what you are about to read are my own conclusions about Christian character and ethics, my own understanding of the meaning of faith, hope, and love, and of the Beatitudes. I wrote this book because I am not satisfied with anything else out there. There are two huge influences on what you are about to read, far more significant than even the teachers I mentioned above. The first influence is the Bible. I *love* reading the Bible, and what you are about to read is the product of my wrestling with it for several decades, trying to figure out what guidance God was giving *me* about my character and my sense of right and wrong. I just can't let it go.

The second big influence is the people I have taught. You are about to read ideas that I presented *hundreds* of times in lectures, classes, sermons and seminars. This material has been debated in uncountable conference centers, living rooms, restaurants and coffee shops. It was the enthusiasm of my hearers that pushed me to write this book. It was their specific questions and suggestions that kept me going back to the drawing board with a new insight or for a better understanding of some point.

Much of the "road testing" of this material took place in my courses at New College Berkeley and North Park University and in graduate student groups associated with InterVarsity Christian Fellowship across North America. Among the churches where I have presented this material, the Evangelical Covenant Churches of Berkeley and Davis, and the First Presbyterian Churches of Berkeley, Burlingame and Evanston have been especially important for me.

As this study neared its final form, I asked several friends to read it and give me their suggestions on how to make it better. Donald Bloesch, Sonia Bodi, John and Marj Erisman, Chip Fisher, Jim Sire, Steve Smith, Susan Sprinkle and Jonathan Wilson responded with many helpful comments. My children and their spouses (Jonathan and Carrie Gill, Jodie and Andrew Hoffman) and, above all others, my wife, Lucia, blessed me with lots of support, encouragement and specific suggestions on this study. I haven't always followed all of this advice, but often I did, and always I appreciated it. The weaknesses, mistakes and eccentricities that remain are, of course, my own responsibility. I know that the very day the book appears from the publisher I will wish I could change the way I said something. Learning is never over!

This book is dedicated to the churches to which I have been privileged to belong. I believe the local parish church is, and is intended to be, the primary shaper of Christian moral character. In particular I want to recognize with gratitude Berkeley Covenant Church (which our family called home for twelve years) and University Covenant Church in Davis, California (where, on a brief break from my academic career, I served two years as interim senior pastor).

I began writing this book in 1994 when North Park University graciously gave me a leave of absence so that I could serve as J. Omar Good Distinguished Visiting Professor of Evangelical Christianity at

Juniata College in Huntingdon, Pennsylvania. I finally finished it five years later in 1999 while again away from North Park, this time as Visiting Professor at our sister school, Södra Vätterbygdens Folkhögskola, in Jönköping, Sweden. I am grateful to all three schools for their encouragement and support.

David W. Gill

Part One

PREPARE

One

ETHICS ISN'T PRETTY

*W*e are living today in an ethical wilderness—a wild, untamed, unpredictable landscape. Wildernesses are threatening, dangerous places where a person can easily get lost or seriously hurt. The stresses of wilderness life do not always bring out the best in people; its explorers sometimes turn on, attack or even abandon each other. Ethics today isn't "pretty"—it is rough, tough and often ugly.[1]

What I mean by "ethics" (or "morality"—same thing) is matters of good and evil, right and wrong.[2] What I mean by "wilderness" is that this subject (ethics) is in ferment and chaos not only among professional ethicists and moralists but among the people.

---

[1]With a nod to Steve Martin who has said about his own field, "Comedy isn't pretty."
[2]"Ethics" terms have Greek linguistic roots; "morality" terms have Latin roots; that is the only significant difference. "Moral philosophy" is the same subject as "philosophical ethics"; "ethical and unethical" mean the same as "moral and immoral"; etc. Some authors *stipulate* a difference in meaning (e.g., "ethics is the field of study, morality is the subject studied"), but such usage is neither implied by the vocabulary nor followed with any consistency by those who write and speak on the topic. I will use these terms interchangeably.

Not just philosophers and theologians, but pastors, politicians, teachers and parents think and speak about ethical matters. Actually, we all do it: We all try to figure out *what we ought to be* (the goodness question) and *what we ought to do* (the rightness question). In ethics, by the way, that word *ought* is central. Ethics is not about what we *are* (in the senses used by biologists, economists, psychologists and sociologists) or what we *were* (in the sense used by historians) or even about what we *will be* (in the sense futurists might use it). Ethics is about what *ought to be*—about the standards by which we judge character and action. And, as we know, what we ought to be and do is often not an easy question to answer.

There is something, of course, that is inviting about a foray into a wilderness. While we might get hurt if we go out there, would we really prefer a life of timid reticence? The ethical wilderness is where the adventure is today—and where our tomorrow is being shaped. There is nothing in life as exhilarating as getting involved in the war of good and evil. Our old, ethical world had its advantages, not the least of which was its familiarity and predictability. When I speak of this "old world" of ethics, I am referring to places and times when the ethical side of life was relatively stable, when virtually everyone in a given community agreed on the basic standards of right and wrong, good and evil. Such moral communities often existed without much significant encounter with (and challenge from) other, different communities. Moral disagreement occurred but within a shared set of basic commitments.[3]

An "ethic" (or a "morality"—same thing) is a working set of guidelines concerning what is good and bad (or evil), right and wrong. "Ethics" (or "moral philosophy") is the serious study of such guidance and its justification.

These older ethical worlds were neither the Garden of Eden nor the New Jerusalem, however; there's little reason to get too nostalgic! They were by no means perfect and had some terrible weaknesses along with their strengths. We want to carry into today's ethical wil-

---

[3]A growing percentage of readers may never have lived in an "old world" like this. If you have lived in a close-knit, more traditional, ethnic or religious fellowship, then you know what I mean. But even if you have been part of a fairly strict, conservative, disciplined church, a full-orbed Christian ethic is rarely a major focus.

derness the best insights of the old ethical world, but we cannot simply huddle together in the old world.

Our situation has dramatically changed. Today we live with epidemic ethical disagreement, confusion and conflict. We experience these conflicts within ourselves (i.e., on a personal level) when we are uncertain what we ought to be or do. Therapists of one kind or another do a booming business among the confused, ashamed and guilt-ridden. Many individuals are truly lost today in the ethical wilderness.

On the social level, the ethical chaos is even more apparent. People disagree with each other about right and wrong. When these disagreements are not merely intellectual but lead to actions that impact others, the wilderness can get downright ugly. Conversation is replaced then by hostile rhetoric, propaganda and accusation. Lawyers and politicians are asked to resolve our disagreements since moral discourse fails.[4] And when even the courts and the state fail to guide us through the ethical wilderness (and fail they must in many cases), the only thing left is withdrawal or violence.

Given our population growth and our increasing economic, political and technological interdependence, such withdrawal and avoidance are unrealistic options. Unless and until there is some kind of ethical renewal, we can expect to see an increasingly fractious, litigious and violent society.

Whether social or personal, ethics is fundamentally about protecting people from harm—and promoting their healthiness and happiness.[5] Sexual ethical guidance, for example, is not intended to spoil people's fun, freedom and sexual fulfillment; just the opposite, this

---

[4]The law can only deal with external behavior (ethics deals with our interior life as well as external behavior); the law can only deal with broad generalities, usually based on precedents from the past and responding to situations already mired in intractable controversy (ethics can be flexible and specific); the law requires force to compel obedience (ethics motivates not just by threat but by promise, not just by physical sanction but by spiritual, psychological and social sanction and by reward).

[5]This is the difference between *etiquette* (manners) and *ethics*. Both use the language of right and wrong, good and bad. But breaches of etiquette do not harm people like violations of ethics. They *offend* but do not *harm*.

guidance is intended to promote fun, freedom and fulfillment. I will not rehearse here the litany of harms and hurts that are occurring in today's sexual ethical wilderness. The fact that lost souls in our wilderness are inclined to think that sexual ethics is repressive and negative is largely because its advocates haven't learned how to understand it or present it any other way. The same sort of case can be made concerning economic and consumer ethics. They should protect us all from getting hurt and promote our economic fulfillment. Few have a clue what this means or how it works.

> **E**thics is fundamentally about protecting people from harm—and promoting their healthiness and happiness.

In short, this "ethical wilderness" of which I speak is not merely an intellectual problem for "thinkers" to wrestle with. Ethics is about people and the planet: Will we continue to hurt them and trash it? If seeing children harmed, friendships betrayed, marriages disintegrate and the earth polluted troubles your conscience and breaks your heart, let me recommend that you give some attention to the sort of ethical renewal this book is about.

All of this is why I say ethics isn't pretty—but we must embrace it anyway.

The Making of a Wilderness

How is it that we have arrived at this ethical wilderness today? One source is the wide range of complex new problems we face, for example, in genetics, healthcare and information technology. We just don't have ready answers to a lot of what we face. Until our era, nobody had to deal with the rights and wrongs of high-tech life-support systems or the potential of genetic engineering. Our newspapers present us with a daily litany of new moral dilemmas and quandaries, many of them related to technological innovations of various kinds. We often have reason to be grateful for the technological changes in our world—but the price of such progress is a vastly growing ethical challenge.

A second factor is our increasing, local and global, interdependence. While it sounds (and is!) great to promote individual freedom, privacy rights and self-determination, the emerging reality is that our lives and choices are increasingly networked into the lives of others. Information technology (the World Wide Web, computer networks, global communications) is the prime example of this interconnectedness. One person's computer "virus" is not merely a local problem but a problem throughout the vast network. So too with business decisions and practices, entertainment products, medical developments, agriculture and energy choices: the impacts are potentially global. In short, a moral agent (little old me and you) is acted upon by far more numerous others than before—and influential upon far greater numbers. These impacts are hard to measure and nearly impossible to manage.

A third cause is the growing diversity of our population. We have a great deal in common with others, but moral conviction is not one of those things. We're not all Catholic or Protestant or in recovery or heterosexual or a hundred other things. Yet these ethnic, religious, therapeutic, sexual and other orientations carry with them deeply held (if not always deeply analyzed) values. When our lives intersect, ethical conflict is inevitable. The situation is even more complex, of course, because most of us identify with more than one value-laden community (e.g., the Catholic attorney who faithfully attends Alcoholics Anonymous and is thus a member of three value-laden groups). Diversity is usually a great enrichment of our lives—but it brings with it a challenge to the ways we do ethics.

Fourth, the speed and intensity of modern life leave little time for deep study and reflection or for honest, tenacious conversation together. We can handle a lot of speed in some aspects of life. Ethical reflection and discernment, however, require time—a rare commodity today. It's just easier to stick with the simple certainties of our "gut feelings" or our little enclave and avoid both self-examination and the rigors of two-way conversation with those of different perspective. We cannot simply stop the world and get off—but we must figure out how to carve out some time and space for deep reflection and moral discernment.

Finally, the wilderness is more menacing because the old moral wisdom has lost much of its power. It's a little as though we have some ethical ghost towns strewn about our wilderness. They attract some tourist interest but are no longer living communities. Some of this is because of inattention and neglect: various preoccupations have undermined people's interest in (say) developing or preserving a robust, vital Christian ethic in the economic arena.

And various attacks on traditional morality have also left it reeling. This is especially true for those who study in schools, colleges and universities. Ethics and "values" education tends to be descriptive, deconstructive and even cynical. The main lesson seems to be that "nobody knows for sure" so "choose your own values." The guardians of traditional values (such as theologically conservative churches and schools) have played into the hands of such attacks by failing to teach their tradition, creatively and effectively, in our new situation.[6] Thus, even if you are a Christian, you probably don't have the Ten Commandments or Beatitudes memorized, much less carefully analyzed and integrated into the warp and woof of a daily life ready to confront pluralism, new technologies and so on.

Factors Creating Our Ethical Wilderness
1. a host of complex new problems
2. the interdependence of our problems
3. growing diversity brings conflicting values
4. life is too intense and fast to think deeply
5. traditional moralities have lost credibility

Lost in the Wilderness
None of the foregoing will come as a surprise to anyone who has thought for ten minutes about our situation. Our ethical wilderness is widely recognized. In response there has been a vast proliferation of new books and articles on ethics. Ethics conferences, institutes and courses of study are rapidly multiplying. Values clarification courses are being aggressively promoted. "Family values" and "medical ethics" are growth industries. Ethical codes are almost a requirement in today's businesses. Leaders from traditionally apolitical and quietistic religious groups are now speaking out loudly on various moral issues.

Much of this is a welcome development. At least our "wilderness" predicament is recognized. But let's look at four different kinds of responses to the ethical wilderness. I am proposing a fifth response in

---

[6]I certainly don't mean to imply that all our churches are complete failures and moral ghost towns. But what we have been good at is personal salvation and the therapy of the soul—not at fully developing the Christian ethic

this book, and perhaps there are others. These four cover a lot of territory, however.

Naive radical individualism. Among moral philosophers, educators, culture shapers and many of our contemporaries, ethical thinking is dominated by what I call "naive radical individualism." By this I refer to the common belief that each individual is the creator and master of his or her own values. This amounts to a sort of "Welcome to the wilderness! You're all on your own now!" approach. Values clarification teachers, for example, bend over backwards to assure their students that no attempt will be made to persuade them to adhere to any particular values, that each person's values are valid by definition and in need only of clarification. Some versions of postmodern thinking on ethics despair of any moral guidance valid beyond an individual or, at most, two people in relation.

This is *radical* individualism because it makes individual preference and whim the ultimate (even the sole) value.[7] In its most extreme form it becomes narcissism, a sort of cult of the self. Something of extreme importance, the individual, is perverted into an ideology, an "ism," a god, an all-embracing critical perspective and philosophy of life.[8]

Such radical individualism is *naive* (innocent, uninformed) for several reasons. First, it is ostensibly a welcoming, "value-free" position: "Whatever you say is okay." In reality it is a normative (not a "value-free") position. Subjectivism becomes a *normative article of faith*, assuming (not demonstrating) that all individuals' values are equally valid (except, of course, those that contest this basic subjectivist assumption). Second, radical individualism in ethics is philosophically naive because it implies that both individuality and morality can survive without the social and community dimensions of our life and values. We never want to undervalue the individual, but individuals are

---

[7]"Radical" is usually a compliment in my vocabulary. Here, however, it is represents extremist folly. Our situation is very much like that described in the Old Testament book called *Judges:* "all the people did what was right in their own eyes" (Judg 17:6; 21:25).

[8]Christopher Lasch, *The Culture of Narcissism* (New York: Norton, 1978). Still one of the more important books of our time.

always, inextricably, part of communities of one sort or another; recognizing this is essential to sound moral philosophy and healthy moral life.

Radical individualism is also sociologically and historically naive in that it ignores people (a substantial minority at least) who are not radical individualists and narcissists. For many, moral identity is decisively shaped by value-laden communities with which they identify. (This process is accelerated, actually, by the poverty of academic ethics—by its incapacity to satisfy our hunger for meaning and direction). Feminism shapes many in this way. Ethnic identity groups shape others. Recovery groups are identity-making. Islam is a powerful force, demonstrating that traditional religious commitment is far from impotent in guiding the whole of life.

Damage control ethics. Hardcore, radical individualism in ethics is, however, not welcome everywhere. When we move into the typical organizational milieu (businesses, schools, churches, government agencies) there is a much different response to our ethical wilderness. Here ethics is a codes and cases affair that insists that you leave your individual moral convictions at the door.[9] Difficult cases and quandaries, and the threat of litigation and gigantic financial costs, force organizations to create ethical codes and ethics committees as a way of protecting their interests and navigating our litigious waters. Ethics is often then reduced to a sort of political/legal technique for deciding what to do and what not to do on a case-by-case basis. This approach to the wilderness is called, variously, "quandary ethics," "dilemma ethics," "decisionist ethics" or "casuistry." It is ethics based on a legal model of reasoning.[10]

I call this sort of approach "damage control ethics." It sterilizes the organizational process of all individual eccentricity, nuance and religious conviction. Then it focuses on putting out fires and on "fire pre-

---

[9]Yes, it is bizarre to promote naive, radical individualism everywhere—but then impose a legalistic behavior code within the doors of institutions. Libertine sexuality everywhere—but sterilized male-female relations within organizations, the slightest breach of which brings charges of sexual harrassment.

[10]Edmund Pincoffs, "Quandary Ethics," in *Revisions,* ed. Stanley Hauerwas and Alasdair MacIntyre (South Bend, Ind.: University of Notre Dame Press, 1983), pp. 92-112, provides an excellent critique.

vention" measures. It is the threat (or the occurrence) of damage that drives the organizational ethics agenda. Sexual harassment and gift and entertainment policies are of this sort. It is not high-minded ethics that puts them at the top of the organizational agenda; it is cover-your-tail, damage control ethics.

What is missing in this codes-and-cases approach is attention to personal *character* and corporate *culture*. The moral life cannot be reduced to a series of discrete problem cases confronted by decision-makers employing abstract moral rules and logic. Damage control ethics needs to be subordinated to (not "eliminated by"!) what I call "mission control" ethics. Mission control ethics pays attention to the organizational mission and purpose (we sometimes use the Greek word *telos* for this sort of "end" or "goal"), and to the culture and character that support (or undermine) its achievement.

All of the foregoing is the good news! In addition to these two responses (naive radical individualism and damage control codes and cases), there are two more ominous possibilities appearing in our wilderness.

Moral barbarism. The first of these is in some respects radical individualism run amok, except that it is just as likely to be represented by some group as by an individual (e.g., by a gang of skinhead predators or a demented, lone, gun-wielding assassin of the innocent). I refer to this response as "moral barbarism."[11] It is a sort of despairing "This is nothing but a stinking wilderness! Let's trash it!" position. Moral barbarians push beyond all limits of livable, sustainable human behavior and relations and explore what might be called animal levels of existence (except that, in all fairness, most animals lack such inventive cruelty). Much of this is expressed in sexual and violent behavior—two of the most powerful urges in animal life.

> The moral life cannot be reduced to a series of separate problem cases confronted by decision-makers employing abstract moral rules and logic. "Damage control ethics" needs to be subordinated to "mission control ethics."

Whence comes this moral barbarism? In a "wilderness" context where people have lost sight of any compelling dream or vision of

---

[11]This may be an insult to the original barbarians who threatened ancient civilizations like Rome. If so, I apologize.

human goodness and meaning, a context in which people are left at the mercy of their own appetites alone, a society that systematically trivializes and damages most relationships—and has usually neglected or abused these very barbarians as they were growing up—in such a society more and more people will display senseless violence, loveless sex, hopeless addictions. Jerry Springer and Jenny Jones, with their guests and studio audiences, are the cheerleading squad for twenty-first-century moral barbarism.[12]

If there is any virtue in this madness, it is that the hypocrisy and flabbiness of conventional life and morality are unmasked, and the urgent need for Christians to wake up and present the gospel in a compelling way is underscored. There is simply no vision of goodness on the horizon today that can compete with the pitiful comforts of barbarian camaraderie and bravado. But these barbarians are men and women made in the image and likeness of God! Not repulsion and condemnation but (nonpaternalistic) compassion and friendship, and a sharing and living out of the gospel is what this situation calls for.

Moral Stalinism. Unfortunately, compassion is not a major strength of the fourth set of responders to the ethical wilderness. Those who prefer the vices of order to those of anarchy are increasingly flocking to the new moral authoritarians, the moral Stalinists I call them.[13] Their angry ranting, pontificating, threatening, hyperventilating as they stomp around their platforms, their omniscient prophesying, is on display on a television channel near you. Why do these maniacal frauds attract such a following? See Jerry Springer. See item five on the list of "Factors Creating Our Ethical Wilderness." The Hitlers and Stalins of the world step in with their answers when the barbarians have had their moment.

I really don't want to overstate any of this. Nor am I trying to

---

[12]I call these shows (which, by the way, are a symptom of moral barbarism, not its leading edge) "prostitelevision": a "pimp" (the show's host) offers a few moments of attention and fame to the vulnerable and foolish to get them to perform intimate, hopefully shocking, acts (i.e., to prostitute themselves) with other guests and with the studio audience. Another audience of "voyeurs" sits in dark anonymity at home, getting their kicks out of watching.

[13]In this case a compliment to Stalin, whose crimes and cruelty against humanity equal Hitler's; none of the moral Stalinists I am thinking of reach these depths, but the mentality and style have scary similarities.

frighten anyone. My purpose is to get people to stop and take a better look at what I am calling the ethical wilderness. But I am not personally very frightened or lacking in hope. After all, Jesus (the best example) and others have lived in times of moral chaos, violence, decadence and confusion—and helped bring about positive and significant change. And as I said earlier, while today's wilderness is pretty bad, what it replaced wasn't all that great in many ways. I certainly wouldn't want to return, for example, to the appalling sexism and racism of the Ozzie and Harriet '50s in America. I'd rather be alive here and now than in any other place and time.

How Will Christians Respond?

What are Christians to do in our ethical wilderness situation? This is the question that has motivated me for the past thirty-five years, since I started my freshman year at UC Berkeley in 1964 (a rather chaotic time itself!).

Huddle and hide? On the one hand, then and now, there are Christians who want to withdraw—"huddle and hide," I might uncharitably call it. I grew up surrounded by such other-worldly, after-life, inner-life saints. Good people! But they only heard the "You are not of this world" part of Jesus' farewell address; they missed the "I am sending you into the world" part. The biblical formula is "in, but not of" (Jn 17).

Four Inadequate Responses
1. naive radical individualism
2. damage control codes & cases
3. moral barbarism & excess
4. moral Stalinism

Dive in and disappear? On the other side have been those Christians who merge into the world and its moral tastes with hardly a ripple—the "dive in and disappear" strategy. I do not for a moment judge their motives, which may, in fact, be a deep love and concern for our world and its outcasts. But it cannot help the world for Christians to do no more than affirm it as it is. We have to contribute something else, something specific and unique, something creative and redemptive, to the table.

Be pulled by compassion for the hurting in our world? It seems to me that Christians should be "pulled" strongly toward such a renewal of their own distinctive ethical thought and life by the need and the opportunity in the world around us. There is a lot of dry and thirsty ground out there; should we not, out of compassion, try to offer something to help our neighbors? Despite what some of my "huddle and hide" Christian friends think, there are tremendous opportunities today for Christians to articulate their moral convictions and suggestions. Yes, there will be some criticism and maybe even some prejudice and persecution—whoever said that *that* should stop the Christian witness?—but it is generally rare. Often the resentment Christians experience is because either (1) they are personally arrogant and offensive in giving their witness, or (2) the persecutor is a closet ex-Christian with a deep psychological need to reassure himself that what he rejected really was a bad thing!

Be pulled by the needs of our churches, especially our youth? If we don't feel the pull from a morally needy world out there, surely we should feel it from our churches, not least our younger people. It is simply not wise, not biblical and in the long run not effective to continue to try to impose a very partial Christian morality consisting of some short list of major noes to our kids: no sex, no booze, no R-rated movies, no drugs, no cussing, etc. For one thing, it's all negative, and the Bible says that we "overcome evil with good"—not with an inordinate focus on the evil (see Rom 12). But it is also too narrow: What about caring for God's earth, and the poor, and standing up for truth and fairness and compassion and for *holy* dancing and partying and celebrating? Can't we see it? Our people (again, especially the young) are in desperate need of the radical, robust, soul-stirring ethical "platform" of Jesus.

> Our people (especially the young) are in desperate need of the radical, robust, soul-stirring ethical "platform" of Jesus.

Be pushed by the commands of our Lord and of Scripture? So will we work at our Christian ethic because we feel the pull of worldly and churchly need? But even more than this pull of compassion, Christians should feel an unavoidable push from their Lord and their biblical commitment to articulate and live a faithful Christian ethic. It is simply impossible to read the Bible (any section of it) and not get the message that God wants to be the leader of a whole new way of life for his followers.

To reduce the Christian life to an affair of the afterlife alone (or even mainly) is biblically preposterous and heretical. To think that God has little or no interest in your business, money, education, politics, family patterns and so on—that he is only interested in your prayer life and attendance at church—this is nuts. It is far, far from what the Bible teaches, from what Jesus and Paul present over and over. So it is not just a question of compassion for a needy world or church out of the goodness of your heart—it is a matter of obedience and fidelity to Jesus Christ that demands our interest in recovering a robust, vital, insightful Christian ethic.

An ethics for evangelical, biblical people.[14] It is for all these reasons that this book will explore a Christian ethic of character. This is a study in ethics for biblical people, for the church and even for the world. It is an evangelical Christian ethics in that it is rooted in the gospel of Jesus Christ (I believe Jesus is the interpretive center of a biblical ethics), but it is intended to bless and benefit all who are touched by its practitioners.

My agenda is not to critique other positions in depth or to engage in an apologetic for biblical Christian commitment. In this sense, my own work here is "naive" because I am assuming something that many people out there in the ethical wilderness will not agree with. But there are multitudes of men and women for whom the Bible is God's message, and as such, the moral and spiritual authority for their lives.

> To reduce the Christian life to an affair of the afterlife or the inner life alone is biblically preposterous and heretical.

My purpose is to assist such people in their reflections on good and evil, on right and wrong. I am not saying that fundamental apologetic or comparative discussions are unimportant but that for my purposes I would be "preaching to the choir." I am writing for a community of faith, grounded in what it believes is the truth of Jesus Christ and Holy

---

[14]I mean "evangelical" and "biblical" in a very broad and inclusive sense: all people of all denominations and traditions who love the gospel (good news, *evangel*) of Jesus Christ and who love Holy Scripture.

Scripture—and for any others curious about what kind of ethics might be implied by such a starting point. My question is: "Where do we go from there?"

Of course, saying that we want a "biblical" ethics raises other questions. Does this mean we want simply to discover the precise details of biblical guidance for Israel in the ninth century B.C.—or the Ephesian church in A.D. 55—and apply it without interpretation to our situation? Not exactly. Even within the Bible, ethical guidance varies somewhat from place to place and time to time. Historical circumstances change and some ethical applications change (not the big stuff but the detailed applications). Far from being a problem, this ethical variety across the biblical canon helps us understand that our ethics also needs to be related to our own particular, historical context. There is no reason to limit the meaning of biblical ethical teaching in some narrow sense to its original setting (or dismiss its relevance to us because our setting is somewhat different).

At the same time, biblical guidance is not infinitely elastic. There is continuity as well as variety in biblical ethics. There is one gospel, one Lord, one history and one humanity created in God's image. We want to understand our steadfast God and his message in Scripture and then apply it faithfully to our situation. We are part of a two-thousand-year-old community of faith that receives and passes on Holy Scripture. Listening respectfully to our predecessors as well as our contemporaries in this vast community, we look for the meaning of God's Word for our ethics in today's wilderness.[15]

It's not pretty, but ethics is a terrific adventure. One final note here: for biblically oriented Christians, life with its ethical challenges is not some sort of heavy-handed obligation, some dreary, negative, legalistic affair! It is, by all biblical accounts and ample historical witness, an exciting adventure in meaning, truth and love. It is not a grim retreat

---

[15]Two excellent general references on Christian ethics (which in turn will point you to other books of help on specific topics) are David J. Atkinson, David F. Field, Arthur Holmes and Oliver O'Donovan, eds., *New Dictionary of Christian Ethics & Pastoral Theology* (Downers Grove, Ill.: InterVarsity Press, 1995); James F. Childress and John Macquarrie, eds., *The Westminster Dictionary of Christian Ethics,* 2d ed. (Philadelphia: Westminster, 1986).

but a challenging advance, not so much an obligation as an invitation, not less but more than ordinary life. It is an adventure that begins and ends in God's grace, his generous and overwhelming drive to love us and bless us. Hearing, seeing, comprehending, believing in and responding to God's grace is the beginning of a healthy life, the first step in the Christian adventure, the first step toward the renewal of our ethics.

For Reflection or Discussion

1. In your opinion, are terms like "ethical wilderness" and "moral barbarism" too extreme? Or do they seem appropriate today? Can you give some examples supporting your view?
2. What about your understanding of Christian ethics? Describe any organized study of Christian ethics that you have done. Describe the informal ways you have learned Christian values and ethical standards.
3. Can you recite the Ten Commandments in order? the Beatitudes? the fruit of the Spirit? the double love commandment? the Golden Rule?

Two

THE BUILDING
OF OUR
CHARACTER

Why do we do the things we do? Why does a young man viciously attack a weak child or elderly person walking through a park? Why does a financial manager steal thousands of dollars from a charitable fund under her care? Why does a man impregnate a woman and callously refuse to help provide for her and their child's needs? Why does a politician, elected on the trust of the voters he represents, accept illegal contributions or ghost payroll his relatives?

On the other side of the ledger, why does a woman with great career prospects choose to put her family before a promotion? Why does a soldier or firefighter risk his life in an unlikely attempt to save someone he doesn't even know? Why did Aaron Feuerstein, CEO of Malden Mills in Massachusetts, decide to keep all three thousand of his employees on the payroll while his factory was being rebuilt following a disastrous fire? Why didn't he simply close it all down, take the big insurance payoff and retire in luxury to the Bahamas as many of his fellow CEOs would do?[1]

---

[1]See *Time*, January 8, 1996, and the *New York Times*, July 4 and December 26, 1996, for more details on this great character

What Is Character?

Why we do the things we do is a huge and complex subject. Our choices of good or evil have many contributing sources. Certainly our mental or psychological state affects our choices. In times of great stress we act and speak differently than in less-pressured times. Certainly our social environment has a lot to do with it; past associations can haunt our present, and those around us now often create pressure or provide support that influences us as well. And there is always "the devil made me do it" (or more commonly, "these voices in my head kept telling me to do it"), and "God told me . . ."

Principles? Often when people do something morally praiseworthy or blameworthy, attention is directed to their (high, low or nonexistent) moral principles. What I mean by a moral principle is a brief statement that serves as an action guide determining the right thing to do (or prohibiting the wrong thing). Principles are broad, general and inclusive—like the Golden Rule ("Do unto others as you would have them do unto you") or the Principle of Utility ("Do what results in the greatest happiness for the greatest number").[2]

But isn't it the case that the problem in our ethical wilderness is something more than a lack of good principles and rules? That kid who attacked the weak probably heard "Thou shalt not kill" in Sunday school. That embezzling financial manager probably knew "Do unto others as you would have them do unto you" and "Thou shalt not steal." For that matter, I'm not sure that great principles alone could explain the saintly CEO Aaron Feuerstein. No doubt there is a decline in moral principle in our era. But plenty of evidence shows that the possession of moral principles does not necessarily, by itself, lead to their observance.

There is something more basic than principles: our character. Principles tend to hover over our existence like abstract, detached formulas and sayings. We subscribe to them; they are sometimes lodged in

---

[2]In comparison to a *principle*, a *rule*, also an action guide, is usually narrower in focus, applying to a sector or dimension of life: for example, "Do not lie" or "Do not copy and distribute other people's products without their permission." The Golden Rule is really, by this distinction, the Golden Principle. This definition is fairly common but not universal

our memory. But they don't always get applied to situations. It takes some motivation and effort to recall, interpret, apply and live out a principle. But your character is always with you, always immediately present in any situation. Weakness of character will thwart or distort the application of the highest set of principles. Strength of character can carry us through situations in which we can't remember a principle.[3]

Principles and rules hover over our existence like abstract, detached formulas and don't always get applied. Our character is always with us in any situation. Weakness of character will thwart the highest principles. Strength of character can carry us through even when we can't remember a principle.

So what is this character? Willow Creek Pastor Bill Hybels says that your character is "who you are when no one is looking"! Character is what and who we are—whether people are looking or not. My character is "the kind of person I am." It is the ensemble of characteristics that make me uniquely what I am.

Everyone has a physical character (short, tall, strong, fast, flexible), an intellectual character (inquisitive, rational, intuitive) and an emotional character (aggressive, romantic, sympathetic, etc.). Obviously it takes some additional categories to fully characterize a person (a football fan, a Republican, an African-American, a lawyer, a poet)—and each time we are saying something about what a person is, not just what he or she does. The communities to which we belong (churches, clubs, gangs) also help define who we are. And character has a dynamic aspect to it: we not only *are* something, we are always *becoming* something.

It is a helpful exercise to ask what someone might say about us at our funeral some day (and also what we would *like* them to be able to say!). Would they say, "Joe was always a guy who was fair-minded, loyal and loving to his family"? (Nice stuff!) In the quiet chitchat later, would people be saying, "Yeah, but I always knew him as a cutthroat

---

[3]"An ethic of virtue centers on the claim that an agent's being is prior to doing. Not that what we do is unimportant or even secondary, but rather that what one does or does not do is dependent on possessing a 'self' sufficient to take personal responsibility for one's action." Stanley Hauerwas, *A Community of Character* (South Bend, Ind.: University of Notre Dame Press, 1981), p. 113.

business wheeler-dealer, and he regularly cheated on his wife!"? (Ouch!) This gets at what we are searching for in this book. We are not asking about the principles or rules people espouse, nor are we asking about their occasional slip-ups or moments of heroism but about what is characteristic of their lives in an ongoing way.

We sometimes talk about someone playing a "character" in a film or theatrical performance. Not just the lines that are said but the mode of dress, movements, gestures and facial expressions depict a certain *role*. A great actor is capable of fully "getting into" a particular character in a believable way. One way of talking about our character is to talk about our various "roles" in life. What is the dramatic narrative of which our life is a part? What is the authentic character that I wish not only to portray but to "be" in this story?

> **Y**our character is not defined by your occasional slip-ups or moments of heroism but by what you are day in and day out.

Values? Our concern here is with *moral* or *ethical* character. A modern way of talking about our ethics is to ask what our *"values"* are. What do we *say* our values are? What values are *actually guiding* us (even if implicit or unanalyzed)? This "values" terminology points to the fact that we view certain attributes of our character as "having worth" to us, as things that we approve.

The problem with "values" language is not what it says but what it doesn't say. It affirms the subjective side of the issue (and surely it is important for us to value certain attributes of character). But it leaves aside the question of whether these "values" of mine are actually worth embracing, actually good![4] We also should note the fact that we have

---

[4]"Values clarification is essentially the following. 'Facilitators' (no longer *teachers*, for there is no longer anything true to teach) encourage students to state and clarify their own personal values by asking questions. . . . These questions are never about the roots or grounds of values, about *principles.* Instead, they are about feelings and reasonings, *calculations.* . . . They never ask questions about virtues and vices, about character, but ask only about what you would do, or rather what you would 'feel comfortable' doing. . . . The one moral absolute in values clarification is that there are no moral absolutes, and the only thing forbidden is for the facilitator to suggest that his beliefs are *true*, or even to suggest that there *is* objective truth in the realm of values, for to do that would mean that some of the students are *wrong*, and that would be 'judgmental,' the only sin. . . . [V]alues, in short, are not facts but feelings." Peter Kreeft, *Back to Virtue* (San Francisco: Ignatius Press, 1992), pp. 28-29.

taken an economic term ("value") and applied it wholesale to character issues. This says something about the consumerization of our perspectives—and it is not very flattering.

Virtues! So it is better to use "values" language sparingly and try to
recapture the great classical language of *virtue*. It was common for
centuries to speak of the attributes or traits of a good character as
being virtues and of the bad attributes as being *vices*. Virtue comes
from the Latin *virtus*, which literally meant something like "power."
(*Virility* retains some of this ancient connotation.) Virtues are thus not
just "values" (traits that I feel are worthwhile) but "powers" (real capabilities of achieving something good).

From this perspective the question is "what are the powers (virtues)
we need to develop in order to live a good life?" (Vices, by contrast, are
the corruptions of our character that contradict and undermine the
quest for a good life). As Peter Kreeft has noted, it is a little ironic that
a word that originally included the capacity of a man to impregnate a
woman (virility) now often means little more than a woman's capacity
to resist a man ("preserving her virtue")![5]

Before the Latin notion of "virtue" was the Greek concept of *aretē*.
(*Aretē* was translated by the Romans as *virtus.*) The ethics of character is often called by philosophers "aretaic ethics" because of this origin. The Greek term *aretē* is probably best translated as "excellence."
But *aretē* is not excellence in all possible meanings of the word; it
means excellence "in light of a given purpose." Thus, the *aretē* of a

---

[5]On the subject of virtue, the outstanding recent philosophical classic is Alasdair
MacIntyre, *After Virtue*, 2d ed. (South Bend, Ind.: University of Notre Dame Press,
1984). Some good theological/philosophical introduction to virtue ethics can be
found in Peter Kreeft, *Back to Virtue* (San Francisco: Ignatius Press, 1992); Gilbert
Meilaender, *The Theory and Practice of Virtue* (South Bend, Ind.: University of
Notre Dame Press, 1984); Robert C. Roberts, *The Virtues: Contemporary Essays on
Moral Character* (Belmont, Calif.: Wadsworth, 1986); Jonathan Wilson, *Gospel Virtues* (Downers Grove, Ill.: InterVarsity Press, 1998); Stanley Hauerwas, *A Community of Character* (South Bend, Ind.: University of Notre Dame Press, 1981); and
The Peaceable Kingdom: A Primer in Christian Ethics (South Bend, Ind.: University of Notre Dame Press, 1983). Hauerwas continues to publish challenging, helpful
books on character- and community-oriented Christian ethics faster than most of
us can read! Mary Ann Glendon and David Blankenhorn, eds., *Seedbeds of Virtue*
(New York: Madison, 1995) have gathered some outstanding essays on virtue in
society.

knife is to cut well; the *aretē* of a horse is to run fast and carry heavy loads. Virtue, then, refers to powers and capabilities we have—not any and all of our powers but those enabling us to achieve excellently our intended purposes. We could also say that such virtues are the *skills* needed to accomplish the task of life.

When such virtues become woven into our character, they become not occasional components of our life experience but ongoing *habits*, *inclinations* and *dispositions*. We would like to possess virtue so that it is almost reflexive. Aristotle argued that if you thoughtlessly or absent-mindedly did something nice, it was not fully an act of moral goodness, because true virtue results from thoughtful choice. Okay, but a consciously cultivated character trait like honesty that becomes habitual and reflexive does not cease being ethically praiseworthy just because we are not wrestling on each occasion with whether or not to be honest! When various challenges arise, then, we don't merely consult our formal principles and values, but we are *inclined* or *disposed* already to react with kindness, fairness or another appropriate virtue—and we have acquired the *skill* and *power* to act in such a manner.

Heart! A biblical account of character includes the notion of *heart*. For biblical people, the heart is the controlling center of one's life.[6] Jesus said, "It is from within, from the human heart, that evil intentions come: fornication, theft, murder, adultery, avarice, wickedness, deceit, licentiousness, envy, slander, pride, folly. All these evil things come from within, and they defile a person" (Mk 7:21-23). We need the new heart that God promises to give us. "I will put my law within them, and I will write it on their hearts" (Jer 31:33). We want, like David, to be men and women after God's own heart (see Acts 13:22). Our heart is the core of our being, of our soul, the controlling center of our character. It is the fountainhead of our motives and our behavior. You can see how closely this is linked to our character. In building (or rebuilding) our character, we want it to correspond to that "new heart," that "new life," that God promises.

In exploring the subject of "being" good, of who we "are," we are

---

[6]By "heart" we don't mean the pump in your chest but rather the orientation of that ensemble of your intellect, will and feelings—physiologically rooted in your brain but triggering responses in your heart/pump as well as in the rest of your body.

temporarily leaving aside the subject of the ethics of decision and action in the face of difficult dilemmas. Of course, we cannot truly, finally, separate our being from our doing. They interact with and influence each other. Being and doing are related something like "potentiality" and "act." In this sense, character and virtue have to do with the development of our *potential*. But potentiality

A Character Virtue
1. a habit, a trait, a characteristic
2. a power or potential
3. a capacity or capability
4. a skill
5. an inclination, a disposition

cannot be developed without action, and action requires potentiality to so act.[7]

Why Is Character Important?

Let me provide three analogies or metaphors to help us think about the critically important role of moral character. You will probably think of some others.

The automobile driver in Europe. First, let's think of someone who wants to make an automobile trip in Europe, say from Amsterdam to Rome. One very important necessity is a set of directions and a map. But the map and directions alone will never get you there. In addition to some material basics (a car, enough gas, money or credit card, etc.), you also need to know how to operate the car (probably a 4- or 5-speed manual transmission since you are in Europe), how to drive on European roads (lots of turnabouts with their own rules, stay-to-the-right-except-to-pass on bigger roads, a free-for-all in most big cities), how to read directions and ask for help (do you know the words for "unleaded gasoline" in Dutch, French and Italian?). And so on. You might make it to your destination with very little of this knowledge or skill in advance. On the other hand, your chances of trouble, extreme inconvenience, anxiety and even disaster rise dramatically without such preparation and skill.

---

[7]"It is obvious that a man cannot just *be;* he can only be what he is by doing what he does; his moral qualities are ascribed to him because of his actions, which are said to manifest those qualities. But the point is that an ethics of Being must include this obvious fact, that Being involves Doing; whereas an ethics of Doing . . . may easily overlook it." Bernard Mayo, *Ethics and the Moral Life* (London: Macmillan, 1958), cited in Christina Sommers and Fred Sommers, eds., *Vice and Virtue in Everyday Life,* 3rd ed. (Orlando, Fla.: Harcourt Brace Jovanovich, 1993), p. 233.

The map and directions are analogous to moral principles and rules; they guide your choices and actions. But by themselves they will never get you to your goal. It takes the other powers, capacities and resources to get there. In the moral life we call that character.

The pianist. Second, let's think about a pianist. My daughter Jodie is a pianist and piano teacher, and I remember well when she started taking lessons at age seven. And I remember a great night in more recent years when I heard her master's recital at the School of Music at Northwestern University. It was quite a journey from her piano playing at age seven to what it became by age twenty-six.

How does a pianist work toward great artistry and performance? Certainly one requirement is finding good compositions. But the musical score by itself doesn't do it. Hours and hours of practicing scales, progressions and sight reading, and other exercises are required to develop the capacities to play the notes and progressions demanded by a musical score. I had enough musical training to read at least some of the score and to know when to turn a page for Jodie while she played. But I couldn't begin to play the music (I tried). I could understand it intellectually, but I didn't have the powers, skills or capacities to carry it off. You can easily see how moral principles and moral character have their analogy here. If you don't develop the basic skills and strengths, you can't play the music. It's that simple.

The football team. My favorite metaphor, however, is American football. How do you build a winning football team? One thing most good football teams do is watch films of their upcoming opponents. They study carefully how the other team plays and the problems their opponents will cause on offense and defense. This activity is similar to the kind of ethics study in which attention is focused on various dilemmas and cases. (I called this damage control ethics in the last chapter). Good enough. But if too much of your attention is focused on such problems caused by the other team, you will not win. Such a focus makes you too reactive, too defensive. Your game plan is set by the other team, not by your own positive mission.

Another thing football teams do is study the "playbook" (full of Xs and Os as some of you will remember). This is where you learn (in your head) your team's plays and your specific responsibility during each play. Games have been lost because players moved the wrong direction, blocked the wrong man or otherwise forgot the play assignment. This is like the role of principles and rules in ethics. It is essential to have great plays and study them if you want to achieve your goals. But it is not enough. Lots of football geniuses lose.

The third factor in winning football is physical fitness and conditioning. Conditioning requires actions that are "of the sort" that will be required in specific play assignments. We must run "wind sprints" to develop the capability of breaking free for a long run late in the game, when the play is called. We must lift weights to build power and strength; we must stretch to develop flexibility and so on. It doesn't matter how brilliant the plays are—or how well you have studied the opponent. If a football team has not developed superb physical conditioning, it will not win—not only will it lose, it will suffer many need-

> **I**f a football team has not developed superb physical conditioning it will not only lose but suffer many needless injuries. Plays will be called, but the players will be too weak or exhausted to run them well.

less injuries. The plays will be called, but the players will be too weak or exhausted to run them well. Of course, superb conditioning without careful study of the playbook or the opponent still might result in a loss. It is not an either-or situation, but conditioning is absolutely fundamental. This is a great metaphor for character building.

There is also a fourth dimension: teamwork. No football program produces winners if they don't successfully teach teamwork.[8] The nature of the game is such that one or two heroic super athletes cannot win games. It takes teamwork. Players need to get in sync with each other, cover for each other, adapt to each other, encourage and discipline each other. This is so true for the moral life as well. It just isn't possible to build character and do the right thing very consistently if you go it alone. Biblical ethics are for communities of faith, not for isolated individuals.

Metaphors and analogies don't prove anything, of course, but they can be very helpful in illuminating truth and reality. (Maybe that's why

---

[8]My pianist example, thus, would be a more complete and accurate analogy if the pianist were part of an orchestra or a jazz ensemble.

Jesus and Paul relied on so many metaphors in their teaching.) Whether by way of metaphors and analogies, or a study of history and biography, or common sense, or by direct argument, the importance of building good character in individuals and in movements and organizations is hard to gainsay. Thankfully, there has been a renewed interest in character ethics over the past twenty years or so. But we have a long way to go. Many are wandering around in our ethical wilderness without decent maps and directions. But what is even more frightening is that most of them are in such feeble condition that they probably couldn't make their way forward even if they did have them.

How Is Character Built?

Enough of parables, metaphors and analogies for the moment. We want to ask now how character is built, shaped and formed. Where does our character come from? Knowing this will begin to help us understand how we might build the best possible character in our kids and how we might change our own where it needs it. There are six basic factors here.

My genetic nature. There is a relationship between our character development and our "nature," although it is impossible to describe this precisely. Nature is not "destiny" in some deterministic way. Researchers continue to look for a genetic basis for things like intelligence, aggressiveness, alcohol addiction, compulsive overeating and sexual orientation, that is, not just physical characteristics but emotional and intellectual ones as well.

At the very least, it seems, our natural, genetic endowment inclines us in certain directions, in various ways and degrees. What we know about genetic "markers" for many physical characteristics and conditions is that these are not necessarily going to "activate" without a stimulus from one's diet, lifestyle, stress level and environment. Our genetic nature, in other words, is a powerful force but not always or necessarily something that operates deterministically. It is not something we should always yield to. The gene for obesity is not a license to overeat irresponsibly; the genetic marker for aggressive behavior is not an excuse to be violent. Genes for intelligence or athleticism do not guarantee anything.

On the positive side, our natural endowment as human beings continues to bear the image and likeness of God. Our natural character is the beneficiary of God's creational goodness, and we are fashioned in his good image. We do not reflect on this nearly enough, that when God made me, he made something good (even allowing for my very real shortcomings). On the negative side, our natural endowment (even our genes) carries the scars of millennia of alienation from the Creator, and of the sinful and stupid patterns of behavior of our ancestors. Our illnesses, physical, mental and social, are not the work of our Creator, and they deserve our strongest efforts to resist and overcome. Might this include some sort of "gene therapy for character disorders"? I doubt it. Some are dreaming of this already, but I think the answer to bad character lies elsewhere.[9]

God's ongoing work in my life. In a Christian perspective, however, our nature is not something just "given" and left alone. Rather, God is at work giving us a "new nature." This is what is meant by phrases like "born again" and "receiving the Holy Spirit." The moral self is composed not only of the "old nature" but is being decisively refashioned and augmented by a new work of God. God is not just our Creator but our Redeemer and Sanctifier. Much of this book challenges Christians to become more proactive in building good character—and yet it must be emphasized that the formation of good character is fundamentally God's work in us rather than our own autonomous effort. "God is at work in you," is a frequent New Testament theme.

Knowing that any goodness we achieve is ultimately because God is at work should lead us to be very humble about anything we "accomplish" and cause us to give credit and thanks to God. It should also underscore for us the importance of prayer in this whole process. If God can sanctify us (make us holy), then let us pray fervently that he will do so. Nevertheless, God invites our cooperation, participation and effort. Character building is neither an accomplishment of autonomous human beings nor something that God

---

[9]In *Doing Right* I will have more to say about the ethics of preserving and enhancing human life and health

imposes on utterly passive subjects.[10]

The way I was raised. In addition to the contributions of nature (our genetics) and God, our character is shaped and nurtured by the people around us—first of all, by our parents and the household in which we spend our early years. It would be impossible to overstate the influence of parents and families in shaping our character for better or worse. Millions go through life deeply wounded, scarred and sometimes twisted by the appalling treatment they received from their parents and family. Others go through life with great resilience, joy, energy and kindness because of the wise, warm and affirming ways they were parented. Most of us are a little of both.

> Character building is neither an accomplishment of human beings by themselves—nor something that God imposes on utterly passive subjects. God invites our cooperation, participation and effort.

Our childhood socialization has a tremendous impact on things like intellectual curiosity, aggressiveness, alcoholism, obesity and sexual orientation—the same list often linked to our genetic nature. If parents always react to disappointment or to difficulty with uncontrolled anger or with pouting and withdrawal—or if their sexuality is badly messed up—their children may well find their own characters misshaped or weak in these areas.

Every time parents (and other significant elders) explain something, answer or fail to answer our questions, our character is being molded. Every time they hug us, pat us on the head, smile at us, compliment or otherwise reward us, they are reinforcing values and behavior patterns. Every time they punish, beat, berate, insult or reject us, they are also shaping our character.

We didn't get to choose these people, these homes or the national, religious and cultural identities that came with them. Yet these are

---

[10]Donald G. Bloesch (*Freedom for Obedience: Evangelical Ethics for Contemporary Times* [San Francisco: Harper & Row, 1987], pp. 82-83; cf. p. 22) cautions us against a simple adoption of the Greek notion of virtue as a human strength of character. "As Christians we are called not simply to a life of virtue but to a life that transcends virtue. . . [to a] life that transcends and defies the humanly possible." Fair enough if we let the Greeks determine the entire meaning of virtue; my approach, following Thomas Aquinas, Peter Kreeft and Stanley Hauerwas is to broaden the definition to include the theological virtues and the biblical graces.

influences fundamentally and dramatically shaping the character we will have to work with for the rest of our lives. We can usually escape (physically) at some point and go in another direction, but it remains a monumental task to overcome poor parental and familial experiences. Those with mostly positive experiences, on the other hand, while not finding success in life handed to them on a platter, do carry tremendous advantages with them into adulthood.

The friends and communities I choose. In addition to the people we didn't choose, who dominate our early character formation, we also live among people we choose, starting with our early childhood friends. We are shaped by these associations, by the individuals and groups with whom we spend time. In the next chapter, "The Reality of Our Communities," we will explore this phenomenon in greater detail.

As human beings we have some basic needs that can only be met by other people. When our parents and family do not (or can no longer) meet these needs, we begin to look elsewhere. These needs change somewhat (though not entirely) as we grow older. People are sometimes relatively satisfied with their group of friends for a few years but then yearn for something more.

We have all seen people change, sometimes dramatically, as a result of coming under the strong influence of new friends. The nice guy we once knew becomes a cutthroat gangbanger or a Wall Street dealmaker under the influence of those two crowds; the tough guy becomes astonishingly sensitive and caring for love of a woman; hanging out in a gym or fitness center profoundly changes someone's appearance and lifestyle; the people we choose to "hang out" with have a profound impact on who we are and who we become.

My cultural environment. Just as there are people we don't choose and others we do who influence our character, so too there are both unavoidable as well as chosen aspects to the culture that influences our character. By "culture" I mean television, film, music, games, language, information and dress. I mean the things we see and hear and touch. Our cultural setting is for the most part inescapable (and much of it is good stuff we do not want to escape). It is impossible to avoid and very difficult to resist a culture that from all directions promotes nonstop consumerism and hypersexualized relationships (to name but two of our leading villains). The critical necessity is to become aware of this cultural environment we did not ask for. Name its components— then evaluate them and decide what to embrace and what to resist.

Nevertheless, a great deal of latitude remains for us to choose the things that will influence us. It is certainly possible to see or hear something (in movies, music, books, etc.) without necessarily affirming and embracing all that is being said! It is possible, I think, to play violent video games without becoming a violent person. It may be possible to watch sordid situations on television without imitating them yourself. It is also possible to read a lot of biographies of great-souled characters and remain personally an un-self-critical wretch!

But it is utterly absurd to suggest that the cultural influences we choose have *no impact* on our character! The character we build (our own and that of those around us) is affected by the cultural environment we choose. Our tastes, preferences, habits, dreams, longings and ideals cannot help but be shaped to a great extent by the literature, music, film, sport, information, dance and other activities and materials we choose to have in our life. We are choosing our character as we choose our cultural environment. We can't blame this one on our parents!

My personal choices. So we move our attention to a look directly in the mirror. Human beings are not just the passive products of nature, God and nurture by others. We have the capacity for "self-transcendence"; that is, we can think about ourselves, reflect on our life and choices, our desires and instincts. We are capable of struggling with, even contradicting, the inclinations of both nature and nurture (and against the commands of God for that matter).

That is where our freedom begins: with our choices to obey or not to obey what our natural inclinations and environmental influences initially prescribe to us. This is where the ethical life begins for individuals: when we consciously do what seems to be right and good, rather than thoughtlessly doing "what comes naturally" or "what everybody expects me to do."

No, we can't do much (if anything) about our genetic endowment (although plastic surgeons are having a lucrative go at it anyway). We do, however, have important choices about the sacred we install at the

...ter of our life, the god we follow and the larger purposes we pursue. These choices are decisively important for our character.

Our choices with respect to our social and cultural environment are limited during the early years of our life. As we get older, however, we usually have more freedom to choose our associations, communities and cultural context. We can choose what music, literature and films we want in our life. We can read the Bible or not. We can keep up with all the celebrity news or watch ballgames religiously. We can choose who we want as our role models and heroes.

With regard to our friends and communities: Who is giving us the acceptance we crave? Who is giving us the approval we need? Who is giving us the help we need? Who makes us laugh—and who will cry with us? Who has the dream that inspires us, the adventure that thrills us? Who has the answers to our questions? Who has the story we want to be a part of and which gives meaning to our role in life? How much are we willing to put up with before we cut off a relationship? These are provocative and difficult questions. Their answers reveal the directions that our character formation is taking.

> Our freedom—and the ethical life—begins the moment we choose not to thoughtlessly follow the crowd or our instincts, desires and habits but instead to figure out and do what is right and good.

These are some of the choices we get to make on a daily basis about how we will respond to life and its challenges. All of this, together, shapes our character.[11]

I don't mean to minimize the difficulty and pain involved in trying to overcome what may be our victimization by parents, former mates or bosses, genetics, or even our own bad choices. But we do not need to let these forces from our past victimize us forever, at least not as much as they would if we rolled over and quit. We do not need to accept a minimal "damage control" attitude toward ourselves. Instead,

---

[11]On character education see Bonnidell Clouse, *Teaching for Moral Growth* (Wheaton, Ill.: Victor Books, 1993); Barbara Darling-Smith, ed., *Can Virtue Be Taught?* (South Bend, Ind.: University of Notre Dame Press, 1993); Craig Dykstra, *Vision and Character: A Christian Educator's Alternative to Kohlberg* (New York: Paulist Press, 1981); William Kirkpatrick, *Why Johnny Can't Tell Right from Wrong* (New York: Touchstone, 1992); and Gilbert C. Meilaender, *The Theory and Practice of Virtue* (South Bend, Ind.: University of Notre Dame Press, 1984).

with the help of God and a few friends, and with some strategic changes in our lifestyle, we can seize every opportunity to rebuild our character and our life.

It all starts with our making a decision to try to change and grow. It will, of course, take a lot more than a decision or a good intention to have it actually happen, but this is where it all starts. Reshaping our minds is critical. Will we develop the wisdom to discern and know what is good and right? Study, critical reflection, imagination and thoughtful analysis are essential. Laziness and a life of superficial distraction (television, etc.) is nobody's fault but our own, and the flaccid character that results is of our own making.

Our opportunity continues beyond our thinking to our actions. Aristotle described well the way habituation develops virtue (or vice). We become generous people partly by doing generous things; we become honest by repeatedly behaving honestly; we become temperate people by repeated acts of disciplining our appetites. Conversely, we become violent people by repeatedly venting our anger in word and deed. Will we make efforts to practice true virtue, to cultivate the fruit of the Spirit? Or will we give in to our vices, to the works of the flesh?

Six Shapers of Our Character
1. genetics, our created/fallen "nature"
2. God's sanctifying work in us
3. the "nurture" of those we didn't choose
4. the influences of those we do choose
5. cultural influences: chosen and not
6. my choice of who I want to be

We usually need to unpack (to some extent anyway) what others have done to us to bring us to where and who we are today. But now it is our turn to call the play. What will we do?

Optimists and pessimists about character change. How much change in anybody's character is really possible? Many people are, frankly, very pessimistic. They point to Bill Clinton's sorry track record of repeated sexual failures, to supposedly "cured" gay people who reverted to the lifestyle, to habitual liars, and (get ready for this) to the way most of us who lose weight soon gain it all back again. Character is very, very tough to change even in minor ways.

But despite this evidence, there are countless other stories of people who have conquered deeply engrained habits in all the areas mentioned above. There are stories of dramatic changes in people's lives and character. Violent hoodlums have become peaceful leaders. Selfish husbands have reformed. Nagging mothers have changed directions. Prodigal sons have come home. The murderous Saul of Tarsus became the apostle Paul.

If you are a Christian, you have to believe in the possibility of dramatic change, of being born again and renewed toward the image and likeness of Jesus Christ. You have to believe it not just because the Bible says so but because almost any church you could be part of has living examples of people whose character has changed. Don't give up.

For Reflection or Discussion

1. Describe the main character traits (or "virtues") you would like to exhibit in your character. Why do you value these above other possibilities?
2. How have people (the ones you didn't choose and the ones you did) influenced and shaped your character into what you are today?
3. Describe (and evaluate?) the ways you have been shaped by your choices of music, literature, film, or radio and television.
4. Can you describe anyone who has undergone a profound change of his or her character? What caused the change?

Three

THE REALITY OF OUR COMMUNITIES

*L*et me put it bluntly: *you cannot build a strong, good character without at the very same time being actively involved in signifi-cant community experiences.* An isolated, community-fleeing, relationship-avoiding character is a weak and deformed one.

A perfectionist quest for friends and communities that meet some utopian standard we set is doomed from the start. We will soon discover that everyone and everything we find is failing and imperfect. Living and coping with the imperfections of others is a criti-cally important aspect of the process of building strong character. Of course, horrible, sick, dysfunc-tional relationships and communities are devastating to individuals who must suffer them. There is certainly a time to flee a given relationship or community! But not *all* relationships, not *all* community.

> **L**iving—and coping—with the imperfections of others is a criti-cally important part of building strong character.

Our individual, personal character and the character of the commu-nities with which we are associated, are interwoven and interactive.

Individuals affect their communities; communities affect their members. If we wish to understand one or the other, we must study both.

More than a few teachers, leaders and authors have tried to reserve the term community only for group experiences meeting a list of criteria they provide (usually in the "perfectionist" mode mentioned above). I think it is better to use the term in its generic sense.

What Is Community?

The basic idea of community (Latin *communis*, Greek *koinonia*) is that a group of people share something in common (Greek *koinos*). *Merely* sharing a common trait (such as left-handedness) does not make a community. The commonality must be *recognized*, *affirmed* and *acted* upon (say, by forming a left-handed club). Communities do not just assemble people with such shared characteristics, they *reinforce* those commonalities. Some minimum amount of communication and activity completes this sketch of basic community.

W hat Is a Community?
1. two or more people
2. some common characteristics
3. some shared purpose, intention
4. time, communication, action together

This is still a definition of "thin" or weak community. A more robust, "thick" version of community increases all of these dimensions: shared characteristics (purposes, beliefs, values, knowledge, tradition, customs, manners), a sense of a collective identity, time together, communication and joint activity.

Why do we form communities? According to Plato and other ancient philosophers, we gather together in communities because of both our needs and our desires.[1] By living and working together, we can better provide for our basic needs, such as food, shelter and protection. And beyond these most basic needs we find that together we can achieve some of our desires, luxuries that would be impossible if we were alone. Education, culture and greater material prosperity are all made possible by community. Community life promotes the common good; our personal good is found in this common good.

The traditional, basic forms of community. Community has meant

[1]See Plato *The Republic* bk. 2.

things as simple as friendships, clubs, neighborhoods and churches. Historically, the most common experience of human community has been based on blood ties. Families, households, clans, tribes and ethnic groups shared an elemental community. This is where most basic needs were met.

Shared language, stories, traditions and customs sustained such community. The perils of leaving such kinship-based communities were considerable. Members were not only *drawn* to be loyal to the community by its obvious benefits—they were *driven* into loyalty by the undesirability of any alternative. It was dangerous to leave one's community.

Why Community Is Crucial to Character

There are two sets of reasons why community is so essential to our character. The first set is functional in nature; it has to do with what communities *do* to us and *for* us. The second set is ontological in nature; it has to do with what communities and individuals *are* in their essential reality and being.

Communities meet our basic needs. We are "herd animals," social (not solitary) beings. We need relationships with other people in order to survive (and thrive). Our basic human needs include food, shelter and protection, but we also need somebody to talk to, someone who will listen to us, and somebody to love. We need to be accepted and approved by someone. As thinking beings we also crave meaning and understanding of the way we are and the way the world is. We need some way of figuring what is right and wrong—and why.

First our parents, family and kin meet these needs for us. Later, other people and groups usually become as important as family in meeting our community needs. Much of this need is met by friendships, but some of it requires larger associations, from clubs and neighborhoods to corporations and nations.

A culture is both taught and "caught." Communities of whatever size and type *socialize* their participants into their particular culture and values. Every community has its own specific "corporate culture"—an ethos, a constellation of mission and values. Communities, like individuals, have habits and customs, traditions and principles.

The way communities arrange and decorate their space, as well as how they act within that space, carries values. The institutions and practices of communities (even friendships) transmit moral values to their members. They all have a kind of structural justice (or injustice). The way decisions are made, the purposes that are held to really matter, the patterns of leadership, all are value laden. Some of this is explicitly taught, some of it is simply "caught" through repeated exposure.

Communities help their members figure out *what is right and wrong,* then they help them carry out *the right thing.*

Communities have a morality. Communities share some kind of agreement on what is right and wrong, on what is morally praiseworthy and what is morally prohibited. Communities help their members discern what is right and wrong in particular cases, and they support and help them carry out the right thing—by their encouragement (or threat and punishment) and by their coming alongside individuals to help out in difficult circumstances.

Approval/disapproval leverages behavior and character. Some individuals in communities serve as role models, heroes and authorities for other members. As members receive praise and reward—or blame and punishment—from leaders (and peers), they are steered into conformity with community values and characteristics. Every time we are hugged, patted on the head, smiled at, complimented or otherwise rewarded, our character traits and behavior patterns are affected. Every time we are punished, beaten, berated, insulted or rejected, our character is being shaped.

Because of our basic human craving for approval and acceptance, we conform to the expectations and demands of friends and communities. We need the security and good feeling of acceptance and approval. Kindness, generosity and compassion often become character traits because they were applauded and rewarded by others. Conversely, we instinctively avoid pain and seek to protect ourselves. This is why disapproval, shunning or insults are effective in socializing us in certain ways.

This process is not always positive or predictable. Negative experiences (too many or too extreme) by members of communities sometimes lead them to reject the values and even the larger purposes pursued by the offending community. Someone may become a habitually violent person as a self-protection mechanism. Passivity or honesty may have been punished repeatedly in this person's experience, so they can only survive by becoming violent and dishonest.

Toughened through tests and trials. Communities make demands on their members—community means sharing life and its tasks in one way or another, after all. It is in responding to these demands that strength of character often results. Courage, patience and wisdom are demanded by some of these tasks and tests. Often we do not have the strength going into a situation—but develop it during the course of the trial.

How does one develop physical strength? By lifting heavy weights, by walking or running up hill. Often we need a coach or (in lifting weights) a "spotter" to help us if we get beyond our current strength. But struggling against resistance is essential for strength. One's intellect only becomes strong through encounter with others who "push back" at us intellectually, forcing us to mount better arguments. We only become psychologically strong if our parents and others push back at us, set boundaries and force us to struggle with them. Always giving in to your children is not protecting and caring for them; it is actually destroying their chances at developing strength of character.

This is why hanging in there with our friendships, marriages, churches and other community commitments is so important. Struggling with the difficult times builds our strength of character. Of course, some relationships may become so destructive that we must get out (a little like someone lifting weights who has a big machine fall on her—this is not a growth opportunity!). But *habitually* letting friendships go, changing churches and running away from family almost certainly points to immaturity and weakness of character.

Communities give us the big picture, a saga. Communities (except for the weakest, thinnest versions) also have histories. They tell and retell their story to their members. This narrative functions as an interpretive saga that makes sense of life, of who we are, and of where we are going. Stanley Hauerwas has often said that our lives are embedded "story-formed communities."[2] Our own personal moral

---

[2]"All significant moral claims are historically derived and require narrative display.

identities acquire a narrative dimension within the broader texture of our community's story. Meaning, direction and value are intimately related to the "story" of ourselves in our communities.

So good communities (not perfect ones) help shape us toward good character. Bad communities reinforce bad individual character. Community stories become our stories, whether of virtue or vice, meaning or meaninglessness, of heroic pursuit of the good or villainous exploitation of others. Reciprocally, our character contributes to the community, adding to the richness or poverty of its texture. Stanley Hauerwas again: "Our capacity to be virtuous depends on the existence of communities which have been formed by narratives faithful to the character of reality."[3]

How Community Shapes Character
1. provides role models, behavior patterns
2. approves/rewards behavior
3. disapproves/punishes behavior
4. helps us discern right and good
5. assists/supports our performance
6. demands, tests and trials build strength
7. story/tradition gives direction/meaning

The essential reality of human and Christian community. There is an even deeper set of reasons why community is crucial to character. For Christians this should be obvious, but it is often not given the emphasis it deserves. It has to do with the nature of God, the way we have been created, the work and witness of Jesus Christ, and the corporate reality of the people of God.

The nature of God: Trinity. The biblical God *is* a community in a profound sense. While we are monotheists who believe there is one God, this one God says "Let *us* make humankind in *our* image, according to *our* likeness" (Gen 1:26, my emphasis). We describe this "plurality in unity" as the Trinity. The *oneness* of God is simultaneous with the *distinctiveness* of the Father, Son and Holy Spirit.[4] In their unity of will, purpose and action, and in their distinctiveness and complemen-

What is peculiar to Christian convictions is not that they involve a narrative, but the kind of narrative they involve. . . . [O]ur first moral question must be Of what history am I a part and how can I best understand it?" Stanley Hauerwas, *A Community of Character* (South Bend, Ind.: University of Notre Dame Press , 1981), pp. 99-100.

[3]Ibid., p. 116.

[4]On the Trinity, see Donald G. Bloesch, *God the Almighty* (Downers Grove Ill.: InterVarsity Press, 1995), pp. 166-204.

tarity of roles, the Father, Son and Holy Spirit are the foundation of our human community.

Humanity is cohumanity. Human beings are made in the image and likeness of this triune God. God created a "them" in his image and likeness. "It is not good that the man should be alone. I will make him a helper as his partner" (Gen 2:18). Solitary, isolated existence is "not good" (everything else in the Creation was declared "good" or "very good"). As Karl Barth has said, "humanity *is* co-humanity." Our need for community is woven into the fabric of our being, our nature. There is a distinction between man (*ish*) and woman (*ishah*), but they are made of the same stuff and even the similarity of their names emphasizes their commonality.

The tasks of being fruitful, multiplying, filling and subduing the earth, receiving and caring for the earth, are given to man and woman in their community and partnership. It is only sin and its curse that alienated and separated man and woman in these tasks (Gen 3).[5] Hardcore, rugged, "Lone Ranger" individualism violates our nature and contradicts God's purposes. It is sin.

Biblical ethics is given to communities. The creation story should be enough evidence that community is essential. But there is a lot more. The great, classic ethical instruction of the Bible is given not to lone pilgrim individualists but to a people, a community. Why on earth would we think today that we no longer need to approach our ethics in community? Where would we get the idea that now it is okay to be individual "moral athletes"? The Ten Commandments were given to the congregation to learn, interpret and apply.

> All the great, classic ethical instruction of the Bible was given not to lone individuals but to groups. Why do we think we no longer need to approach ethics in community and can succeed as individual "moral super-athletes"?

Jesus gave his Sermon on the Mount to a band of disciples. He sent those disciples out two by two, not one by one, and promised forever to

---

[5]A careful reading of Genesis 1—3 indicates God's intention for men to be involved in parenting and women to be involved in the world of work beyond parenting. From the point of view of God's creation, it is crucial to a fulfilled humanity for both men and women to work in both domains together.

be present "where two or three are gathered in my name" (Mt 18:20). His farewell prayer (Jn 17) stressed the importance of being united, not divided.

We are members of the body of Christ. Paul's greatest extended ethical text, Romans 12—13, was written to a church and early on warns "not to think of yourself more highly than you ought to think, but to think with sober judgment." At just this point Paul brings up a theme that appears elsewhere in the New Testament: You are one member in the body of Christ. You have value, you have gifts and a role to play, but you are not self-sufficient. You need the larger body, and it needs you. Paul asks us, How can we say to another brother or sister "I have no need of you"? The members that appear lesser are even more necessary to the healthy functioning of this body (1 Cor 12:14-26). We are a *koinonia,* a fellowship, a community; that is the basic reality of what Christians are.

Deeper Reasons for Community
1. God is three-in-one: made in God's image
2. "not good to dwell alone"
3. biblical ethics given for group practice
4. Jesus sends out two-by-two
5. "wherever two or three are gathered"
6. members of body of Christ

While God does reveal his goodness one-on-one to individuals, his presence is at least as much a corporate, community reality as an individual one. If we are not living out our Christian life in community with other Christians, building a good character will be much more difficult; it may even be impossible.

So it is not just for good sociological or psychological functional reasons that character building needs community, it is because of the basic reality of our being—what we are made of. We cannot become what we were meant to be, unless it is in community. That is the bottom-line reality.

Community is an imperfect necessity. Those early communities, whether Israel in the Old Testament or the churches of the New, were most certainly not great places to be much of the time. Every problem imaginable in a community (bone-headed leadership, sleep-inducing teachers, sexual and financial scandal, racism and sexism) is there, well-reported in the Bible for our inspection. And yet community remains the place of reality, the place where God is at work and where we must remain. That's the way it is.

Community Today: Bad News/Good News

But let's return to our situation today. Meaningful community is not
something we can take for granted. A century ago observers began
noting the disappearance of traditional communities. Clubs,
churches, associations, neighborhoods and extended families were
declining in their power and significance. Large-scale institutions
were increasing in their importance for people's lives. The "nuclear
family" (two parents alone with their children) was more commonly
standing alone, lacking traditional supports. Individuals were often
now detached even from their nuclear families and left floating in
large-scale "mass" society (the "crowd" we could call it). Why was
this happening?

Causes of community disintegration. Beginning in the nineteenth
century, and really gathering momentum in the twentieth, the stan-
dardization of work in large-scale business and industry, the growth of
the bureaucratic nation-state, the rising dominance of mass media and
the global development of technology drove this social change. The
authority and relevance of traditional communities (such as churches
and fraternal organizations) were steadily diminishing. The specter of
individual "atoms" bouncing around in an impersonal mass society
became common by mid-twentieth century.

Mobility, not stability. The mobility of people has been steadily
increasing. It is very difficult to sustain meaningful community when
we change jobs, residences, friends and even families so easily and frequently. Ease of good transportation is fundamental to this mobility.
For the most part, we have also been liberated
from kinship dependence; we can usually break
away from our families and roots and "start a
new life" somewhere else. There is little or no
social disapproval of divorce or of failing to live
near one's aging parents—forces that used to
inhibit mobility. Our basic needs for jobs, food,
shelter and education can be met without family
or traditional community help—usually by the

> It is very difficult
> to sustain meaningful
> community when we
> change jobs, resi-
> dences, friends,
> churches and even
> spouses so easily and
> frequently.

bureaucratic institutions of the government if we can't make it on our own.

A growing social mobility has meant that our economic and social classes are not stable but fluid. With hard work and the right circumstances, people can live in radically different styles and environments from those in which they grew up. Not all of this mobility and change is fully chosen by those who experience it. Employers have sometimes transferred their employees to other locations, or forced changes in employees' personal appearances or schedules.

For these many reasons, deep community and long-term loyalty are in decline. Owners and players in major sports, for example, are loyal to their own individual financial interest—not to their fans or to each other. Employers and employees show little loyalty and community in the era of downsizing. Our commitment to community rarely seems able to survive a challenge from our personal self-interest.

Affinity groups. Of course, we are still herd animals. It is still embedded in our nature to seek fellowship, belonging, acceptance and approval. Even if our basic physical needs do not require it, our psychological needs for some kind of community remain. We do find a degree of community today, although its forms tend to be structured primarily by technological possibilities (i.e., what e-mail, cell phones and transportation can support). Usually it is based on shared interests, tasks, desires or needs. Modern community tends to be based on what we do and what we want, not on who we are or on a longer-term shared vision transcending today's desire. It tends to be transitory and superficial, not enduring and multidimensional.

Isolated conformists. Even a superficial level of interpersonal association requires some time and effort. You have to actually go spend some hours in the bar or health club—or go through all those responses to your personals ad, then go out and meet your prospects, eliminate the insane and so on. We constantly lament that we do not have enough time for quality in our relationships. And even when we are physically present with each other, the television often competes with meaningful conversation. Loyalty is generally minimal; our fleeting relationships will be severed the moment they cannot be justified in terms of either measurable success or personal gratification.

Relationship building usually takes a back seat to our work and travel schedule. Since a person's career advancement is so competitive and demanding, multitudes opt to sit alone for hours daily, watching television programs before falling asleep exhausted.

The joys of mass "community." Lacking substantial, persisting community, we are prone to drift toward an artificial, lowest-common-denominator "community" created by mass media, shopping malls, big organizations and anonymous Internet chatter. This sort of "community" reinforces a jaded, conformist dullness of character—which does not become more admirable just because more people are developing appetites for it!

Mass, technological society isolates us as faceless atoms (as consumers and as "data") from deep human community. At the same time it promotes the illusions of community (some television viewers have said they really feel that Oprah is their best friend!). The mass media (and business monopolies) standardize our individually atomized experiences. We are propagandized with the gospel of the sacred, autonomous self and its desires—at the very same time we are being integrated as faceless (but not numberless!) atoms in the crowd. A standardized "McDonalds/CNN/USA Today/WalMart/Blockbuster" identity molds individuals into a mass today. We are shaped into self-serving narcissists, doomed to slavery to our appetites and to frustration at their never-quenched demands.

> An artificial, lowest-common-denominator, jaded, conformist dullness of character is not admirable just because more people are developing appetites for it.

Lost characters. Max Weber, Emile Durkheim and the early sociologists warned that the very meaning of life was endangered by this loss of community. They worried that a condition of anomie, of lostness and chaos, would result. People who have no meaningful community and are told only to gratify the self as fully and immediately as possible, are people who will not be able to sustain their vows of marriage and friendship when they become unsatisfying. They may neglect, abuse or abandon their children (and sick and elderly) when it becomes inconvenient. They may avoid all sacrifice and trample over anyone who gets in their way. A modern mass society is a society of users and takers, a society of narcissists in a faceless mass culture of loneliness, violence, despair and suicide.[6]

Community persists. Of course, this grotesque picture is painted with overly broad, rough strokes. There are exceptions to my picture at every point. Despite the generalizations about mass media, there are movies (e.g., *Life Is Beautiful*) and television programs of depth and substance. Some popular music reinforces deep commitments among people. Despite the generalizations about large organizations, some corporations (e.g., Herman Miller) work hard to create cultures of personal caring and growth for both their customers and employees.

There are still many examples of meaningful, even sacrificial, community building today. Many adults volunteer their time in coaching and caring for youth soccer or baseball teams. Many parents invest time as volunteers in local schools, churches and neighborhood organizations. Kids still have best friends to whom they are often passionately loyal. Some newer forms of community, such as 12-step and recovery groups, Internet "chat" groups, radio talk shows, and computer-user groups, can support (although not replace) our need for genuine community.

> We are not called to return to either a nostalgic or an oppressive past! The way is forward—bringing with us the best wisdom of the past.

Not nostalgia but hope. Much has been lost that was good, and we should try to learn from the past as we rebuild community and friendship. However, traditional community should not be viewed as an idyllic lost utopia. Plenty of extended families, churches, neighborhoods and labor guilds were oppressive; some were threatening. This book is not a call simply to return to an oppressive past! The way is forward, but bringing with us the best wisdom and relationships of the past.

The good news is that the mobility that has allowed us to flee our relationships also allows us to return. The freedom that allowed us to neglect our old communities allows us to build new ones.

---

[6]On these cultural trends see Robert Bellah, et al., *Habits of the Heart: Individualism and Commitment in American Life* (Berkeley: University of California Press, 1985); Christopher Lasch, *The Culture of Narcissism* (New York: Norton, 1978); and David Riesman, *The Lonely Crowd: A Study of the Changing American Character* (New Haven, Conn.: Yale University Press, 1950).

Rebuilding Our Communities: The "To Do" List

But enough of this handwringing! Our project is to build good character. To do this we must rediscover or rebuild the kinds of community experiences that are conducive to the process. Notice the term "conducive"; we are not looking for perfection, nor are we looking for freedom from trial and conflict. Neither of those is really an option anyway, but even the search for them, as alluring as it may be, is a distracting waste of time from our objective.

Community with God. It could easily be overlooked, but the first practice of Christian community is with God. Developing a personal relationship with God is the first and decisive way of breaking out of our isolation and entering into meaningful relationship. God strengthens and guides us as we devote time to our relationship with him in prayer, meditation and listening for his living Word to us as we read his written Word, the Bible.

As any longer-term Christian knows, community with God is not always easy! Like Peter, James and John in the Garden of Gethsemane with Jesus, we sometimes have trouble staying awake and engaged. We fall into the doldrums of routine and our relationship with God gets stale and predictable—not at all the vital adventure God offers to us. Like Jacob, we sometimes wrestle with God; like Job, we argue; like David, we cry out.

Whatever our past experiences of speaking to God in personal prayer, trying to hear God speak to us as we read Scripture and meditate on it, or as we open ourselves to God's creation ("The heavens are telling the glory of God" [Ps 19:1])—we must keep on trying to make community with God a daily experience. Practicing the presence of God as we go through our daily life is a character- and life-changing strategy. Of course, God also indwells his people, and we seek his presence with them. This is one reason why participation in a church is so important.

Friendship. A second elementary form of community essential to building good character is *friendship*. One of the most common terms for love in the New Testament is *philia*, the Greek word for friendship and brotherly/sisterly love. The relationship of Adam and Eve is fundamentally about friendship and partnership in life.

Jesus told his disciples, "I call you my friends." He taught them that friends *choose* each other (it isn't just a casual thing), love each other sacrificially (not just when it feels good), instruct each other (not just passively affirm each other), share with each other and call on each other to do important tasks (Jn 15:12-18). Jesus sent his friends out on their mission two by two, not one by one, so that they would have a friend alongside at all times.

Jonathan and David are a model of good friendship. They had much in common as young warriors and were fond of each other. They made an explicit covenant of commitment to each other (and repeated it more than once) and to care for each other's families no matter what might come. They spent time together, shared possessions, listened to each other, encouraged each other in hard times, warned each other of approaching trouble, acted as advocates for each other and strengthened each other spiritually (1 Sam 18—20; 23).

Ruth and her mother-in-law, Naomi, both tragically widowed, also model great friendship. Their language is often used in marriage ceremonies, but it concerned their friendship when Ruth said "Where you go, I will go; where you lodge, I will lodge; your people shall be my people, and your God my God" (Ruth 1:16). Ruth and Naomi, like David and Jonathan, built on a shared experience. What made their relationship more than a just casual acquaintance (like the occasional coffee or round of golf we have with our friends), was an intentional commitment to each other, a covenant.

In a friendship-poor era, churches need to teach, bless, celebrate and support covenants of friendship. Our era is friendship poor. Part of the cause is the busyness and mobility of life. But most of the problem is that we don't understand or value friendship enough. Our churches (and schools and families) need to teach friendship and even create some liturgies and celebrations blessing and confirming covenants of friendship.

Aristotle explained that there are basically three kinds of friendship. The first is based on pleasure: we are friends because (and as long as) we enjoy each other. The second is based on utility: our friendship is based on what we can do for each other. The third is based on goodness, on a shared virtue or excellence. It is this third kind of friendship that can endure difficulty and last over time. Of course, this third form includes (at least at some times) the pleasure and utility of the first two forms. Unfortunately, our world knows mostly the friendships of pleasure and utility, and those are just not enough for character building.

Our agenda is straightforward: invest in deep, long-term friendships. Call up your "prospects" and test the waters; who is interested in giving your friendship more time? Who will commit to get together weekly? We need a couple of friends with whom to schedule regular time together for sharing the burdens and celebrating the joys of our lives, for encouraging and admonishing each other, holding each other accountable, loyally nurturing each other's growth in character. Get on the phone! Don't be discouraged if it takes a few tries before you find the committed friends you really need and want.

Households. The word "family" rarely appears in the Bible, which prefers to speak of "households." The "nuclear family" is a modern phenomenon in which parents and children attempt a life isolated from their extended family. The biblical pattern was for "nuclear families" to be inserted into the broader texture of the household, which may include more than just blood relatives.

Certainly husbands and wives, fathers, mothers, and children are at the core of most households. Spouses have roles to play in loving and caring for each other as they develop a common life (and hopefully become each other's best friend). Parents have their roles to play in producing and nurturing children. But we cannot do without the wisdom and counsel of grandparents, the richness added by other relatives, and the blessing and challenge of the guest and the stranger in the household.

This is a risky subject, I know. But I think that the trend toward living alone bodes ill for character. Everyone needs some private space to be healthy, but that place is healthiest when it is within a larger household wherein we regularly eat together, share the tasks of life and our stories and daily challenges. Such household community is healthiest when there is multigenerational interaction. Tending only to the self is not good for our character. It goes back to the earlier argument about why community is crucial for character. It is not good for one to dwell alone. Practically speaking, we are going to need to be very inventive here. Some of us may be able to move closer to our relatives and begin to work, rest, converse and eat together with some regularity. For others, the best we can do is more aggressive e-mailing, telephoning, writing and traveling.

In the absence or impossibility of reestablishing household community with our kin, perhaps we can invent an alternative household community by "adopting" parents, grandparents, brothers, sisters and children into our life and care. We cannot fulfill our agenda for character building nearly as well without some household dimension. Living together is partly what it is about.

Churches. The local parish church is also a crucial form of community involved in character building. Church is where that deeper "ontological" reality of community we discussed above can be acknowledged and built upon. Church reinforces our community with God, and it should reinforce our friendships and households in a healthy way. The church is the *koinonia* (the "community") created by God's Spirit.[7]

Jacques Ellul has written that it is

> in the Church [that] we might possibly discover a new style of Christian life, voluntary and true. . . . Such research is necessarily a corporate act. It is impossible for an isolated Christian to follow this path. I believe, in fact, that one of the essential conditions for its realization is . . . a true solidarity among Christians (a solidarity voluntarily created by obedience to the will of God). . . . In order to undertake this search for a new 'style of life,' every Christian ought to feel and to know that he is supported by others. . . . It will evidently be necessary to engage in a work which aims at rebuilding parish life, at discovering Christian community, so that people may learn fresh what the fruit of the Spirit is.[8]

Stanley Hauerwas also emphasizes how crucial the church is:

> As Christians we are at home in no nation. Our true home is the church itself, where we find those who, like us, have been formed by a savior who was necessarily always on the move. . . .
>
> They [the church] must, above all, be a people of virtue—not simply any virtue, but the virtues necessary for remembering and telling

---

[7]On the ways church was community in the New Testament era, see Robert Banks, *Paul's Idea of Community* (Peabody, Mass.: Hendrickson, 1994).

[8]Jacques Ellul, *The Presence of the Kingdom* (New York: Seabury, 1967), pp. 148-50.

the story of a crucified savior. They must be capable of being peaceable among themselves and with the world, so that the world sees what it means to hope for God's kingdom.[9]

The church is the community that carries and retells the grand, epic story in which our personal (and household) narratives have their place and meaning. The church is the community that takes us beyond the bounds of our friendships and households to embrace Jew and Gentile, slave and free, male and female—the wonderful diversity of God's kingdom. Church puts us in relationship with the full gamut of the spiritual gifts and ministries, the callings and burdens of the whole people of God.

The church is a hospital for the sick and a gym for the healthy. It is a laboratory for testing out the new life and a school for the creation of new character. Even its weakness, mediocrity and failure form the important lesson that God does not abandon us but stands by us in solidarity even in our weakness and failure. As Dietrich Bonhoeffer has written so powerfully, we must not let some ideal dreams of Christian community blind us to the reality and value of what God is doing in the church that already exists.[10]

> The church is a hospital for the sick, a gym for the healthy, a laboratory and a school for character.

Churchly community needs to be experienced at three levels. First, there is our experience of the local parish church as a whole—for example, in large group, usually multigenerational, worship. Many churches today are dividing their congregations according to worship- and music-style preferences, and this often means generational division. I think this is a terrible mistake, saying exactly the wrong thing both to Christians and to observers outside the faith. The world is fraught with divisions over musical tastes and personal preferences of one type or another. Our character is built by learning another more inclusive and richly diverse way of life. We want Pentecost, not Babel, as our model.[11]

---

[9] Stanley Hauerwas, *The Peaceable Kingdom* (South Bend, Ind.: University of Notre Dame Press, 1983), pp. 102-3.

[10] Dietrich Bonhoeffer, *Life Together* (London: SCM Press, 1954). A classic little book on community.

[11] Pentecost had diversity in its unity experience. Part of the reason why many today

Second, smaller or more specialized group fellowships are important to allow for more intensive relationships, study, prayer, caring, worship and service. This (not the large-group church gathering) is where affinity and perhaps even taste might have some legitimacy. Community with others challenged by the same sort of parenting or work or trials can be an important criterion at this second level.

Third, to be sure that we experience the broader dimensions of Christ's universal church, we need to be sure to have experiences of fellowship with Christians in other churches, other neighborhoods, other ethnic and theological enclaves. Joint worship services, retreats and service projects, pulpit and choir exchanges, and occasional visits to other church services—these are ways of overcoming the tendency of the churches to become isolated, homogeneous enclaves.

What shall we do about church? This is an extraordinarily difficult question. In general, I think we should try hard to be faithful members of a church close to where we live so that it is easier to (1) participate regularly and fully, (2) have people in for dinner and (3) be part of a living witness to the neighborhood. In general, I think we should not church-hop around but make a commitment and stick with it through thick and thin, unless the church becomes clearly unfaithful or clearly destructive to us and to our families.

Somehow we need to find our place in a churchly community, or our character will suffer. That's not the primary reason for church, but it is an important consideration for this study.

Neighborhood and workplace. Christians also need to seek a form of community with the *world* around them. Such community lacks the same spiritual foundations as the preceding examples. Nevertheless, it has a foundation in our common creation as people made in the image of God, and in the universal love of God for the world. We must not seek to live our lives in some kind of Christian fortress or ivory tower.

What I am thinking of is, for example, intentionally (not just casually) trying to get to know some people at our gym, in our office or

---

insist on having their taste for "contemporary" worship satisfied is because of the narrowness of the traditionalists—who are just as misguidedly narrow as any contemporary praise music addicts.

school, in our neighborhood—eating with them, working with them, listening to them, caring for them as we are able. Part of this includes reaching out to the weak, needy, and unloved—not just to the beautiful or powerful. Remember how Jesus was criticized: "This fellow welcomes sinners and eats with them" (Lk 15:2).

We need to listen and ask questions, not just talk and "witness." Good character gets built through encounter with the world, not just in Christian enclaves. In our places of work as well as our places of residence, there are important and valuable opportunities to build community. There is a great deal of interest today in corporate culture. Will we help create or improve it?

Our tendency, abetted by our society's propaganda, is to invest most of our time in our self and our interests. If Christians get beyond this, it is usually the church and maybe the family that next get some attention. But we are in the world as ambassadors for Christ, and this requires some significant efforts to build relationships with people outside the community of faith. Their language, interests and lifestyles may be far different from ours. If Jesus is our guide, however, we will be able to remain true to the character God requires of us—while we enter into relationships with some whose character is far different.

Rebuilding Your Community Life
1. commitment and time for God
2. build some deep, long-term friendships
3. help create/sustain a good household
4. vital participation in church and small group
5. one neighborhood/community group
6. a serious effort for community at work

This is an ambitious agenda, and yet if we are interested in building good character, we cannot pass over the critical importance of having a multidimensional community life.

For Reflection or Discussion

1. What has been your experience of friendship? Can you describe any ways your character and values were ever affected—for better or worse—by your friends?
2. Has any church you have ever been part of seemed to be a good place for its participants to develop strong character? How could churches improve on this, in your opinion?
3. What has been your experience of building better community in your school, workplace or neighborhood? What have you learned from this?

Four

THE GOODNESS OF GOD

*W*hat precisely is goodness in matters of character (and community)? How do we define, recognize and evaluate good character? What are the traits, attributes, values and virtues that make for goodness? We can move toward a satisfactory answer by first considering four basic options.

Goodness as our approval. In simplest terms, of course, "good" is our basic term of positive evaluation. Saying "that's good," means the evaluator is pleased and approves of something. Goodness, then, is a property or experience of an evaluator—a positive feeling, an intellectual affirmation or a value judgment. Certainly, there is some truth in this perspective. Furthermore, we all need a certain amount of acceptance and approval from others. It would be nice to have the sort of character that people around us approve of. It may surprise some Christians to discover that Paul argues (Rom 14:17-18) that those characterized by righteousness, peace and joy not only please God but have "human approval." This is only one of many biblical texts promising that, ordinarily, good godly character is admired and approved by others. (Proverbs is full of such comments.)

Some philosophers (called *emotivists*) took this position one step further and argued that approval is *all* that goodness means. "Good" *only* means that I approve of something, that "I like it"; "bad" only means "I disapprove!" This reductionist position is called *subjectivism* or *relativism*—a denial of any sort of intrinsic, transhistorical, transcultural or absolute goodness.

So goodness as approval is an incomplete concept. It is, of course, desirable to have that feeling of approval for the good and the right, but that feeling by itself is not a reliable guide to the good or right. And if the extreme position of emotivism were really true, there would be little point in wrestling together about ethics. Ethics would be an irrational, nonrelational waste of our time.

Goodness as God's decree. If the preceding position appeals to secular individualists, the next position appeals to conservative believers. In this position Christian ethics is simply a matter of "divine command" from God. A related (but not equivalent) notion has been called *nominalism* (as opposed to *realism*): something is good because God designates (names, denominates) it as such. In this view, God does not *recognize* the good and label it as such; rather, he *names* something good, and, because he's God, that's what it is. We may not be able to see why this something is good, but aware of our fallenness and finitude we obediently yield to God's prerogative.

Jacques Ellul comes as close to this position as we should go. He writes that to say that there is a good apart from God

> would mean that God is not God, that he is not sovereign, since he is determined by an excellence higher than himself. If God is God, it is he who determines the good. . . .
>
> Sin is not the failure to obey a morality. It is the very desire to determine that morality independently of God. . . .
>
> Let no one object that if the good is nothing other than the will of God the moral life becomes unadulterated incoherence, actions which succeed one another disconnectedly, blind and contradictory obediences. To say that is to form a strange concept of God! . . . God is one. There is no division or change in him, no contradiction. It is because he is one that his will is coherent and our moral life is coherent. . . . This will of God which gives

content to the good is not arbitrary. God does not call evil good.[1]

A nominalist-divine command approach seems to preserve the absolute authority of God against humanistic reason and presumption, and that's good (Ellul's primary audience for the quotations above was modern theologians sprinting away from the transcendence and authority of God). But we need to be very careful. A full-scale nominalism actually is akin to a sort of divine emotivism. God says "that's good" about something—and that's what it is, irrespective of its nature or characteristics or effects. God has every right to be an emotivist or nominalist as the Creator of all things! But I do not think he has done so. I think God created a world that is in no sense morally arbitrary. As Ellul says above, God does not call evil good. When God says something is good, that's because it really is good—good for him, good for us, good for the universe.

Goodness as effectiveness. In the classical Greek account of character, virtues (indeed all moral norms) are dependent on their *telos* (the goal or mission they serve) for their legitimacy and persuasiveness. Moral virtues, in a generic sense, guide and assist behavior to some end, be it happiness, pleasure, unity, rationality, the glory of God or something else. Goodness, on this reading, means effectiveness or usefulness. It is instrumentally justified.

For Plato and Aristotle, virtues are related to purposes. The purpose of the knife is to cut—so the virtues of a good knife are to be sharp, cut well and not get dull or break too easily. The purpose of a horse is transportation—so its virtues are strength, speed, endurance, gentleness and the capacity to carry heavy loads.

This sense of "goodness" is based on the objective or goal we wish to achieve. A classic distinction in modern moral philosophy has been between *deontological* and *teleological* norms. Deontological principles, rules and traits are *intrinsically* right (right irrespective of consequences or factors external to the act); teleological principles, rules and traits are *instrumentally* right (justified by the consequences they produce).[2]

---

[1]Jacques Ellul, *To Will and to Do: An Ethical Research for Christians* (Philadelphia: Pilgrim, 1969), pp. 10, 13, 23.

[2]I will explore this distinction more fully (but not too fully, I promise!) in *Doing Right*

This distinction is important on a practical decision-making level, but what it obscures is the fact that *all* ethical guidance is ultimately related to a *telos* (Greek for "end," "goal" or "purpose"). This is just as true for divine command moralists and for Immanuel Kant (king of the deontologists) as it is for any explicitly consequentialist thinker, like John Stuart Mill. For Kant, the *telos* that justifies all legitimate morality is universality and rationality. It is to satisfy this goal (i.e., to end with rational, universal ideas governing our behavior and our world) that Kant's ethics labors. Divine command nominalists also have a *telos*: a relationship of obedient submission to the Commander. That's the meaning of life: everyone and all creation is in obedient submission to God. This *telos* trumps all other contenders. But are these the best (or only) purposes our ethics can serve? I don't think so.

The primary challenge for "goodness as effectiveness," "instrumentalist," "consequentialist" views of ethics is how to determine the appropriate end or purpose of human life.[3] If the purpose of human life is expressed by the cynical phrase: "He who dies with the most toys wins"—then the "virtues" will be things like cunning, aggressiveness and sagacity in finance. One can easily see what the "virtues" would be for lives dedicated to fame, power, sex, money or possessions.

Our society tends to reduce human purpose to things like consumption and production. In our technological era there is a tendency to evaluate everything (and everybody) in quantitative terms. The vocabulary of goodness tends to merge with the language of success and measurable effectiveness. In short, good character does mean *effective* character—but we need more than that to have a satisfying position on what makes for good character.

Our modern, technological society tends to evaluate everything and everybody in terms of effectiveness, measurable success and quantifiable results. "Good" character must be evaluated by another standard.

Plato, Aristotle and their philosophical tradition considered and

---

[3]The second great challenge is coordinating means with ends; it is notoriously difficult to predict or control consequences. This has been one of the strongest arguments against teleological approaches

rejected such superficial pandering to our appetites and argued that *happiness* (for both individuals and their communities) was the final good, the final purpose of human life. Happiness is good in itself, intrinsically good; it is not pursued because it leads to something else. The Greek word for "happiness," *eudaimonia,* literally means "good-spirited." It has to do with human fulfillment, well-being and contentment, with both "doing well" and "faring well." Ethical systems that say that happiness is the ultimate good are called *eudemonistic.* Good character is thus constituted by the virtues and traits most likely to achieve happiness (and they thought justice, wisdom, courage and self-control were these central requirements).

In the nineteenth century, Jeremy Bentham, John Stuart Mill and the utilitarians argued that *pleasure* was a better way of describing the good. "Hedonism" is the name for ethical systems that propose pleasure as the good. In either case, *eudemonism* or *hedonism*, we need to remember that these older discussions of happiness and pleasure were not intended to justify excess or imbalance, for example, as in today's narcissistic "playboy" philosophies. Great place was given to the happiness and pleasure of knowing the truth, and of living a moderate, balanced existence. It may be fair to say that those who pursue the modern gods and goods that I disparaged above really are seeking happiness but just don't know what true happiness is.

Goodness as a property or attribute. In a fourth sense, goodness may refer to things that are *intrinsically* good. Something might be good in itself, good per se, good as an *end*, not just good as a *means* to something else. In this sense, goodness is a sort of property, almost like color (e.g., red or green), weight, size and so on are properties of things. Some philosophers have argued that we recognize such goodness through our reason or our moral intuition. Beauty, life, friendship, honor, peace, happiness, pleasure—many have argued that these are intrinsically good, moral realities, even if some twisted characters disagree and act differently. But there remain irresolvable disagreements about the list of intrinsic goods as well as the method for compiling the list.

A Christian perspective can say that when God created the world, he created it good—and he called it good. It was intrinsically, really good. Yes, of course, things got very bad with the Fall; moreover, part of this badness consisted of our human dimness of vision in even recognizing what goodness persists! But neither all the goodness nor all the capacity to recognize it was lost.

Many theologians have argued that God has planted some sort of moral sense or reason in his creatures (the "law written on the heart," or "written in nature") so that they can recognize such natural goodness. All Christians, however, should affirm that God has revealed this goodness in Jesus Christ and in Scripture. This theological view of goodness and its perception need not totally cancel out the alternatives. Rather, it governs, clarifies, corrects and illuminates our understanding of goodness in its various senses.

> God has not arbitrarily designated things as good and bad, right and wrong. God's moral guidance points the way to what is truly, really good in human life.

In summary, my position is that while God certainly has the power and the right to be an arbitrary dispenser of moral commands, I don't think that he has done so. God certainly could be a nominalist, but I don't think he has gone that route. I don't think God has played any games with us. The moral guidance of God is guidance on how to experience and achieve what is truly, really good in human life. A fundamental part of our task then will be to try to understand the *telos* we should pursue. What is God's ultimate purpose for us in life? We simply cannot understand or properly appreciate the biblical virtues without seeing them in intimate relationship with the great purposes of God for our human life.

> What Is "Goodness" of Character?
> 1. something we can approve of
> 2. what God approves or designates
> 3. traits/powers that enable us to achieve the ultimate good purposes of life
> 4. intrinsic, real, positive attributes

Deeper into the Meaning of Goodness

Defining goodness in terms of approval, divine fiat, effectiveness and intrinsic worth helps us see four angles on God's goodness. Two other points of orientation need to be given here.

Goodness is primary; evil is secondary. In the Bible "good" and "goodness" (Hebrew *tov*, Greek *agathos*, *kalos*) are frequently applied

to God as well as to human life. The vocabulary refers to a moral quality, an excellence, a harmony or a pleasing condition. Goodness is one
of life's main objectives: "Seek good and not evil, that you may live;
and so the LORD, the God of hosts, will be with you" (Amos 5:14). In a
wonderful passage, Paul says: "Do not be overcome by evil, but overcome evil with good" (Rom 12:21). It is not by becoming experts on
evil that we will acquire a good character. We must be aware of evil, but
our central task is to seek, understand and live out the good.[4]

Goodness is God's gift. In a profound sense we can not make ourselves into good characters. Paul says that "all have sinned and fall
short of the glory of God," and it is "God . . . at work in you, enabling
you both to will and to work for his good pleasure" (Rom 3:23; Phil
2:13). God causes us to be "born anew," gives us his Spirit and
remakes our character. "Goodness" is not, first of all, one of our works
but rather a gift of God and a "fruit of the Spirit" (see Gal 5:22-23).

Some theologians have feared that an ethics of virtue and character
will be a threat to biblical discipleship in two ways. First, they have
suspected that it smuggles a "works righteousness" back into the
Christian life. Certainly in the classical Greek tradition, virtue was an
achievement of human reason and will. But in the biblical tradition it
is not. Our virtue is wholly based in the gracious work of God and the
response God enables us to make in the gift of faith.

Second, they have suspected that an emphasis on virtue might
undermine the dynamic, existential nature of biblical ethics. Some
theologians (such as Jacques Ellul) argue that Christian ethics is not
about any sort of permanent change in our character but rather about
the obedient responses of a disciple standing before God in each
moment. But such an existentialist ethics of decision might be guilty of

---

[4]I have been told that workers in the United States Treasury Department do not
study counterfeit money nearly as much as the precise details of the real, authentic
thing—because the best way to be able to detect the bad, the counterfeit, is to be
expert in the real and the true. Studying and being absorbed in contemplation of
the good contributes to our becoming good. Since I've never been a "dog guy," I
also have to rely on hearsay that if you want to get a bone out of a dog's mouth, it is
better to throw down a steak next to him than to try to pull the bone out of his
mouth. Chapter eleven will look at some counterfeits and bones in the moral life,
but the major emphasis of this book is on the real thing: goodness.

selling short the power of God if it assumes that God cannot remold the content of the character of that disciple who stands before him. Furthermore, character is a dynamic notion: we can improve or we can backslide. Character and virtue ethics are not alien concepts imposed on Scripture—they are an account of growth and maturity in the Christian life.

> **A**n existentialist ethics of decision and of the in-the-moment guidance of the Spirit may be guilty of selling short God's power and desire to remold our character.

This dependence on God to give us goodness as a gift is both humbling and liberating. We are humbled in that whatever goodness we may achieve must be attributed to God's gracious work within us, not to our having become accomplished "moral athletes" on our own. We are liberated in that we do not have to bear the ultimate burden of reforming ourselves: we move forward, we try and try again, but we know our lives are given to God and are not to be taken back. In the end it is God's business to remake us.

The Way We Learn About Goodness

In chapter two (above) we considered the way our character is built. You will notice some repetition of those themes as we now ask how, if God is where we find the truth about goodness, we can learn about it.

With and without God? For Christians, the search for the good always retains its connection to God.[5] In his *Ethics Without God,* the atheist philosopher Kai Nielsen argues at length that this cannot be so. "We call God good because we have experienced the goodness of his acts, but in order to do this, in order to know that he is good or to have any grounds for believing that he is good, we must have an independent moral criterion that we use in making this predication of God."

---

[5]In my essay "Ethics With and Without God" in David W. Gill, ed., *Should God Get Tenure? Essays on Religion and Higher Education* (Grand Rapids, Mich.: Eerdmans, 1997), I argued, against Nielsen, that it is important for our pluralistic society to consider God- and religion-based approaches to ethics alongside the secular options. In a remarkable essay in *The Atlantic Monthly* ([December 1989]: 69-85), Glenn Tinder answered his title question "Can We Be Good Without God?" with a strong no; not just our church but our culture needs "transcendental backing" for its human values or we are in trouble. My purpose here is more modest: I would just like Christians to get their views of goodness from God!

"Morality cannot be based on religion. If anything, the opposite is partly true, for nothing can be God unless he or it is an object worthy of worship, and it is our own moral insight that must tell us if anything at all could possibly be worthy of worship."[6]

Blaise Pascal is often credited with saying, "There is a God-shaped vacuum in every human heart." I often add that there is also an ethics-shaped vacuum in every human heart. The need, if not also a faded memory, of the goodness of God persisted in the human race after eviction from Eden. All human beings, all cultures, have some kind of a morality or ethics. Just as people find or create gods and religions to try to fill the "God space" in their lives, so we create moralities to try to satisfy that "ethics space" in our lives, which has been empty since Adam and Eve rejected God in favor of seeking their own "knowledge of good and evil" from the forbidden tree.

Part of the allegedly innate "moral standards" that Kai Nielsen points to are really the residue of a historical and social conditioning we have all received to a greater or lesser degree. Especially in what was formerly called Christendom, we still benefit from some true insights into the good (though contaminated by many other influences, to be sure). That is part of why we recognize that God is good. It is not an independent morality but a remnant of God's creation (he shaped what is now our "ethics space" and gave us a conscience and some capacity to read the moral lessons of nature; see Rom 1—2) and a memory of God's activity in our history. Nielsen has not started with a sterile, blank slate but with some cultural/historical formation in the truth.

What does this mean for our Christian ethics of good character? It means that ethics must never be divorced from theology, nor discipleship from worship, nor study from prayer. We just don't "do" ethics without God centrally involved.

Hearing and telling the stories. The Bible is the true *Book of Virtues.* The stories in the Bible are character-forming moral instruction. To begin with, we learn about good character by immersing ourselves in biblical stories—of Adam and Eve, Cain and Abel, the Tower of

---

[6]Kai Nielsen, *Ethics Without God,* rev. ed. (Buffalo: Prometheus Books, 1990), pp. 56-57, 65.

Babel, Abraham and Sarah, Joseph, Ruth, Saul, David and Goliath, Daniel, Peter, Priscilla and Aquila, Paul and the early churches, and all the others. Biblical illiteracy is a tragedy for our civilization, but it is a *scandal* as well as a tragedy for biblical people. Reading, rereading, discussing and mulling over these stories, personally and in the community of faith that "owns" them, is a crucial exercise in character formation.

> **R**eading, discussing, and mulling over the biblical stories—over and over and over—is a crucial exercise in the formation of a good, godly character.

Most important are the stories of Jesus: his birth and youth, his travels and encounters with children, women, Samaritans, political and religious leaders, the poor, hungry, oppressed and lost, with his small band of men and women disciples. This is our Lord and Leader, God in our history. The story of the final days, the trial, death and resurrection of our Lord is told in detail by four different Evangelists: this is *the* story of God's goodness, in light of which all the other biblical stories take on newer, fuller meaning.

The Bible stands above all other literature, of course, but it is also valuable to hear the stories of people outside of the scriptural canon. Reading biographies or watching portrayals of the faithful and courageous can shape us toward those same character traits. The sleaze assault in so much of today's film and television needs to be contested and replaced in our lives by more edifying fare.

Studying the teaching. The counterpart to these narratives is the teaching of the Bible. The laws and principles of the Pentateuch, the meditations of the Psalms, the counsels of the Proverbs, the proclamations of the prophets, the sermons and letters of the apostles, the revelation of John—these are instruction in God's goodness. Reading, studying and discussing the biblical teaching, memorizing classic passages—this also must be at the foundation of our character instruction.

As in the case of the biblical stories, so in the case of the direct ethical teaching of the Bible, Jesus' contribution must be at the center. The parables, sermons, prayers, discourses and conversations of Jesus are the interpretive anchor of our search for instruction on biblical character. The question of which ancient reports and records of Jesus' teaching to accept and which to reject as apocryphal was decided for

Christians by the early church councils. Nothing that has been discovered by technical biblical scholars should (or need) dissuade us from receiving the New Testament as an accurate, multifaceted report of our Lord's teaching. This is our canon, our book; we are convinced that it is God's story, God's book—reliable, persuasive and illuminating.

Can we recite the Ten Commandments? Psalm 23? The Beatitudes? The Lord's Prayer? Sorry, but one out of four isn't good enough if we want to know God's will.

The Bible stands above all other instruction for us, but it is also valuable to read the ethical ideas, analyses and counsel of others (as we have already been doing with Plato, Aristotle, Ellul, Hauerwas and others). We all have decisions to make about how we use our time and what we will read. Increasing the virtue input and diminishing some other inputs can have an impact!

Practices: imitation and obedience. The goodness of God is a gift. It is not just a set of stories and ideas. We receive this gift with open hands, and it is ours. However, a gift needs to be unwrapped, taken out of its package and integrated into our daily life. Unfortunately, for many Christians the gifts of God remain on the shelf. This is a terrible mistake. "Discern" what is good; "hold fast" to what is good; "work for the good of all"; become a "lover of goodness" (Rom 12:2, 9; Gal 6:10; Tit 1:8).

We have an activist role to play in the process. God gives us the gift of his life and goodness, we read the biblical stories and lessons on goodness and character, but then we must put them into practice. Goodness cannot be truly known or learned without practicing it. Christians are called "to put away your former way of life, your old self . . . and to be renewed in the spirit of your minds, and to clothe yourselves with the new self, created according to the likeness of God in true righteousness and holiness" (Eph 4:22-24; cf. Col 3:9-10).

Two ways we put on this new self are "imitation" and "obedience." In our self-absorbed era it is not popular to speak of the "imitation of Christ," and still less of "obedience to God." Mother Teresa was the exception rather than the rule, in her joyful imitation of Jesus, but everyone imitates some model or other. We all obey one authority or another. Bob Dylan put it this way: "You may be a rich man, or you may be a king, but still you gotta serve somebody."

The Bible gives us *examples* of the good, above all in Jesus Christ, and we need to understand these and "mimic" them (the literal meaning of "imitate"). Jesus' example in telling the truth, in serving the disciples (e.g., washing their feet), and in reaching out to the sick and the outcast is part of this model for our imitation. The Bible also gives us *instruction* in goodness, and we need to understand this and obey it. If we don't practice the ethical guidance of Jesus and Scripture, we cannot truly know it.

Cultivate community. Finally, in this pedagogy of Christian character, it is essentially impossible to learn about good Christian character without some significant friendship and community. I won't repeat all that we said in chapter three about the importance of community and its various forms, but our friends and communities can pray with and for us, prod and encourage us to faithfulness, and help us understand and interpret what we study and experience. Communities are the places where the great story of God's goodness gets told, updated and celebrated. Our communities help us remember the story and the lessons, figure out what they mean and then apply them to our daily life.

> **L**earning About Good Character
> 1. live in relationship with God
> 2. hear and tell the stories
> 3. study the teaching
> 4. imitate and obey
> 5. cultivate the community of faith

The Content of God's Character

In the Christian view, God is the origin of the true good. Any notions we have of goodness need to be supplemented and rigorously corrected by the goodness of God. God is Good in itself. God is entirely Good.[7] "Give thanks to him, bless his name. For the LORD is good" (Ps 100:4-5). We will need God's self-revelation, presence and help to know, to be and to do the good, just as he promised Moses, "I will make all my goodness pass before you" (Ex 33:19) and as he delivered to Micah "He has told you, O mortal, what is good" (Mic 6:8).

---

[7]Two excellent studies of the goodness of God are Donald G. Bloesch, *God the Almighty: Power, Wisdom, Holiness, Love* (Downers Grove, Ill.: InterVarsity Press, 1995); and Thomas L. Trevethan, *The Beauty of God's Holiness* (Downers Grove, Ill.: InterVarsity Press, 1995).

The content of a good character is the content of God's character. Goodness is godliness (literally, "God-like-ness"). Human beings are made in the image and likeness of God, and they are destined to be conformed to the image of God's Son. God, especially as revealed and incarnated in our history in Jesus Christ, is our model of goodness. So what is the character of God's goodness?

Naming goodness. The content of God's goodness is revealed, first of all, by his *names*. In biblical tradition one's name reveals one's character. When God reveals himself to his people through the name "Yahweh" (Ex 3:14—connected to the verb *hayah*, "to be"—often represented in English Bibles as "the LORD"), he is showing himself to be existence—the self-existent one, the source of all being, existence and life, past, present and future. So the first thing we can say about the goodness of God is that he is life, and he is for life. He brings his life to the world and the people.

> The content of a good character is defined by the content of God's character. Goodness is the same as godliness.

God is also the Lord (the leader), the Almighty, the Everlasting Father, the Prince of Peace, the Wonderful Counselor, the King of kings and the Good Shepherd, to recall some of his better-known names. *Jesus* means "Savior"—a concept every bit as central to the character of God as the prolife "Yahweh." All of these aspects of God's goodness displayed in his names have their counterparts in our own goodness of character. If God is the Prince of Peace, then I want to be a (Lieutenant) Prince of Peace; as a father I want to be like the Everlasting Father; I want to be a stubborn voice for life like Yahweh.

Creative goodness. We understand God's goodness, second, as it is demonstrated in his creation.[8] "In the beginning when God created the heavens and the earth, the earth was a formless void and darkness covered the face of the deep. . . . Then God said, 'Let there be light'; and there was light. And God saw that the light was good" (Gen 1:1-4). The

---

[8]On the ethical implications of creation, see Karl Barth, *Church Dogmatics,* III/4, trans. G. W. Bromiley (Edinburgh: T & T Clark, 1961); Henri Blocher, *In the Beginning: The Opening Chapters of Genesis* (Downers Grove, Ill.: InterVarsity Press, 1984); Dietrich Bonhoeffer, *Creation and Fall: Temptation* (New York: Macmillan, 1959; orig. pub. 1937).

God who is, creates. By his word and acts he shapes what is formless, he fills what has been a void, and he illuminates what has been in darkness. And then he sees that "it is good."

But what, more precisely, is this creative goodness? Here is a brief, whirlwind review: Creation has life and the power to reproduce life; beauty as well as usefulness; variety and harmony, diversity and unity; individuality in balance with community; partnership in the care of the earth and the reproduction of human life; good, meaningful work and good sabbath rest; vast freedom within wise boundaries. The only thing that God declares "not good" is for one to dwell alone (Gen 2:18). Humanity must be lived out in cohumanity and relationship. These are some of the major characteristics of God's creative goodness.

Before moving away from the Creation story we should note carefully the prohibition of taking of the fruit of the "tree of the knowledge of good and evil." The Fall of humanity from its created state of goodness occurs precisely when the knowledge of good and evil is sought outside of an obedient relationship with God. Much of the history of moral philosophy is a continuation of this desire to grasp the fruit of the "ethics tree" (the tree of the knowledge of good and evil)—without the God who created it.

This Fall and its consequences tell us a lot about the basic character of evil: (1) alienation (running and hiding) from God, (2) alienation from each other (accusation, isolation in tasks intended for partnership), (3) alienation from nature (thorns and thistles, pain and toil), and (4) an interior alienation from the true self (shame and fear). It is but a step to the jealousy, competitiveness and violence of Cain and Abel, and then the unfolding of the whole story of the subjugation of women, the practice of polygamy, the resort to warfare and the despair of individual life without God.

The Garden of Eden is behind us, and there is no going back. The creative goodness of God is scarred but not defeated. The word of God that created and identified the true good is not withdrawn but is reexpressed, recalled and retold through human history. We often find biblical texts such as "The heavens are telling the glory of God; and the firmament proclaims his handiwork" (Ps 19:1). The first of two great themes in the worship described in the Apocalypse (Rev 4) is the worthiness and glory of God as Creator.

Thus the lessons on goodness from the creation should not be over-looked. How could this goodness of God the Creator guide our own char-acter formation? Our first lesson must be to reject any ill-fated quest for an ethics without God and instead hear what God himself says is the true good. Then we focus (like the Creator) on the good—not on "the knowledge of good and evil." We try to overcome evil with good, not with our knowledge of good and evil. We also see that good character is inclined to teamwork and partnership among both men and women, to beauty as well as usefulness and effectiveness, to caring for the earth as stewards of God's possession and so on. The Creation accounts of Gene-sis are not just to tell us where we came from, they intend to guide our character and ethics as well. A basic part of the goodness of God's char-acter is that he is always at work creating something that truly, recogniz-ably, is good. That has to be our objective as well.

Redemptive goodness. Since the ejection from Eden, human history has been laced with (but by no means limited to!) violence, corruption, lies and slavery. People are in bondage, injured, alienated and hungry. Thus God's goodness is expressed since the Fall not just in creating good things but in his *redemption* (buying people out of bondage into freedom), *salvation* (saving the lost and condemned) and *reconcilia-tion* (restoring relationships of peace and well-being).[9]

Israel's prophets and sages recalled God's goodness in creation but spoke even more of God's redemptive, liberating goodness. Israel's exo-dus from slavery in Egypt and then her return from exile in Babylon much later are two pivotal examples of God's salvation and redemp-tion. David's psalms speak continually of the greatness and goodness of God's redemption and deliverance from distress.

The lessons of God's redemptive goodness for our character building include the virtues of realism (about the suffering, self-deception and bondage in our world), hope (for a better tomorrow), compassion and justice (for the poor and downtrodden). Our character is not launched

---

[9]On the ethical implications of redemption, see John Howard Yoder, *The Politics of Jesus* (Grand Rapids: Eerdmans, 1972); and Richard B. Hays, *The Moral Vision of the New Testament* (San Francisco: HarperSanFrancisco, 1996)

into an Eden of possibilities but into an Egypt or Babylon with all of its challenges. Understanding and imitating God's redemptive goodness is essential. I summarize it by saying that I want my character to be one that is always thinking about how to help, heal, free and reconcile people. That's a central attribute of God's ongoing character—and thus part of our standard of goodness.

Incarnational goodness. Jesus is the clearest, fullest revelation of goodness of God. Hebrews says that Jesus is "the exact imprint of God's very being" (Heb 1:3). Paul says that Christ is both Creator and Redeemer and that in him "the whole fullness of deity dwells bodily" (Col 1:14-16; 2:9). John reports that Jesus has "manifested the *name*" (describing the character) of God, has not just spoken his own *words* but the words of his heavenly Father, and has not just *acted* on his own but that God has acted in him (Jn 17:4, 6, 8).

In his proclamation of truth, good news and forgiveness, in his actions to heal the sick, exorcise the demon-possessed, feed the hungry, teach the ignorant, reconcile the alienated, and love, serve and finally die for all those in need, Jesus models and reveals the goodness of God. We are destined to be "conformed to the image of his Son" (Rom 8:29).

It cannot be stressed enough how central Jesus must be to our character building. He is the charac-

> Jesus centers our understanding of what God's goodness looks like in our fallen world. When life's issues get very complex— or when the Bible gets confusing or unclear— he is the solid anchor to which we always return.

ter we would like to be like. We would like his values and his virtues. When life gets very complex (or when the Bible gets confusing or unclear!), he is the anchor and center to which we return. Jesus stands at the beginning, center and end of Christian character development, as our teacher and as our model. We might say that *ontologically* (i.e., in terms of ultimate "being") God's goodness resides in the Trinity (Father, Son and Holy Spirit), but that *epistemologically* (i.e., in terms of our "knowledge") it is available most fully and clearly in Jesus.

The Incarnation was God bringing his goodness close to us, right into our history and our daily, ordinary life. Thus, one of our traits and habits must also be to bring God's goodness right into our relationships, our workplaces, our neighborhoods, our political life, and so on. Bringing goodness into people's daily lives—that's good character.

Eschatological goodness. Another critical perspective on God's goodness comes from eschatology—the doctrine of the "last things." Jesus is called the "bright and morning star" of the new day that is dawning. This new day will only be fully here in the future. The apocalyptic and eschatological writings of the Bible provide the outlines (often in very colorful imagery) of that final day when God's goodness reigns everywhere in heaven and on earth. Paul says, even though not here yet, the "day is near," we should live now "as in the day," assisted by the Holy Spirit, who is the "the pledge" (down payment) on the future (Rom 13:11-14; Eph 1:14).

The final, ultimate good at which a Christian character aims is not personal happiness, pleasure, or fulfillment in any narrow sense but rather the robust vision of God's goodness in an eternal day to come. The means we use must conform to that end; the means should be congruent with and exhibit the character of the end. God's end not only "justifies the means," it "specifies the means," which must not violate or contradict the goodness of the end. If the end is a peaceable kingdom, we must now employ peaceable means; if the end is a kingdom of truth, we can never justify deceptive or fraudulent means.

This eschatological goodness of God affects our character first by disposing us always to be the bearers of hope in our world, as Jesus was. We believe our good God will have the last word on human history and struggle, and it will be redemptive and liberating. Our character should follow God's example in bringing hope into daily life. From what we can tell, swords will be beaten into plowshares, peace will reign, and the nations will each and all bring their glory into God's eternal kingdom. We cannot pretend that our present world is the New Jerusalem, but we can try to have a character that bears witness to this great future, rather than to ways that are mired in the past.

Historical goodness. Let's keep in mind two important realities. First of all, nobody but Jesus could ever be consistently or wholly good in our history. The biblical saga clearly shows that God takes people where they are and that in their lives they experience the cosmic struggle of good and evil. Mistakes are made, sins are committed, and ignorance is triumphant more often than we would like. But God does not abandon us despite the scandal this represents. Christianity, I like to say, is a religion with very low admission standards—unlike most other religions.

> **F**our Themes in a Godly Character
> 1. Creation: always create something good
> 2. Redemption: try to heal and free others
> 3. Incarnation: bring goodness into daily life
> 4. Eschaton: bring hope alive, lean forward

Second, God does his good work not just through "card-carrying" Christians but through others as well. There is, after all, some approximation of God's good to be had from the "ethics tree," even though it is incomplete and inadequate. The goodness of God's creation persists, in spite of everything. The apostle Paul says that even the hostile Roman political authorities can be the servants of God's good (Rom 13:3-4). The reach of God's redemptive love is not confined to the length of Christians' arms! So when we see creative and redemptive goodness displayed by non-Christians, we should not be surprised or reject it or minimize it. Rather, we should give thanks to God and affirm it.

For example, if a company introduces a flexible scheduling or job-share program to enable employees to better fit parenting into their life and work—if it sets aside resources to assist homeless or jobless people get back on their feet—these moves ought to be applauded as true goodness. They are reflections of creative and redemptive goodness, whether their instigators are conscious of it or not. Christian ethics is not about criticizing and undermining others—nor is it about pride or arrogance. We receive God's word and help as gifts, seek to be faithful to what we have been given, and humbly share these gifts with others.

For Reflection or Discussion

1. When you say that someone is a "really good man" or a "really good woman"—what do you mean? What makes for such goodness in your view?

2. Is it too distant (and thus impractical) for us to hold out God's own character as our primary model for what a good character should be like?

3. What personality or story in the Bible has made a positive impact on your life? What virtues were especially impressive? Any negative examples?

Five

POURING A NEW FOUNDATION

*S*o we come to the question of ultimate purpose. What is the meaning and purpose of our life? What is the ultimate goal or telos? When we figure this out, we can then progress to a delineation of the virtues that will empower and assist us in achieving that telos. Happiness, pleasure, complete rationality, personal salvation, eternity in heaven and total submission to Almighty God—these are among the nominees. But none adequately capture the purpose of human life as Jesus and Scripture present it.

The Mission of A Good Character
I want to propose that we think of the purpose and mission of human life as having three tightly interwoven aspects. The first and most important of these purposes has to do with our relationship with God: knowing, loving and glorifying our Creator, Redeemer and Friend. The second purpose concerns our relationships with other people. This part of the mission needs to be elaborated in several directions because these others may be near or distant, enemies or friends, and so on. In

short, our mission is to love these neighbors, to promote conditions in which they can know truth and experience life, and to retard or ameliorate conditions that harm them. Third, our mission is to be blessed personally, to experience the fullness and wholeness of life as God intended for us and our intimate companions.

The "interweave" is that it is impossible to separate these three aspects from each other. Our personal flourishing depends on our relationships with God and others. Our mission to love others cannot be achieved without the sustenance of the relation with God and the growth of a self sufficient to serve others. Our ultimate purpose in relationship to God cannot be achieved if the mission to self and others is forsaken.

Knowing, loving and glorifying God. The ultimate purpose of human life is to achieve (or "restore") a certain relationship with God. Already in the Creation, humans were made in the image and likeness of God. They spoke with God, shared in his work and lived in his presence. The history of redemption since the Fall is a history of God calling us back into relationship with himself. "You shall be my people and I will be your God" is an often-repeated refrain in the Old Testament. God wishes human beings to be in communion, not alienation, with himself. "The LORD your God has chosen you . . . to be his people, his treasured possession. . . . The LORD set his heart on you and chose you . . . because the LORD loved you" (Deut 7:6-8). Jesus chose the disciples not just to do things but "to be with him" (Mk 3:13-14). "If I go and prepare a place for you, I will come again and will take you to myself, so that where I am, there you may be also" (Jn 14:3). So when I say "knowing" God is part of the *telos,* I mean in the personal sense and not in some abstract sense.

The whole law and prophets are summarized in the command to "love the LORD your God with all your heart, and with all your soul, and with all your might." This is from the opening of the *shema* in Deuteronomy 6, and it is the first half of Jesus' great double-love commandment. "Loving God" follows directly from knowing God. God first loves us; we then love him. Yes, to love means to serve and to sacrifice, but it also means to feel affection and deep friendship. God wants our love in all of its dimensions.

And finally, we glorify God. We glorify him by words and actions pointing to who he really is. Glorifying God is honoring him with the truth about himself, celebrating his greatness. The truly virtuous life draws attention and bears witness to its source, to God, the fountain of all goodness. It cannot do otherwise for this is a rare goodness not invented by humanity, not arising from the wisdom of the world and not exhibited or practiced by human strength alone. God is honored and glorified when this character is displayed.

Knowing, loving, glorifying God—this is the first component in the good *telos* of good character. It is a great purpose for our lives. Pursuing this mission gives meaning and adventure to life in ways that the pursuit of money or even happiness cannot. The virtues of a good character, then, are the powers and capabilities, the habits and dispositions, which help us to know, love and glorify God. If they don't help us toward that goal, they are not virtues but vices.

Salt, light and neighbor love. The second component of the *telos* of a good character has to do with our neighbors around us—including our family, our church, those we work with, and those who are distant from us. It even includes our enemies. The goal is to love our neighbor as our self. Both Jesus and Paul taught that this neighbor love is the summary and the fulfillment of the whole Old Testament law. John asked how we could possibly say we love God if we don't love our neighbors. In his Sermon on the Mount, Jesus makes sure that we understand that this includes our enemies and those who repay us evil for good.

Part what this entails is building up the Christian community. The biblical virtues are taught, and the blessings promised, to disciples in community. It is impossible to achieve good character without the community. In the community gathered around Jesus, this new, blessed life is possible. Good character begins by coming to Jesus and learning from him. But it requires a community of faith in which to be learned and practiced. Chapter three gives the full argument.

But our character is intended not just for the community of faith but to benefit the larger world around us. In fact, going out into the world and loving our neighbors with God's creative and redemptive goodness is essential for our growth; it is not just for the world's benefit. To return to my football metaphor from chapter one, no team will experience what it is to be good without playing against other teams in the league. Intrasquad scrimmages and locker-room talk is fine and necessary, but if that's where it ends, something essential is lost, not just to the other teams but to our own players. Christian character is intended for presence, service and witness in the world. We are called just as decisively to be "in the world" as Jesus was, as to be "not of the world" as Jesus was not (see Jn 17:14-18).

We could describe this part of the *telos* as having two components: the Great Commission and the Great Commandment. The first represents the mission to tell everybody the truthful good news of God's new kingdom. The second would make it our goal to reach out in love to everybody. Good character then would be composed of the virtues that empower and guide us to those two accomplishments/goals.

> When Jesus says "you are the salt of the earth" and "you are the light of the world," he is referring precisely back to the Beatitudes character he has just presented.

Another way to describe the neighbor side of our mission is to use the great phrases of Jesus, who said that those who are characterized by the eight Beatitudes are the "salt of the earth" and the "light of the world" (Mt 5:13-16). These are powerful metaphors based in daily life experience. Salt has the impact of seasoning and of preserving (e.g., meat) from decay. Salt retards the growth of evil. Light makes it possible to see clearly what is around us, and it also is an essential condition for growth (photosynthesis) and life. Following hard on the Beatitudes, I believe that Jesus was saying that men and women with the Beatitudes' character traits would have this salting and lighting impact on the world. Restated, if part of our *telos* and mission is to salt the earth and light the world, the character traits of the Beatitudes are essential to empower such an achievement.

So even though Christian ethics is for disciples, it is not self-serving. Just before beginning the Sermon on the Mount and the Beatitudes, the text says that Jesus "saw the crowds"—and then taught his disciples. But the crowds were looking on, listening, observing—and would eventually benefit from this salt and light. The biblically virtuous life blesses others around us.

Not happiness but makarios. Finally, the good *telos* includes our desire to be "blessed," personally and with our intimate family and friends. More than "happiness" (which is too subjective), this goal is "blessedness" (Greek *makarios*)—an objective condition of "well-being." Several aspects of this blessing are described in the second part of each of Jesus' Beatitudes: having the kingdom of heaven, being comforted, inheriting the earth, being satisfied, receiving mercy, seeing God and being called a child of God. The biblically virtuous life is the truly good life in spiritual and material, and present and future terms.

Psalm 1 famously begins "Blessed are those." The Lord, on giving the Law to Moses and the people, said that if the people lived out its guidance, it would "go well" with them and they would "live long in the land" the Lord your God was giving them (Deut 4:40; 5:29; 6:18). It is God's will that we be blessed. Despite the suffering and difficulty of life and relationships in our fallen world, the traits of a good, biblical character are intended to maximize your likelihood of having a blessed life. These virtues will sometimes help us to achieve the good, in other cases they help us cope with the bad things in ways that minimize their negative impact or convert a negative into a positive.

It is biblical and faithful to want God to bless you and your loved ones. The character traits we explore in this book will help lead to such blessing. But we must be careful at several points. First, the most virtuous person in history was betrayed by his closest friends and crucified at age thirty-three. In our broken world there is no formula for automatic good times, approval or other blessings. Our "formula" is the best we can do in such a world. It is worth our commitment, even knowing that things may sometimes go badly in this life.

Second, because of the sickness of our self-centered, narcissistic culture we must take special care not to forget that in an authentic Christian ethic there can be no personal blessedness without it being interwoven with blessing our neighbors and blessing God. We will face constant temptations to make ourselves the top priority again and even to detach our self from God and our neighbors.

Third, we must be vigilant about not confusing God's version of the blessed life with that promoted by our media. There will be some overlap, undoubtedly, but God's blessing is not much like what they give out on *The Price Is Right* or *Wheel of Fortune*, nor is it the lifestyles of the rich and famous. The blessed lifestyle of the faithful and loving is much better—and much different. (You will have to decide whether you agree with me after finishing the book!)

The Virtues That Support the Mission

Finally, we are ready to look at the good virtues that serve the good *telos* described above. We will focus on two accounts of character traits in the New Testament. Actually, the biblical material is immense. Think of how often the Proverbs commend certain character traits, like wisdom, diligence and honesty. Throughout the New Testament there are several vice and virtue lists telling us what kinds of people and what kinds of traits are good and pleasing and part of the new life, and which traits are bad and offensive and worthy of severe condemnation and judgment. The "fruit of the Spirit" and the "works of the flesh" are a famous example (Gal 5:19-23).

The Goals of Christian Character
1. God is known, loved and glorified
2. your neighbors are loved
3. the earth is salted = evil is restrained
4. life, light and growth in the world
5. you and yours are fully blessed

We will focus on the two most famous and influential accounts of character in the New Testament: the three Pauline or theological virtues of faith, hope and love—and the eight (or nine) Beatitudes at the beginning of Jesus' Sermon on the Mount, augmented only by holiness, wisdom, joy and courage—four other virtues prominent in both testaments.

Faith, hope and love. I am drawn to faith, hope and love as an account of good character most of all because of their prominent place in the New Testament. Jacques Ellul also organized his theological ethics around these three themes. Long before Ellul, Thomas Aquinas explicated these virtues in his *Summa Theologica*, and long before him Augustine wrote his *Enchiridion on Faith, Hope, and Love*. Many other writers and teachers of ethics and discipleship as well as biblical commentators have contributed to our understanding of the centrality of these virtues as an account of Christian character.[1]

---

[1]On the theological virtues, see Augustine, *The Enchiridion on Faith, Hope, and Love* (Chicago: Regnery Gateway, 1961); Thomas Aquinas, *Treatise on the Virtues* (South Bend, Ind.: University of Notre Dame Press, 1966); Emil Brunner, *Faith,*

Faith, hope and love are sometimes called the "Pauline" virtues because of their frequent recurrence in Paul's writings. Here are some examples: "And now faith, hope, and love abide, these three; and the greatest of these is love" (1 Cor 13:13). "We have heard of your faith in Christ Jesus and of the love that you have for all the saints, because of the hope laid up for you in heaven" (Col 1:4-5). "We always give thanks to God . . . remembering . . . your work of faith and labor of love and steadfastness of hope in our Lord Jesus Christ" (1 Thess 1:2-3).

The letter to the Hebrews, probably written by an associate of Paul, and Peter in his writings also use faith, hope and love as an account of Christian discipleship (Heb 10:22-24; 1 Pet 1:3-9). Jesus doesn't provide faith, hope and love in a one-sentence account of character, but these three terms (or concepts) are often on his lips, and the ideas they represent pervade his message. The language of faith and belief is everywhere, along with the language of love, in Jesus' teaching. The hope and the promise of God are never far from sight, even when the word "hope" is not used.

We will examine each of these virtues in detail in coming chapters. A few general comments are appropriate before looking at the details. These virtues were called the "infused" virtues by Thomas Aquinas, in contrast to the natural virtues of justice, wisdom, courage and self-control. Aquinas believed that faith, hope and love were infused in us by the Holy Spirit, whereas the four cardinal virtues were accessible to reason. He also believed that the theological virtues guided us to our supernatural end, to see God while the cardinal virtues guided us to our natural end, happiness.

In my opinion, all seven of these virtues are to some extent understandable to reasonable human beings, and all seven require some infusion by God's Spirit. The cardinal virtues are not alien to the New Testament. Justice/righteousness is everywhere and is no less the gift of God than is faith, hope or love. The natural-supernatural "end" distinction is also too much of a dichotomy. Faith, hope and love are intensively related to our this-worldly existence, not just to a supernatural, beatific vision. Justice, courage, wisdom and self-control are of major relevance to the life with God as well as the life of earthly affairs. I value Thomas Aquinas's insights very much, but I do not agree on these issues.

Jonathan Wilson has a fine discussion of faith in relation to knowing and education, hope in relation to being and worshiping, and love in relation to doing and hospitality.[2] Other commentators have argued that faith relates us to God's great works in the past (e.g., we believe in the resurrection of Jesus), that hope relates us to God's work in the future (e.g., we hope for the return of Christ), and that love relates us to God's work in the present.[3] But faith is as much a virtue orienting us to the present as it is to the past. Hope affects our present as much as our future orientation. The past-present-future distinction has some appeal but doesn't completely hold true.

It could also be argued that faith primarily restructures our relationship to God, love primarily restructures our relationship with others, and hope (the most subjective of the three) primarily restructures the self. This is close to the message of Hebrews 10:22-24 (draw near to God in faith . . . provoke one another to love . . . hold fast your hope without wavering) and Colossians 1:4-5 (faith in Christ . . . love for the saints . . . hope for you laid up in heaven). I believe this perspective is true but still insufficient to understand the full meaning of these virtues. How could one possibly say that love is not as much a restructuring of our relationship to God as it is to our neighbor—or that faithfulness and hopefulness don't fundamentally change our relationships with others?

We need to think not only about each individual virtue but also their interrelationships and the ways they concentrate on, or cut

> **C**ultivating and practicing the four classical, cardinal virtues of justice, wisdom, courage and self-control requires just as much infusion of God's Spirit as the theological virtues of faith, hope and love.

---

[2]Jonathan Wilson, *Gospel Virtues* (Downers Grove, Ill.: InterVarsity Press, 1998).

[3]"We live in the past by faith; we live in the future by hope; we live in the present by love." Brunner, *Faith, Hope, and Love*, p. 13. Brunner means that in faith we are related to what God accomplished at the cross and empty tomb—and in faith we believe that God has forgiven our own past.

across, categories like past/present/future, God/neighbor/self, Father/
Son/Spirit and so on.

Jesus' Beatitudes. Our second focus in constructing this account of
character will be the Beatitudes.[4] Although Jesus
often returns to various components in the list
(notably in the "Sermon on the Plain" in Lk 6),
the opening of the Sermon on the Mount gives the
complete account. Why should this list of virtues
be so dominant in this book on building moral
character? First of all, it is because these are the
teachings of our Lord. I don't mean to imply either
that Paul was not speaking for this same Lord
when he wrote about faith, hope and love or the
fruit of the Spirit—or that Matthew and his assistants had nothing to
do with the literary presentation of the Sermon on the Mount. But the
church has received the New Testament as the Word of God, and we
view the Sermon on the Mount as an accurate account of our Lord's
teaching.

The Pauline,
Theological Virtues
1. faith: trust,
 loyalty, commit-
ment
2. hope: confident
expectation
3. love: sacrificial
service; friend-
ship

In his historical setting I believe Jesus probably taught the Beatitudes *dozens* if not hundreds of times during his three years of public
ministry, to large crowds outside and to small gatherings in homes. Do
we know any good teacher who doesn't do this? So the fact that Luke
has "Blessed are you poor" and Matthew has "Blessed are the poor in
Spirit" is not a problem at all. He probably said both (and several other
variations!) many times.[5]

---

[4]Among the most helpful studies of the Beatitudes are Robert Guelich, *The Sermon
on the Mount: A Foundation for Understanding* (Dallas: Word, 1982); D. Martyn
Lloyd-Jones, *Studies in the Sermon on the Mount* (Grand Rapids, Mich.: Eerdmans, 1971); Alphonse Maillot, *Les Beatitudes* (Paris: Librairie Protestante [le
christianisme au vingtieme siecle], n.d.); and John R. W. Stott, *Christian Counter-
Culture: The Message of the Sermon on the Mount* (Downers Grove, Ill.: InterVarsity Press, 1978).

[5]I don't mean to say that all apparent discrepancies can be resolved this way (e.g.,
the differences in the accounts of Peter's denial of Christ are a more difficult historical puzzle). But in the case of stories, parables and Beatitudes told by an itinerant
teacher, I am baffled by the total lack of imagination of many biblical scholars
(although this imagination runs wild about the fifth evangelist Q [Quentin, I think
it was]).

The Beatitudes we will study are at the beginning of the Sermon on the Mount (Mt 5:3-11). As with faith, hope and love, let me make a few general introductory comments before exploring the individual virtues in coming chapters.

First, the context is set up by the following statement: "When Jesus saw the crowds, he went up the mountain; and after he sat down, his disciples came to him. Then he began to speak, and taught them, saying . . ." (Mt 5:1-2). Jesus is teaching his *disciples*—so this is an ethic for people in relationship to him, not directly transferable to those without such a relationship. The symbolism of Jesus going up on a mountain to teach and of this discourse (the whole Sermon on the Mount, Mt 5—7) as the first of five great teaching blocks in Matthew—all of this looks a lot like a new Moses with a new Law/Pentateuch! So at the outset this is an authoritative ethic for the people of God.

And yet, it was on "seeing the crowds" that Jesus taught these disciples, first about character, what kind of people they should be. This was a needy, hurting, confused crowd: Jesus' answer to this need was to call together a small community and work on rebuilding their character. There is a lesson here! That Jesus had this impact on the world in mind in teaching the Beatitudes is also clear from his concluding remarks: "You are the salt of the earth. . . . You are the light of the world. A city built on a hill cannot be hid. No one after lighting a lamp puts it under the bushel basket, but on the lampstand, and it gives light to all in the house. In the same way, let your light shine before others, so that they may see your good works and give glory to your Father in heaven" (Mt 5:13-16). It is "Beatitudes-type" people who will serve as the salt of the earth and the light of the world. No one else can do it.

A *beatitude* is a saying that pronounces a "blessed" for being or doing something. The word is related to *beatific*, which means "blessed." The Greek word translated "blessed" here (*makarios*) means more than just happiness. Versions of this text that say "happy are . . ." are a little misleading (e.g., "Happy are you who mourn"?). The word *happiness* is too indeterminate and too much related to our feelings. *Blessed/makarios* carries a deeper sense of "well-being." We could almost translate "*Good for you*, you poor in spirit because . . ." or "*Good for you*, you meek, because . . ."

There are actually *nine* Beatitudes in the opening of the Sermon on the Mount—but I will follow a common practice of treating the ninth one as a repetition and personalization of the point made in the eighth Beatitude. Finally, I want to stress how important is the *order* of the Beatitudes. John Chrysostom (ca. 347-407), an early church leader, wrote that the Beatitudes are like "a sort of golden chain" in which "in each instance . . . the former precept make[s] way for the following one" by careful design.[6] Not every commentator pays attention to the order, but in this book you will see that I find the order crucial. This is not an arbitrary melange of proverbs but an inspired design for a good character.

The Beatitudes
1. poor in spirit
2. mourning
3. meek/gentle
4. hungry for righteousness
5. merciful
6. pure in heart
7. peacemaker
8. persecuted for righteousness

In the next five chapters we will study the building of an ethical, good character under five headings. I argue that we have five, organically connected, roles, exhibiting a fivefold character. The order in which I am treating these virtues is determined first by the order of the Beatitudes. Faith, hope, love, holiness, wisdom, joy and courage are positioned around the Beatitudes in a way that makes sense of the whole picture, in my judgment. This is not the only possible order, of course.

In chapter one we noted briefly that character is often related to the roles we play. For example the virtues appropriate to my role as father are a bit different than those required in my role as a faculty employee. The New Testament often describes various roles that Christians are called to play. I have included five of these—disciple, servant, leader, peacemaker and ambassador—as ways of drawing together some of the threads in this account of character. I have not used our roles as brothers and sisters or pilgrims or many other possibilities. Again, there are many possible approaches to our topic. But it would be easy to get lost in the details, so my instinct as a teacher

---

[6]John Chrysostom, *Homily XV on the Gospel of Saint Matthew* in Nicene and Post-Nicene Fathers, ed. Philip Schaff (Grand Rapids, Mich.: Eerdmans, 1956), 10:96. My understanding of the Beatitudes, on the whole and in the parts, is very close to that of Chrysostom.

is to attempt some summaries as we go along.

First, we look at our role as "faithful, holy, and wise disciples" of Jesus Christ as the foundation of everything else. Second, we will look at the first three Beatitudes as they shape us into "open, responsible, and gentle servants" of God and others. Third, we will look at the next two Beatitudes in our role as "righteous, just, and merciful leaders" for God in the world. Fourth, we will study the sixth and seventh Beatitudes and the great virtue of love under the heading of "loving, sacrificial, and genuine peacemakers." Finally, we will look at the eighth Beatitude and the virtue of hope in our role as "hopeful, courageous, and joyful ambassadors."

This fivefold description (see figure 5.1) will enable us, I believe, to account for the "trees" (the details) while not losing sight of the "forest" (the great themes and contours).

Our role	Paul's virtues	OT/NT virtues	Jesus' Beatitudes
1. disciple	faith	holy, wise	
2. servant			poor in spirit
			mourn
			meek
3. leader			righteousness
			mercy
4. peacemaker	love		pure in heart
			peacemaker
5. ambassador	hope	joy, courage	persecuted

Figure 5.1. Building a good, ethical, Christian character

The Grace That Gets Us Started

Just after World War II, an American soldier was on foot, patrolling a bomb-devastated part of an English city. As he walked past a bakery that had resumed operation, he noticed a poorly dressed young boy with his face pressed up to the window. The soldier stopped and commented to the boy: "Those donuts look pretty good in there, don't they?" The kid answered, longingly, "Yeah, they sure do." The soldier said to the boy, "Wait here for a minute," and entered the store. A few minutes later he came out and handed the boy a bag with a half-dozen warm donuts in it and said, "Here, take these, I want you to have some of those donuts." The amazed and grateful, hungry little boy took the bag and, as the soldier began to leave, looked up at him and asked: "Hey mister, are you God?"[7]

There is nothing more central to the good character of God than his grace, his unmerited favor. We are never more godly than when God's grace is expressed through us. Everything in the Christian life begins with God's grace. In the New Testament Greek vocabulary, grace (*charis*) is related to "joy" (*chara*) and to "gift" (*charisma*). God's grace is his favor toward us. It is his determination to delight in us and to give to us. Grace includes the mercy of forgiving our sins, but it is much more than that alone.

God does not just "hold his nose" and reach out in pity to rescue us from our pit. "You know the generous act of our Lord Jesus Christ, that though he was rich, yet for your sakes he became poor, so that by his poverty you might become rich" (2 Cor 8:9). Not just rescued but rich! God is characterized by a "glorious grace that he freely bestowed on us in the Beloved" and in the ages to come he will "show the immeasurable riches of his grace in kindness toward us in Christ Jesus" (Eph 1:6; 2:7). God's goodness includes this amazing grace.

Adopted, loved and liked by God. The character of biblical people has God's grace and choice as its point of departure. At the baptism of Jesus, the voice from heaven says "This is my Son, the Beloved, with whom I am well pleased" (Mt 3:17).[8] In a similar way, our Christian life begins with God declaring (1) that we are now his sons and daughters, adopted into his family forever; (2) that he loves us, to the extent of dying for us and redeeming us; and (3) that he is pleased with us, enjoys us, delights in us and likes us.

Naturally, what we are and do does not always please God, but the bottom line is that God likes us and people such as David and Peter and Mary Magdalene. David could write, "He delivered me, because he delighted in me" (Ps 18:19). Jesus chose disciples (a fairly motley

---

[7]I heard this story from my friend Jamie Crook, who was nowhere near WWII.

[8]As Karl Barth put it, in Jesus Christ we see simultaneously the perfect God for man and the perfect man for God. Hence, the experience of Jesus at his baptism is the paradigm from which our Christian life derives its initial and fundamental structure.

crew) not just to go out on missions for him but "to be with him" (Mk 3:13-15). And for all eternity he wants us to be with him where he is, and he prepares his heavenly mansions accordingly (see Jn 14:3).

It is a tragedy that our churches have not done a better job of stressing God's gracious choice, his love and affection for his disciples. Many Christians go through life wondering if God really has chosen them, doubting that God really loves them and ignorant of the fact that God likes them. No wonder that our character remains so damaged sometimes. We serve a gracious, not an angry, God, a God of infinite compassion and grace. The anger of God at our sin was exhausted at Calvary. We are free to step forward as the children of his love and affection.

> We serve a gracious, not an angry, God. A God of infinite love, compassion and patience beckons us to offer him, in freedom and joy, our whole character, so he can renew and strengthen us.

Think about how this works in human relationships. I have sometimes been motivated to improve by someone's criticism or disapproval. Fearing rejection or a negative reaction has sometimes made me work harder. But, frankly, that is nowhere near as powerful as the positive force of being loved and approved. I have been massively energized by love and gratitude, by a relationship of grace. Weariness, hesitation and inadequacy fade away, and I work doubly hard in response to someone's unconditional love and affection. How much more is this true of us when we recognize and experience God's amazing, unbounded, unchanging grace to us!

Grace gives. Grace is sometimes defined as "unmerited or undeserved favor." God's grace is his endless reaching out to us and for us. Psalm 65 gives a long list of these gifts of God: God hears our prayers, atones for our transgressions, chooses us and brings us near to live in his courts. God fills us with good things, answers us with awesome deeds of righteousness, stills the turmoil of the nations, calls forth songs of joy, cares for the land and enriches it, provides our food and surrounds us with bounty and goodness. This list ought to make it plain that God's grace is so much more than his pity and mercy.

We are the raw material in need of character development. God is our source and standard of goodness. Our gracious God reaches out to us to launch us on our journey. In the great Hebrews text cited earlier, the basic movements of the Christian life are outlined: "Therefore my friends, since we have confidence to enter the sanctuary by the blood of Jesus, by the new and living way that he opened for us . . . and since we have a great priest over the house of God, let us approach with . . . faith . . . hope . . . love" (Heb 10:19-24).

The first movement is by God, graciously making a way into his living presence. He now stands as the living priest and leader over a household in which we are now members. It is on this basis, this grace, that we are called to respond. To accept God's gift but then fail to respond in faith, hope and love is a threefold tragedy. It is a *tragedy for us personally* to choose to remain as born-again infants in our cribs—when we could have a robust life experiencing the adventure of Christian growth and maturity. It is a *tragedy for our neighbors* when we choose to remain ignorant and infantile in our Christian crib while our world so desperately needs the salt and light God wishes us to represent. It is a *tragedy and an affront to God* for us to ask for God's protection and nurture but refuse to grow up. Dietrich Bonhoeffer refers to this as the Christianity of "cheap grace": grace without discipleship.[9]

Still, the bottom line here is not a scolding and a duty—it is an invitation to fly free in God's grace and embark on the (re)construction of your character so that you will be blessed, the world salted and lighted, and God glorified in your life. Here is a way to begin today: try to be generous and gracious to others, to a fault, to excess.

For Reflection or Discussion

1. How would you describe the mission, goals, or ultimate purpose of your life? How has your purpose affected your lifestyle and major decisions?
2. Of all the Christian virtues you know, which are the hardest to make a part of your character? Why do you think this is?
3. Do you feel accepted, loved and liked by God? Why? What do you think it would it take for you to get excited about God's amazing grace for you?

---

[9]"Cheap grace is the deadly enemy of our Church. We are fighting today for costly grace." Dietrich Bonhoeffer, *The Cost of Discipleship* (New York: Macmillan, 1963), pp. 45ff.

Excursus

From Classical Virtue to Postmodern Emotivism
A Brief Review

It would be difficult to overestimate the value of a review of two ancient and two medieval teachers on character. Our focus for the rest of this book will be on the biblical material but, outside of that source, there is very little that remains as valuable as the ethical works of the Greek philosophers Plato and Aristotle and the medieval theologian/ philosophers Augustine and Thomas Aquinas. Their perspectives on the basic questions of ethics and virtue and, for Augustine and Aquinas, the relation of philosophical perspectives to biblical theology are well worth study by any serious person.

The Classical-Christian Virtue Tradition

Plato's *Republic* set the stage for the ancient and medieval discussion of character. For Plato (ca. 422-347 B.C.), the ideal character has developed his or her human capacities to the full and lives in a personal and social harmony oriented toward the transcendent Good, True and Beautiful, which is God (not the living God of Judaism and Christianity, of course, but the supreme reality). This is the *telos,* or purpose of human life and community, and therefore of ethics and character development.

Four virtues dominate Plato's account of character. *Justice* is the supreme virtue and means that everything is in its proper place, in harmonious integration, fulfilling its purpose. It has some sense of fairness but little to do with "rights" in the modern sense. Justice is the virtue of the whole. *Wisdom* (prudence, discernment) is the virtue of the mind, connecting the intellect with our behavior. It is the capacity to make good practical judgments on how to apply the requirements of justice to particular circumstances.

Courage (fortitude, bravery) means literally "the readiness to fall in battle." It is the virtue of the heart, the "spirited part" of our being. It is the capacity and disposition to do what is right and just despite our fears. *Self-control* (temperance, moderation) is the virtue of the appetites (sex, food, etc.). It is the capacity and disposition to do what is right and just despite our desires.[1]

These four came to be known as the "cardinal" virtues (from the Latin word for "hinge"—life's happiness and goodness hinge on one's possession of these character traits). People can know and understand these traits through the exercise of their reason, and they can embrace them as their own with the help of education and a commitment to practice them.

Aristotle (384-322 B.C.; Plato's most famous and accomplished student) in his *Nichomachean Ethics* developed these four cardinal virtues at some length but added to them a great discussion of friendship and friendliness (and less persuasive, shorter discussions of generosity, ambition, wittiness, modesty, high-mindedness, righteous indignation, gentleness and other attributes appropriate, at least, to a cultured Athenian intellectual).

Aristotle's major contribution to the ethics of character, in addition to his marvelous analyses of friendship and justice, was in his discussion of how character is built through habituation (practice), the importance of thoughtful deliberation and choice, and the argument that all character virtues are a "mean" between two vices, the "extremes" of deficiency and excess. Thus, for example, generosity is the mean between stinginess and prodigality, the vices, and courage is

---

[1]Plato *The Republic* bk. 4 contains Plato's famous discussion of virtue in the city and in the soul.

the mean between cowardice and recklessness.[2]

The two greatest Christian philosopher/theologians from the second century to the sixteenth, Augustine (354-430) and Thomas Aquinas (1225-1274), continued to take this classical Greek account of character with the utmost respect and seriousness. While they saw both Plato and Aristotle as "pagans," they nevertheless believed that God was at work bringing truth to (and through) them by means of his general revelation in nature. Augustine preferred Plato; Aquinas preferred Aristotle. Both tried to integrate the classical wisdom with the biblical tradition.

> The Four Cardinal Virtues
> *Justice:* fairness, harmony, orderliness, wholeness
> *Wisdom:* discernment, prudence, practical judgment
> *Courage:* fortitude, bravery
> *Self-control:* temperance, moderation

Augustine's *Enchiridion* ("Handbook") *on Faith, Hope and Love* relied on Paul's "theological" virtues as the best account of Christian life and character. Augustine saw the four cardinal virtues as four forms of love. Justice was "love distributed fairly and rightly," courage was "love persisting in its good works," and so on.

Thomas Aquinas viewed the four cardinal virtues as "natural" virtues that help us achieve our natural end (happiness). In addition, there are three "supernatural" virtues (faith, hope and love) that are necessary to achieve our supernatural end (to see and know God). The natural virtues are knowable to human reason; the supernatural virtues are knowable through God's revelation and illumination. The natural virtues may be acquired through habituation and effort; the supernatural virtues must be "infused" by God's Spirit.[3]

Modern Ethical Systems

With the sixteenth-century Protestant Reformation, the classical-

---

[2]For an outstanding introduction to Aristotle's ethics, see Nancy Sherman, *The Fabric of Character: Aristotle's Theory of Virtue* (New York: Oxford University Press, 1989).

[3]Augustine, *The Enchiridion on Faith, Hope, and Love* (Chicago: Regnery Gateway, 1961); and *Of the Morals of the Catholic Church* in *The Works of Aurelius Augustine*, ed. M. Dods (Edinburgh: T & T Clark, 1892); Thomas Aquinas, *Treatise on the Virtues* (South Bend, Ind.: University of Notre Dame Press, 1984). Thomas's discussion of virtue is in questions 49-67 of his *Summa Theologiae* 1-2

Christian emphasis on character formation as the foundation of the moral life began to lose its dominance. Martin Luther, in particular, disliked the Thomistic approach and anything that could be interpreted as a righteousness resulting from human effort. Luther was a fan of William of Ockham's nominalism: things are so because God names them so, not because of any reality that exists outside of God. In ethics this undermined the quest for character improvement.

More important for the long run was the rising influence of modern science and the philosophical Enlightenment associated with Immanuel Kant and others. Scientists sought universal laws, based on reason and empirical data, to describe the workings of the universe and nature. Moral philosophers, in turn, sought for universal laws of morality, independent of particular character, community and purpose. Kant's Categorical Imperative was intended to be the fundamental moral law for the whole world in this way. "Modernity" is what we now call this whole epoch from the seventeenth century to 1960 or thereabouts. It was an era dominated by confidence in scientific procedures, in reason, in universal truths. Ethics (moral philosophy) was dominated by a quest for systems of principles and rules. Questions of character were distinctly secondary for these centuries.

Postmodern Emotivism and Its Alternatives

Already by the mid-nineteenth century, philosophers like Søren Kierkegaard began questioning this confident, rationalistic, abstract philosophical system building. Kierkegaard was not paid much attention in his lifetime, and Friedrich Nietzsche fared little better fifty years later as he also boldly and vividly (and profanely) attacked modernity and its ethics. But by the 1960s the grand edifice of modernity began to crumble. In the end it was less the philosophical critics who brought it down than the voices of women, African Americans, Hispanics and others.

It rapidly became evident to many scholars and culture shapers that what had been presented as the universal truth of all rational citizens of the world was actually the particular expression of a provincial scholarly guild of European males. Their rationalism and abstraction was most certainly not a universal characteristic of morality. They had committed a major category error in believing that morality could be detached from historical communities, traditions and purposes as easily as could physics and mathematics.

"Postmodern" ethics today has only one unifying feature: a rejection of modernity. Postmodernity is a wilderness without a common language or conception of ethics. There are spokespersons for the radical moral individualism I discussed in chapter one. And there are countless other moralists seeking to articulate guidance for one or another religious, cultural, behavioral, regional or other affinity group. The ethical landscape reveals an incredible potpourri in our time. Much of what we do when our lives intersect is muddle through—and seek legislative answers when muddling through isn't enough.

But also rising from the ashes in this postmodern climate is a vigorous new movement "back to virtue" led by Alasdair MacIntyre, Peter Kreeft, Stanley Hauerwas, Gilbert Meilaender, Christina Sommers and other philosophers. On a more popular level, William Bennett and others are pressing the character and virtue agenda. This book aspires to make a modest contribution to that renewal.

It would be wrong and simplistic, of course, merely to glorify earlier eras or unfairly take cheap shots at our own. For one reason, there is always a difference between theory and practice. The best wisdom of Plato, Aristotle, Augustine and Aquinas was contested by some voices at the time and ignored by still others. There was plenty wrong with the practices of the ancient and medieval worlds, not the least of which was a lack of individual freedom for many (slaves, serfs), and a fairly consistent demeaning of women.[4] The freedom of choice we experience today is worth the chaos that comes with it. Still, our ethical wilderness is wilder than most have been in the past. To make progress on character we must be aware of this terrain.

---

[4]For some introduction to the history of ethics, see Alasdair MacIntyre, *A Short History of Ethics* (New York: Macmillan, 1966) and *Three Rival Versions of Moral Enquiry* (South Bend, Ind.: University of Notre Dame Press, 1990). Steve Wilkens gives a good popular introduction to ethical theories in his *Beyond Bumper Sticker Ethics: An Introduction to Theories of Right and Wrong* (Downers Grove, Ill.: InterVarsity Press, 1995).

For Reflection or Discussion

1. What, in your opinion, can philosophy, sociology, psychology, biology and other fields of study outside theology contribute to our understanding of Christian ethics? Can you give an example of a thinker or insight that we should pay attention to?

2. Is postmodernism a friend or a foe of biblical, Christian ethics today?

Part Two

BUILD

Six

FAITHFUL, HOLY & WISE
The Disciple

F *aith is our first and fundamental response to the grace of God.* Even if love is "the greatest" of all the virtues (1 Cor 13), it is so as the culmination of faith. In the New Testament, the language of faith is used twice as often as the language of love. Faith is the starting point in the transformation of our character. The Christian life moves from faith, in hope, to love.[1]

The First Character Virtue: Faithfulness
Probably the most memorized verse in the Bible is John 3:16: "For God so loved the world that he gave his only Son, so that everyone who believes [has faith] in him may not perish but may have eternal life." God's grace calls for our faith. But faith is not just about getting born

---

[1]"There are two kinds of order, one of generation and the other of perfection. Faith is first in generation; love is first in perfection." St. Thomas Aquinas, *Treatise on the Virtues* (South Bend, Ind.: University of Notre Dame Press, 1984), p. 123. From the *Summa Theologiae* 1-2, Q. 62, Art. 4.

again or guaranteeing eternal life, it is a characteristic required for all of life and its struggles. With faith "all things can be done" (Mk 9:23). Jesus' great question for the future was "When the Son of Man comes, will he find faith on earth?" (Lk 18:8).

Faith was central not just for Jesus but in the teaching of the apostles: "Believe [have faith] on the Lord Jesus Christ and you will be saved" (Acts 16:31). The connection of faith to grace was also stressed: "By grace you have been saved through faith, and this is not your own doing; it is the gift of God" (Eph 2:8). Faith is crucial to the whole of life: "In the gospel a righteousness from God is revealed, a righteousness that is by faith from first to last, just as it is written: 'The righteous will live by faith' " (Rom 1:17 NIV, citing Hab 2:4). In fact, "whatever does not proceed from faith is sin" (Rom 14:23) and "without faith it is impossible to please God" (Heb 11:6).

These well-known statements are just a small sample of the claims made for the centrality and foundational importance of faith. The basic New Testament word for faith (Greek, *pistis*) means "steadfastness, fidelity, faithfulness, trustworthiness, belief, firm conviction." In English we express these ideas primarily with two words, "belief" and "faith," which we use almost interchangeably.[2] Faith is a "fruit of the Spirit" and a "gift of God"—but also a virtue to be practiced.

The virtue that shapes our relationship with God also shapes our relationships with others and with our self. This is because people are made "in the image and likeness of God." While we can't ignore our brokenness when we relate to others (and to our self), we must nevertheless concentrate our attention on the image of God that we still bear. We must respond to and nurture the creative and redemptive grace of God in others and in ourselves. Faithfulness is not just about God but about all of our relationships.

Faith as intellectual affirmation. Many people first think of faith and belief in contrast to reason and knowledge. Where reason and

---

[2]These two words are interchangeable in meaning and application. Some (e.g., Jacques Ellul) wish to stipulate a difference, but it is not the etymology of the terms that justifies such definitions.

knowledge end, faith and belief begin. *Some* justification for this perspective comes from biblical statements such as "We walk by faith, not by sight" (2 Cor 5:7) and "Blessed are those who have not seen and yet have come to believe" (Jn 20:29). In this definition, reason affirms what we can "see" (what is available to our sense perception). Faith, however, is required to affirm anything beyond that horizon. Example: I *know* I have two legs; I *believe* they will one day walk on heavenly "streets of gold."

This popular understanding, however, is inadequate. It is too narrow to say that we only know what reason (or sight) can establish. We know some things in other ways and on other grounds. It is not reason (rationality) but *rationalism* that seems to exclude faith.[3] Reason and faith often work on the same side—not just in separate domains or in opposition.

Faith is also sometimes contrasted with doubt: you can have one or the other. Where reason finishes its work and can go no further, we are left to choose faith or doubt, belief or skepticism, credulity or uncertainty. But this popular understanding is also too simple; in reality, the relationships of faith, reason and doubt are much more complex and interesting.[4]

Taken as a whole, our intellectual commitments (our beliefs, opinions, ideas) often *follow* the exercise of our reason, but they also *precede* reason's activity in the form of assumptions and presuppositions we must make about truth and reality. We should, of course, examine and modify these assumptions and presuppositions with our reason, but we can never operate, even in the most closed rational system, without faith of some sort. If we insist that our commitments will be based exclusively and entirely on what human reason can demonstrate (an impossible position actually), then in a basic sense we have placed our faith *in* reason.

Everybody is thus a believer in one way or another. Some of our

---

[3]Being a rationalist is itself an act of faith.

[4]The French title of *Living Faith* by Jacques Ellul is *La Foi au prix du doute,* or "Faith at the price of doubt." In Ellul's view, "beliefs" are held with certainty; true Christian "faith" comes only with a degree of doubt and uncertainty.

contemporaries enjoy announcing their unbelief and cynicism, but, on closer examination, a lot of this is posing and posturing. Despite such protests, Jacques Ellul says, "never have people believed as much. . . . The modern world is . . . loaded with religions—communism, Maoism, nationalism, revolution—all are purely and specifically religious attitudes. . . . Technology belongs to the domain of the sacred, and science even more so."[5] It is ridiculous to suggest that only Christians or religious people demonstrate faith.

Thus, faith is in part an intellectual operation. This first kind of faith is expressed by the phrase "believing *that.*" Faith is affirming, thinking and believing that certain things are true. Christians believe *that* God exists, *that* God created and is redeeming the world, *that* Jesus Christ (crucified, dead, buried, resurrected and ascended) is Savior, Lord and God, *that* the Bible is God's Word, *that* the church is God's redeemed people, *that* the world is loved by God and so on (creeds, confessions and statements of faith summarize such beliefs).

Jesus said, "You will die in your sins unless you *believe that* I am he" (Jn 8:24, my emphasis). Paul wrote, "If you confess with your lips that Jesus is Lord and *believe* in your heart *that* God raised him from the dead, you will be saved" (Rom 10:9, my emphasis). "Without faith it is impossible to please God, for whoever would approach him must *believe that* he exists and *that* he rewards those who seek him" (Heb 11:6, my emphasis).

Christians have reasons for believing these things, but the truths we affirm often take us beyond the limits of our ordinary human science and reason. We don't just believe any old thing, of course. Our faith is not a mindless credulity and gullibility. But neither are Christians so arrogant as to believe that truth and reality are confined to the boundaries of their own finite reason and intelligence. There is always some doubt, uncertainty, mystery and paradox in what we believe. But *all* human thinking terminates in some mystery of this sort; Christian thinking is distinctive in that it terminates in the mystery of Jesus Christ.

---

[5]Jacques Ellul, *Hope in Time of Abandonment* (New York: Seabury, 1972), p. 78

What, then, is distinctive about the Christian version if others demonstrate faith in one way or another? The first and decisive difference for Christians is not the *presence* of faith but its *object* and *content:* it is centered in Jesus Christ. Second, Christian faith ought to be distinctive in its *honesty* and *humility*: we do not affirm our convictions because we are smarter than others, nor do we claim some imperial scientific certainty about them, without any mystery or doubt. We do not deny that our intellectual commitments are based on faith as well as reason. Third, Christian faith ought to be distinctive in both its *constancy* and its *vitality*. We embrace our central ideas and convictions firmly, not being tossed around by every passing fad or critical question. At the same time, our minds are alive with a thirst to know more and know better. The implications of our faith and life view require a lifetime of exploration.

> Everybody is a believer in one thing or another. What distinguishes true Christian faith is its focus on Jesus Christ, its honesty and humility, and its constancy and vitality.

This sort of faith is a character virtue. It is seen best in its paradigmatic form as it relates us to God. It is the capacity to believe in God's great acts without having all of our cravings for demonstration, proof and sensory evidence fulfilled. But what is true in this primary way about faith concerning God is true in a secondary sense about human relationships. We can never know everything about other people, even those closest to us. We do accumulate some evidence, experience and knowledge, but we do not and cannot know everything.

It is disastrous to go through life always harboring doubts about what others did, said or meant. We don't want to be gullible and stupid, but we cannot be cynical and suspicious either. We simply cannot demand continual, at will, demonstrations and evidence. We cannot maintain constant surveillance. We must believe *that* they will do as they promised, *that* they will maintain their commitments, *that* they will be today as they were yesterday, and so on. There is a risk involved in all relationships, of course. There are doubts and mysteries, but faith refuses to allow these to paralyze us and ruin our relationships. So not just with God but with others, our thinking and our character must proceed in faith (in a *believing that*) as well as in reason.

Faith as relational commitment and loyalty. Faith is not, however, merely an intellectual virtue. Even more important than *intellectual affirmation* is *relational commitment*; not just believing *that* but believing *on* or believing *in*. We *believe that* a jumbo jet can get off the ground and fly across the country—but we only *believe in* the jet when we get on board! You believe *that* someone loves you; you believe *in* her or him when you get married. I believe *that* my son is very strong; I believe *in* him when he spots me while I'm bench-pressing to my maximum.

All people have faith in this second sense (believing *in*—not just *that*). Some believe in the government, or in technology, or in their stock broker. Their attitudes of confidence and their actions of concrete commitment demonstrate this faith. Others believe in their local militia, or in their race, or in some guru or leader, or in education. This is what they trust to solve their problems and meet their needs (for meaning, protection, healthcare or whatever).

For Christians this second sense of faith is utterly crucial and central. This, not the intellectual form, is the primary emphasis in the Christian faith.[6] A good Christian character not only believes that certain ideas about God are true—it *attaches itself* to God and his activity. If our faith is only an intellectual affirmation of certain truths, it is far short of the genuine Christian virtue. Faith is commitment, trust and reliance on God. It is an embrace by the heart, mind, soul, emotions and body. It is an act of the will as well as the intellect.[7]

Paul described it to Timothy this way: "I know the one in whom *I have put my trust* and am sure that he is able to guard until that day

---

[6]"Faith is a history, new every morning. It is no state or attribute. It should not be confused with mere capacity and willingness to believe. Of course, it may result in and involve all sorts of faithfully held convictions. . . . All the same, willingness to believe . . . certain points is not yet faith. Faith is no *credere quod* but rather a *credere in*, . . . not a belief 'that . . .' but a faith 'in . . .'—in God himself." Karl Barth, *Evangelical Theology* (Garden City, N.J.: Anchor, 1964), p. 92-93.

[7]My visual image of God's grace is his pursuing us, reaching out, seizing us, drawing us close to him, caring for us and giving us his gifts. Grace is God saying "I will not let you go." Faith, then, is our turning around to seize on to God, wrapping our arms around and embracing this gracious God who is pursuing us. Faith is our saying to God "I will not let you go "

what *I have entrusted* to him" (2 Tim 1:12, my emphasis). In faith we "draw near to" or "approach" God (Heb 10:22). Faith is our drawing near to God even though we can only see "in a mirror, dimly" (1 Cor 13:12). We cannot prove everything. We may have some doubts and fears, some unanswered questions and mystery. We walk not by sight (we can't see this Christ next to us) but by a faith that links us firmly and actually to this unseen but very real Jesus Christ (2 Cor 5:7).

> Faithfulness is the first and foundational character trait because it initiates and loyally sustains a relationship —and a faithful relationship with Jesus Christ is what transforms our character.

It is because our relationship to God is the core issue in life that faith is the primary virtue to be developed. The Fall in Eden occurred when Adam and Eve stopped seeking after God and gave themselves to another. The first commandment is "You shall have no other gods before me" or "between you and me" (Ex 20:1-3). "Do not follow other gods, any of the gods of the peoples who are all around you, because the LORD your God, who is present with you, is a jealous God" (Deut 6:14-15). Faith is the virtue that sustains this relationship, that insists on keeping it alive and real. An absence of faith undermines every other possible character virtue.

When faith becomes more than just an occasional act, when it becomes an ongoing habit, an inclination, a disposition, a trait, a mark of our basic character, it is then "faithfulness."[8] Faithfulness is loyalty, steadfastness and reliability in a relationship. The model here is God's unwavering faithfulness to his covenant with the people: "I will be their God, and they shall be my people" (Jer 31:33). Though this covenant has been threatened and broken by the people, God refuses to quit. God's "steadfast love" is one of the chief characteristics of his faithfulness. It is the archetype and ideal for our faithfulness.

A good character, then, exhibits faithfulness and loyalty as an ongoing disposition and stance, habitually, dependably, sticking by Jesus Christ. But this is not just a character trait shaping our relationship with God—it also shapes our relationships with people. We stick with

---

[8]See Gilbert C. Meilaender, *Faith and Faithfulness: Basic Themes in Christian Ethics* (South Bend, Ind.: University of Notre Dame Press, 1991).

our relationships and commitments to others. That's the way we live. When tested, we want to remain steadfastly loyal. Many people today have great difficulty making and keeping covenants, commitments and promises to others. It has become routine and casual to break such covenants that do exist—in marriage (half end in divorce today), in child rearing (a third of all children in America are raised by single parents today). Loyalty and fidelity to employers, employees, churches and neighborhoods is almost a thing of the past. Its absence hardly attracts any attention anymore.

For a Christian ethic, however, steadfast faithfulness is the basic trait of a good character. Faithfully caring for aging parents, vulnerable children, struggling spouses, friends—even faithful loyalty to our neighborhood, colleagues and employers—these are the things we want to stand for in our lives, not neglect, infidelity, betrayal, treachery and abuse.[9]

> **F**aithfulness becomes a part of our character in its relationship to God—but it must also characterize our relationships with people.

Faithfulness as time together. Let's push the faith as relationship aspect one step further. Faithfulness is not just a stance but an activity, the habit and inclination to invest in time together. One aspect of this is conversation. Faithfulness involves *listening* and *speaking*. Listening is more than just overhearing, and speaking is not just spouting off. Both are intentional, focused, active and expectant. Without conversation, relationships wither. Faithfulness is about relationships sustained by conversation, not sporadically but habitually.

Faithfulness means making time for conversation with God. What might God be trying to say to us (as we read Scripture, for example)? What will we say to God (in prayer, for example)? Jacques Ellul has written,

---

[9]Being faithful also means fidelity to my self, to the person God has called me to be. It is easy to be diverted from the identity that God has given us as his sons or daughters, to begin to undervalue that person whom God loves and likes. Our culture constantly propagandizes us to reject our self in favor of some popular image or other. We must learn to be faithful to the self that God has created and is redeeming and not to despise the work of God in us. The foundation of a healthy self-image is to see our self as God sees it. This is not narcissism because we are not exalting the autonomous self, detaching it from others.

faith consists in heeding God's questions and risking ourselves in the answers that *we* have to give. Questions run all the way through the Bible, with three high points. The first question asked of us is a double one: "Adam, where are you?" and "Cain, what have you done to your brother?" . . . The second . . . is the one Jesus poses to the disciples: "And you, who do you say that I am?" . . . And the third, in the last days, after the resurrection of Jesus Christ: "Whom do you seek?" . . . All through Scripture these three questions serve as a framework for the questions that God asks us and that faith is called to answer.[10]

In these questions God confronts us about where we are in life, about our opinion of him, and about what is of paramount importance to us. Faith is expressed and sustained by a living conversation.

Second, and more generally, faithfulness means seeking ("practicing") the presence of God. Relationships don't cease when conversation stops. When alone, we seek to be aware of God's presence within and beside us. When together with other believers, we recall Jesus' promise that "*where* two or three are gathered in my name, I am *there* among them" (Mt 18:20, my emphasis). When we move about in the world, we look, as the Quakers used to say, for the "light of God" in others. Faithfulness thus means clinging to Jesus Christ in all of our daily activities—in our classrooms, laboratories, libraries, sales offices, banks, daycare centers—everywhere.

What is true for the relationship with God is also true for relationships with people (made in God's image and likeness): investing quality and quantity time together is an expression of faithfulness. Faithfulness in marriage or friendship or parenting is not expressed only by avoiding infidelity and betrayal! That is far too negative. The primary mark of faithfulness is the positive act of choosing to spend time

---

[10]Jacques Ellul, *Living Faith: Belief and Doubt in a Perilous World* (San Francisco: Harper & Row, 1983), pp. 101-2. "Faith is neither belief nor credulity . . . neither a reasonable acquisition nor an intellectual achievement; it is rather the conjunction of an ultimate decision, which I have to make and for which I am responsible, and a revelation. . . . I am summoned by a Word that is eternal, here and now, universal, personal. And I accept this summons. I am willing to act responsibly; I enter upon an illogical adventure . . . marked out by a succession of more new questions, more new impossibilities, which are resolved and fade away with each new step I determine to take" (p. 125).

together. Faithfulness means carving out and guarding time for regular conversation as well as just "hanging out" together.

Faith at work. Faith creates a life that points (or witnesses) to a relationship. Faithfulness is a powerful, transforming orientation that deeply colors, affects, and guides what we do. If not, we can ask whether such faithfulness is real. This is certainly the case with faithfulness to God: "faith by itself, if it has no works, is dead" (Jas 2:17).

No one can truly encounter God in faith, without their life changing in response. "Faith is the demand that we must *incarnate* the Kingdom of God now in this world and this age. . . . From one end to the other the Bible shows us that there's no faith without the test of reality."[11] Faith in Jesus Christ expresses itself in ways that point to its object.

Specifically, faithfulness to Jesus Christ produces *holiness* and *wisdom* as character traits (to be explored in the next two sections below). Faith in God shows itself in *hope* and *love*, in *righteousness* and *justice*, and in many other concrete ways. "By faith we understand" (Heb 11:3)—it produces a whole new way of thinking and reasoning, a worldview and philosophy. "By faith Abel offered to God a more acceptable sacrifice" (Heb 11:4)—faith produces good worship. "By faith Noah . . . built an ark" (Heb 11:7)—faith helps us discern the signs of the times and build something helpful, and of true witness to God. "By faith Abraham obeyed when he was called to set out . . . not knowing where he was going" (Heb 11:8)—faith empowers and guides pilgrims and adventurers who pursue God's will and spread his love across the planet.

In the same way, faithfulness in human relationships expresses itself away from the presence of those to whom we are committed. Loyalty and fidelity affect the kind of people we are. The way we behave and talk outside of the presence of our best friend should be consistent with, and witness to, that relationship.

The community of faith. What does it mean for the church to be a community of faith? What is decisive is how the church relates to Jesus Christ. Is its fellowship and unity based on a common faith in Christ—or is it based on social compatibility, political orientation, eco-

---

[11]Ibid., p. 120.

nomic class or cultural preferences? Is Jesus at the center, guiding the life and decisions of the community—or is the church really guided by tradition, social science, psychology or management techniques? Building a faithful character is not intended to be accomplished without the support of a community of faith. It is a lot harder to cultivate faithfulness as an individual if churches do not practice the virtue! For churches, as for individuals, the four key characteristics of faithfulness that we must value, pursue and cultivate are the same.

Faithfulness
1. "believing that"—standing firm on the truth, even when and where it cannot be fully proved
2. "believing in/on"—staying loyally committed to the relationship, even when out of sight
3. investing quality and quantity time together
4. displaying actions that point back to the relationship

Holiness: Knowing How to Be Different

There is a direct link between faithfulness and holiness. Faithfulness leads to holiness in our character. God is holy: over and over we read "Holy, holy, holy is the LORD" (e.g., Is 6:3; Rev 4:8).[12] And over and over we encounter the follow-up message: "Be holy as I am holy, says the LORD" (e.g., Lev 19:2; 1 Pet 1:15-16).

What is holiness? As in the case of ethics and morality, and faith and belief, we have two word families in English for the same original concept. In addition to "holiness" we have the terminology of "sanctification." "Saint" means "holy one" and "sanctification" means "to be made holy." There is no difference between the concepts of being holy and being sanctified.

Holiness as purity. First, holiness (sanctification) means "purity." To be holy means to be clean, pure, and free of sin, vice and contamination. God is holy in that he is completely separate from sin and evil. God is completely good. The elaborate hand washing and purification rituals in Old Testament religion were symbolic reminders to the people of how much God cannot stand sin and evil. It is God's determination in the end to have his people "without spot or blemish" and holy in his sight (Eph 5:27; 2 Pet 3:14).

---

[12]On God's holiness, see Donald G. Bloesch, *God the Almighty: Power, Wisdom, Holiness, Love* (Downers Grove, Ill.: InterVarsity Press, 1995); and Thomas L. Trevethan, *The Beauty of God's Holiness* (Downers Grove, Ill.: InterVarsity Press, 1995).

Our era neither understands nor values purity and holiness. Little is said about it in our churches; nothing is said in the broader culture. Our conscience and our sense of impurity are extraordinarily dull these days, and it is rare to find ourselves revolted by the lies, violence, corruption and moral degradation of our culture. How did we get to this point? The answer is complex, but it didn't help that the most ardent proponents of purity and holiness in the past often confused their own cultural conservatism with divine holiness. And a theology that was so imbalanced toward the anger of God at sin could be predicted to swing eventually to the other extreme.

O ur culture knows very little about faithfulness, loyalty and trustworthiness— but its knowledge of holiness and purity is zero.

But this has got to change. In a Christian ethic we cannot build good character unless holiness has a place of honor among the virtues. To begin with, we cannot be people of faith without being people of holiness. Faithfulness means drawing near to God in loyal relationship; I called it "clinging" to God. But the God we wish to embrace is a holy, pure God and cannot accept the embrace of self-justifying, persistently impure, sinful people.

Remember that passage in Hebrews: "Let us approach [God] with a true heart in full assurance of faith, with our hearts sprinkled clean from an evil conscience and our bodies washed with pure water" (Heb 10:22). Approach (draw near) in faith—but clean up your inner life (heart) and outer life (body). Faith and purity go together. We cannot walk closely with God in faith unless we acknowledge and get rid of our sin. Of course, we realize that "If we say that we have no sin, we deceive ourselves, and the truth is not in us" (1 Jn 1:8). But such realism cannot serve as a license to excuse or justify our poor behavior.

Holiness, in the sense of purity, begins in a renewal of our mind and conscience. We begin to abhor sin, injustice, vice and unrighteousness, reacting to it as we react to cancer in the physical realm. The only way such a huge shift in consciousness can happen is by a compelling vision of the goodness and purity of God. It is a little like the discovery of my tennis shortcomings when I hit some balls with a great tennis player for the first time. I didn't fully understand my weakness until I met strength. So too, we will not fully recognize corruption until we meet the incorruptible. This change in consciousness is the first step toward purity.

But there are other steps. Holiness requires honest self-examination and self-criticism, followed by confession and repentance to God. "If we confess our sins, [God] . . . will forgive us our sins and cleanse us from all unrighteousness" (1 Jn 1:9). Paul urges radical action: "Put to death . . . whatever in you is earthly: fornication, impurity, passion, evil desire, and greed (which is idolatry). . . . Get rid of all such things—anger, wrath, malice, slander, and abusive language from your mouth. Do not lie to one another, seeing that you have stripped off the old self with its practices" (Col 3:5-9).

Holiness as purity requires us to learn how to say no—how to "put to death," "get rid of" and "strip off" vice and impurity. In classical ethics, self-control was one of the four cardinal virtues—the capacity and strength to say no to our appetites and desires, even when they are begging to be satisfied. Fasting (choosing abstinence or self-deprivation for a time), one of the disciplines taught in Jesus' Sermon on the Mount, is also a strategy in the quest for purity and the conquest of temptation. Thankfully, self-control is also a fruit of the Spirit—we are not "on our own" without God's help (see Gal 5:23).

Holiness as distinctiveness. In a second sense, a broader one than purity, holiness refers to God's "otherness" or "differentness." Some theologians have stressed this by referring to God as the "Wholly Other." God is not just different because of his sinless purity; his being and action transcend all our categories. "My thoughts are not your thoughts, nor are your ways my ways, says the LORD. For as the heavens are higher than the earth, so are my ways higher than your ways and my thoughts than your thoughts" (Is 55:8-9).

God constantly confounds the conventions and expectations of the world. In God's approach to war, he will use Gideon's lamps and trumpets. In his choice of prophets and apostles, in his economics and poli-

> I woke up to the truth about my weak tennis game only when I hit some balls with a great player for the first time.
>
> We wake up to our acute need for holiness only when we truly encounter the Holy One, Jesus Christ.

tics, in his ethical teaching, above all in the death and resurrection of
the Messiah, God is and does other than the ordinary. Jesus' teaching
confounded tradition and expectation: "You have heard that it was said
. . . but I say to you . . ." His listeners often reacted, "No one ever spoke
like this." His actions also contrasted with people's expectations: the
disciples marveled that he spoke with the Samaritan woman, that he
ate with "publicans and sinners," that he called children to him. Jesus
is, in these ways, our model of holy "otherness."

As God is holy, we are called to be holy. Jesus commissioned his disciples to be "in but not of" the world *just as* he was "in but not of" the
world—present in the world, but with a clear difference guided by
Jesus' distinctiveness (Jn 17). Christians are called to be the *salt* of the
earth, not just more earth, the *light* of the world, not just more world
(Mt 5). Christians are to "not be conformed to this world, but be transformed by the renewing of your minds, so that you may discern what is
the will of God—what is good and acceptable and perfect" (Rom 12:2).
Christian "citizenship" is elsewhere, in the kingdom of God, not in any
earthly political kingdom. Christians are pilgrims and strangers, never
quite at home in the world.

A Christian character is to be holy in the sense of being non-con-
formist—not fitting into the normal categories of our world. It is not for
us to decide simply between Republican or Democratic conformity,
nor between liberal or conservative, nor between traditionalist and
progressive. Of course we will be in the world and share to some extent
in its various identities, but these are always provisional and secondary
for us. We must not allow cultural, political, national, ethnic, educational or any other identities to dominate and then divide,us.

Such holiness and distinctiveness are only possible with God's help.
God causes us to be born again and then "sanctifies" and nourishes our
new character. Sanctification (becoming holy) is a supernatural work
of God in us. Nevertheless, sanctification is not imposed on us by
God—we are invited to cooperate. As aggressively and intentionally as
he called Christians to "put off" or even "put to death" the old life and
its impurities,the apostle Paul puts the positive challenge: "As God's
chosen ones, holy and beloved, clothe yourselves with compassion,
kindness, humility, meekness, and patience. Bear with one another

and . . . forgive each other. . . . Above all, clothe yourselves with love . . ."
(Col 3:12-14).

Holiness as distinctiveness is dependent on faith. By binding us to
the transcendent God, faith separates us from the world and situates
our identity outside of our culture. No one has described this better
than Jacques Ellul:

> Faith separates people and makes each of them unique. In the Bible
> "holy" *means* "separated." To be holy is to be separated from everyone
> else, from the people, from the world, the group, to be made unique *for
> the sake of a task* that can be accomplished by no one else, which one
> receives through faith, after being awakened to faith by the creative and
> distinctive word.[13]

> Because faith refers to the Absolutely Other, because it places us in a
> qualitatively different universe, it will never let us be assimilated into any
> group or cause or person, into any idea or reality whatsoever. Faith situ-
> ates us at a literally infinite distance from all that.[14]

> Holiness as separation, service, and witness for God . . . expresses the
> distinctiveness of incarnate Christianity, but separation has a place only
> for the sake of mission. The break has to come first, but it implies redis-
> covery of the world, society, and one's neighbor in a new type of relation-
> ship. Holiness in isolation is inadequate. It demands relationship.[15]

The world suffers from closing in upon itself and yielding to the
forces of nature, technology, politics and the economy rather than
experiencing genuine freedom. Our culture limits its options to common sense, realism or "muddling through." Many of our problems
seem intractable and inevitable. Christians have a unique role to play,
a unique standpoint from which alone it is possible to introduce a
Truth that can break open this closure and fatalism. A holy people fired
with faith in the God of the empty tomb refuses to be confined to the
world's limits and sense of inevitability. Holiness as distinctiveness is,
thus, not just for our own sake or just for God alone; it is an essential
part of our witness to the world.

---

[13]Jacques Ellul, *Living Faith* (San Francisco: Harper & Row, 1983), p.107.

[14]Ibid., p.183.

[15]Jacques Ellul, *The Ethics of Freedom* (Grand Rapids, Mich.: Eerdmans, 1976), p. 7.
Ellul drafted but did not edit and publish his long "ethics of holiness."

Faithful, holy disciples must never trade their distinctiveness and uniqueness for relevance or approval. Accommodation is betrayal. The "salt of the earth" loses its saltiness. Christians must plunge into the world and be fully present, but they begin by stepping away from the world and decisively toward Jesus Christ. Then, and only then, from this starting point, God sends them back into the world as the bearers of hope and love.

Holy character does not mean an unguided eccentricity, weirdness or negativity for its own sake. This is because the content of holiness is specified by God's character, not by our genius or creativity. Any holy uniqueness and creativity we have comes from the character of God, from the resurrected Christ, not just by way of a negative rejection of the world but by a positive embrace of the Wholly Other God. Being holy in sexual relationships, for example, means not only repudiating sexual sin and impurity but introducing a *godly eros* and *agape* into that domain. It is not just a no but a yes. Holiness does not mean just opposing abortion or welfare dependency but introducing *godly* creative and redemptive perspectives and actions into these arenas. If we only say no, we are only half holy, which is unholy.

> Holiness is not just purity. Because of their link to the Wholly Other God, holy Christians should be an inexhaustible source of creative, life-giving alternatives to a world closed in on itself.

Holy Christians should be an inexhaustible source of life-giving alternatives to our troubled world. The fact that we see Christians lining up and shouting behind various worldly movements is a sign of the impotence of our faith. If we must line up and shout, at least we should not drag the name of Christ into it. What we are seeing in today's partisan Christian politics and economics is not the rising power of the gospel but its weakness and betrayal, its co-optation by Christian dupes of worldly interests. We are desperate for true holiness today—not just the name of the concept but the biblical and spiritual reality.

A holy community in the world. As with faithfulness, so with holiness: this is not merely an individual character trait. The people of God are collectively a "holy people," a "holy priesthood" and a "holy nation" (cf. Deut 7:6; 1 Pet 2:5, 9). Not just in our personal lives but in our communities of faith, we must seek holiness. This means that we are communities of discipline and purity. Every person is welcome in the community of God's grace, but not every behavior or attitude is welcome. In particular, we need holy leaders. The church is going to have an increasingly tough time maintaining its commitment to purity on some of its favorite issues when it tolerates major violations of God's standards in other areas.[16]

Holiness in our communities also means that our organizational style, structures, policies, operations, decision-making and communications are not patterned according to the culture but strive for a holy uniqueness. We *learn* from this world—but its psychological, social and managerial techniques must never be the main pattern for our community's character. When will the church stop chasing the latest techniques in our culture and return to its own unique character and culture? Until we do, we have precisely *nothing* of interest or help to give to our world (except an encouraging slap on the back).

The Amish are an example of a Christian community that tries to be faithful and holy in a thoroughgoing way. Their approach to farming, to technology, to dress and to the education of their children is in stark contrast to the world around them. They refuse to be accommodated. Even if the Amish version of holy nonconformity is today guided more by an agrarian, preindustrial model than by biblical themes, they deserve our admiration for their determination to be holy. The Christian Conciliation Service of the Christian Legal Society also exemplifies holy nonconformity—offering a creative, biblical alternative to the American system of adversarial court proceedings.

> **H**oliness
> 1. knowing when and how to say no—getting pure and staying free from sin
> 2. knowing when and how to say yes—being distinctive and different in the ways that God is distinctive

---

[16]I am not personally a hard-nosed legalist on these matters, but I do find it strange that many Christian folk don't worry much any more about divorce and remarriage among their leaders but have a fit about homosexuality. Greed, selfishness and gluttony are also widely acceptable, though abortion is not (at least publicly). I'm afraid our sense of what makes for a holy church today doesn't match up very well with what the Bible says. Our list looks pretty self-serving.

Wise: Learning to Be Discerning

Wisdom was one of the four cardinal virtues for Plato and Aristotle, and it is a recurring theme in the Old and New Testaments. We will not be building good character unless wisdom is one of its traits. Wisdom is not the same thing as knowledge, intelligence, cleverness or being smart. Wisdom is practical. It is the capacity to have good discernment and judgment, to give good counsel and make good decisions. Prudence is an older term for this character trait.

In a basic sense, wisdom is the counterpart to foolishness. The Proverbs often contrast wisdom and folly in this way. The fool blunders stupidly forward, failing to learn from experience, making decisions based on short-term desires, refusing to learn from others, incapable of self-discipline. Wisdom is undermined by thoughtlessness.

The biblical and classical traditions part company not on the importance of wisdom but on its sources and content. "The fear of the LORD is the beginning of wisdom" (Prov 9:10). "For the LORD gives wisdom" (Prov 2:6). This is the linkage to faith and faithfulness. Wisdom is a character trait that cannot be cultivated apart from close and constant attachment to its source: God. Faith attaches us to God; wisdom is one of its corollaries. It is not possible to be wise merely through human education and experience or through nature's gifts to us. True wisdom requires God's presence and guidance.

Biblical wisdom is different from worldly wisdom. "God's foolishness is wiser than human wisdom" (1 Cor 1:25). The wisdom of God is "not a wisdom of this age or of the rulers of this age" (1 Cor 2:6). In other words, the wisdom of God is holy—free from both the corruption and the limitation of the world. It brings a distinctive message, uncorrupted by selfish, partisan interests, unimpeded by the narrowness of the world's vision.

It is crucial to note that the Bible does not invite Christians to repudiate all wisdom but rather to seek the true wisdom that comes from God. It is not unusual to find well-meaning Christians who blunder their way through life claiming that God's Spirit has led them to do or say this or that. "God led me," "the Lord told me," and "the Spirit moved me" are all great phrases, and we want them to be true in our lives. I don't question that there can be a sort of mysterious, interior, divine guidance on occasion. But when you see well-meaning Christians making boneheaded, foolish decisions over and over, impervious to the counsel of others, and then piously claiming God's guidance—this is neither God's guidance, nor God's wisdom at work.

The Bible is full of commonsense advice and respect for the lessons of experience and nature. Biblical teaching and wisdom "make sense" of life and its challenges. And yet biblical wisdom always has something greater, something distinctive and different from the wisdom and counsel of the world. This distinctiveness comes from God's character and word. True wisdom is rooted in God's values, opinions and standards. This means that there will be a richer, deeper, broader texture for our thought and decision. God's perspective is not narrow but takes into account other people near and far, the past and the future, the spiritual, economic, psychological, and moral realities of situations. It is this kind of perspective in which true wisdom is rooted.

> The wisdom of God may appear as foolishness to the world but that is not a license for Christians to justify or excuse their foolish decisions by claiming "The Lord told me . . ."
> The wisdom of God is greater than that of the world, not less.

How do we become wise? We must come to know the mind of God by careful and ongoing study of Scripture. We must seek out, observe and listen to others wiser and more experienced than ourselves. We must learn how to listen, how to observe, how to reflect on life. Wisdom does not consist of processing data. It cannot be found in rushing around frantically. It cannot be given by those who only know how to talk. Wisdom needs experience, study, quiet, prayer and courage. Wisdom grows from faithfulness and holiness.

As with all character traits and virtues in a good Christian character, wisdom is not detachable from the work of God's Spirit in our lives. At bottom, it is a gift of God, not a human accomplishment. So we pray for it as well as study and work for it. And we hope we will also be helped toward wisdom by a church which is a community of faith, holiness and wisdom. How good to have a mind that is mentored by wise friends and elders in such a community. How tragic that our churches often do little or nothing to pair people up in such mentoring relationships where the more experienced and wise could pass on what they have learned.

The Virtues and Habits of the Disciple

Character virtues and traits are related to the roles we carry out in the drama of life. Everyone is in the role of "disciple." "Disciple" (Greek *mathētēs*) means "learner" or "trainee." Everyone invites influences into their lives. But of whom or what are we disciples? Who is our teacher and discipler? In the Christian faith we invite the central influence of Jesus Christ. To become a Christian is to take on the role of—to become—a disciple of Jesus Christ. The term is used hundreds of times in the Gospels to describe the foundational role and relationship of people to God.

Wisdom
1. able to make sound, practical decisions
2. faithfully rooted in the wisdom of God
3. appropriate to particular circumstances

Here is the standard pattern: Jesus shows up in some neighborhood or house or business. He works; he eats; he talks; he listens; he heals. He invites those interested to follow him and learn about a new way of life and thought under the rule of the living God. Those who decide to follow are exercising faith. They attach themselves to Jesus, following, clinging to him, pursuing him, trusting him. That is *faithfulness*. They have lots of questions, some doubts, intermittent fears. But they also have some life-changing knowledge. They are gripped by the truth and life that they find in Jesus Christ.

When disciples follow Jesus in faithful, loyal commitment, they necessarily are leaving something behind and embarking on something very different from the previous phase of their lives. They leave behind (repent, turn from, disavow, repudiate) the sin, impurity, unrighteousness and injustice of the past—and embrace a radically new way of life. And this is *holiness*—in the dual sense of purity and distinctiveness. Faithful disciples are holy. All of this is "Discipleship 101"—the most basic, foundational realities.

Faithful and holy disciples become wise disciples. They are taught how to be wise stewards of their master's interests. As disciples they are "learners"—and they are learning a new kind of truth and wisdom from their leader. Their perspectives on life are being changed, deepened and enriched; they are learning to sit and listen; they are sent out two by two to practice what they learn, and then they return for debriefing and for further teaching and encouragement.

The basic, foundational role our character is called to fulfill is that of a disciple of Jesus Christ. God's grace "directs" and enables our performance. Faithfulness is the habitual, foundational master trait of the good disciple in this drama. Holiness and wisdom are two other key character traits that accompany faithfulness from the opening to the final scene.

For Reflection or Discussion

1. What are some of the ways we could better practice faith and faithfulness in today's world? Can you share an example of faithfulness that inspires you?

2. What are the key indicators of true holiness in the Christian life today? Is conformity to the world a problem among today's Christians? Who in the church (present or past) has been a good example of true holiness ("saintliness") for you? Why?

3. What are some of the situations and challenges you face today where wisdom is going to be especially needed? What steps can you take to find this wisdom?

Seven

OPEN, RESPONSIBLE & GENTLE
The Servant

*T*hink back to the scene at the beginning of the Sermon on the Mount: there in Palestine, at the crossroads of the world, surrounded by the crowds, Jesus shows up. This is God's grace: pursuing humanity, showing up in our midst as the healer, teacher, redeemer and friend. The disciples follow Jesus up on the mountain and sit at his feet. This is faith: pursuing God, attaching ourselves to God. And as they attach themselves to Jesus in faith, they are pulled away, separated from the crowd and from their previous way of life. This is holiness: separation, purity, otherness. Jesus then teaches them. This is the beginning of true wisdom. What happens next clashes with our expectations, and it is certainly a "holy" contradiction of the spirit of the world. The first lesson for faithful, holy and wise disciples is that they are blessed if they are poor in spirit, if they mourn, and if they are meek and gentle.

He Restores My Soul
In holiness disciples step away from the aggressive, domineering, con-

trolling attitude of the world. We step back from the "will to power" and the competitive urge. In our activist, "let's just do it" era, our inclination is to want to "get with the program" and immediately begin serving God in the world. But that's not the way it works.

There *is* an activist agenda in this adventure, but the active life of Christians only grows out of what we might call the contemplative life. "Be still, and know that I am God" (Ps 46:10). "Those who wait for the LORD shall renew their strength" (Is 40:31). Knowledge and strength come out of stillness and waiting.

The famous twenty-third Psalm clearly sketches the same pattern as the Beatitudes:

> The LORD is my shepherd, I shall not want.
>> He makes me lie down in green pastures;
> he leads me beside still waters;
>> he restores my soul.
> He leads me in right paths
>> for his name's sake.

Everything begins with the relationship of faith—we attach ourselves to the Lord as our Shepherd. Our activist "make it happen" inclination would follow this opening statement immediately with an aggressive pursuit of the "paths of righteousness" and then boldly onward, swashbuckling into "the valley of the shadow of death" and the "presence of the enemies."

This is a crucial illustration of holiness: God's way is different. This is a wisdom that appears as foolishness to the world but in reality is the truer, higher wisdom of God. We simply cannot be ready to walk, climb or run the paths of righteousness until we are first made to "lie down" where God can pasture us and restore our soul. Remember how Moses was prepared for forty years? how Paul was quiet for three years after his remarkable conversion? how Jesus himself drew away from the crowds to be alone quietly with God?

This pattern of contemplation before action is one that cycles through the authentic Christian experience. There must be a quiet period of time (though not an *empty* time!) at the beginning of our discipleship before we become activists. As the years pass we will need to return to such sabbath rests from time to time, when we back off from our busy-ness and invite God to restore our soul.

Even in our daily lives we need to practice this pattern of quieting ourselves before God. Our most energetic activism must never be separated too far from quietness, waiting, contemplation and humility. There is a kind of rhythm to this. In our most aggressive activism we remain "contemplatives become active," not "activists who were formerly contemplatives." The Beatitudes begin, then, with the step of faith: the disciples come to be shepherded by the Lord—and proceed to the three virtues of the contemplative life: poverty of spirit, mourning and meekness. One flows from the other. And together they prepare us for the "righteousness agenda" of the fourth through eighth Beatitudes.

Openness and Poverty of Spirit: Where We Must Begin

"Blessed are the poor in spirit, for theirs is the kingdom of heaven." God is holy—wholly other than what we ordinarily expect. The wisdom of God appears as foolishness to the world; the strength of God appears as weakness. The first Beatitude perfectly illustrates this otherness. Who on earth would say that it is blessed to be poor in spirit? In the parallel text of Luke, the statement seems even more radical: "Blessed are you who are poor" (Lk 6:20). How can poverty be a happy or blessed condition?

> The active Christian life is only possible if it is rooted in the contemplative life, the basic virtues of which are openness, responsibility, gentleness, quietness and humility.

Rich and poor. Remember that Jesus said, "I came that they may have life, and have it abundantly" (Jn 10:10). Paul said: "You know the generous act of our Lord Jesus Christ, that though he was rich, yet for your sakes he became poor, so that by his poverty you might become rich" (2 Cor 8:9). In the larger biblical picture, poverty is certainly not a self-sufficient end, not an intrinsically good goal of life. God's intention for us is a rich, abundant life.

Nevertheless, there is also a consistent pattern of warning about wealth and riches. Jesus said, "Woe to you who are rich . . . to you who are full now" (Lk 6:24-25). "How hard it is for those who have wealth to enter the kingdom of God! Indeed, it is easier for a camel to go

127

through the eye of a needle than for someone who is rich to enter the kingdom of God" (Lk 18:24-25). ("What is impossible for mortals is possible for God," he then added, so this is not the final word on the rich.)

Paul continued these warnings against striving to become rich. "Those who want to be rich fall into temptation and are trapped by many senseless and harmful desires that plunge people into ruin and destruction. For the love of money is a root of all kinds of evil, and in their eagerness to be rich some have wandered away from the faith and pierced themselves with many pains" (1 Tim 6:9-10). The church at Laodicea is severely criticized in John's Revelation because: "You say 'I am rich, I have prospered, and I need nothing.' You do not realize that you are wretched, pitiable, poor, blind, and naked" (Rev 3:17). The Laodiceans were rich by some standards, but this masked a profound poverty. The least we can say is that it is very risky to be rich, self-sufficient and full. Sometimes it is fatal.

Wealth and poverty have many dimensions. Material possessions come to mind first, but it is also possible to be rich or poor in time, health, personal appearance, education, intelligence, reputation and relationships. At the core of our lives is our spirit—the basic force that moves our life and being, the wind that is in our sails, driving our life. To be "rich in spirit" in this sense means pride, the condition of being "full of our self." In a profound sense *pride* is the enemy, the exact opposite of poverty of spirit. Pride is the great sin, the sin that keeps us from God.[1]

Our technologically developed world is embarrassingly rich in possessions, power, food and many things. Some of this we can recognize as God's blessing for which we should be grateful, but we need to be careful and self-critical. Is our wealth leading to pride and self-congratulation? Is our wealth coming at the expense of others who must remain poor? Does our wealth give us a false sense of security and dis-

---

[1]"The deepest reason God hates pride, the reason pride is so hellish, is that it keeps us from knowing God, our supreme joy. Pride looks down, and no one can see God but by looking up." Peter Kreeft, *Back to Virtue* (San Francisco: Ignatius, 1986), p. 102.

tract us from important issues? Is some of what we treasure actually worthless? The fact is that we are all, in a profound sense, truly poor. Our culture is poor in time, in meaning, in friendship, in relationships. We are living in ways that will increasingly make us poor in safety and poor in our environment. Most of all in the secularized West, we are poor in God's spirit.

God gives to the poor. The Greek word used in the Beatitude is *ptōchos,* which means "empty, needy, poor." This is a condition, a state of being. And yet it can be a blessed condition—if God is in the neighborhood. "When the poor and needy seek water, and there is none, and their tongue is parched with thirst, I the LORD will answer them, I the God of Israel will not forsake them" (Is 41:17). Mary, in her Magnificat, said "He has filled the hungry with good things, and sent the rich away empty" (Lk 1:53). Jesus announced at the beginning of his public ministry: "The Spirit of the Lord is upon me, because he has anointed me to bring good news to the poor . . . release to the captives and recovery of sight to the blind, to let the oppressed go free" (Lk 4:18, citing Is 61:1). It is to the poor, the needy, the sick, the disabled, the oppressed, the social outcast, the prisoner, the sinner, that the gospel is especially directed and among whom it is especially effective.

Certainly, the list includes the materially poor, but it is a constant in the Bible that those poor in reputation, poor in performance, poor in relationships, are also included. From cover to cover the Bible describes God's love and desire for the poor, the widows, the orphans, the outcasts and the losers. To be convinced of this a person has only to look at biblical characters like Jacob (a conniving cheat who was chosen to become "Israel"), Peter ("Get behind me, Satan," was the way our Lord had to rebuke the "Prince of the Apostles"), poor Mary and Joseph, and the list goes on.

But why is it the poor who are blessed? How can this be? Why would God seek out the poor in spirit? The answer is that only those who are empty have room to receive what God has to give. Only the poor in spirit have room to receive God's spirit. Think of a dinner party. The host brings around some fresh, hot coffee; what a shame if your cup is already full of something else or with some lukewarm stuff. What a shame if your glass is full of some generic, mediocre punch when the host brings around the '82 Bordeaux! What a shame to be so full of the hors d'oeuvres that you have no room to take in the spectacular main course. How blessed to be empty and receptive at those times of opportunity.[2]

So the poor in spirit are blessed now, as they come to God in faith and receive the kingdom of heaven. Their empty hands are opened to the God who will fill them. They are blessed with God as their king, with the Lord as their shepherd. Emptied of their own spirit, God's Spirit becomes the wind in their sails, driving their lives. He becomes the bread and the wine that nourish, satisfy, and give life and health. Poverty is, thus, not an *intrinsic* good (good in and of itself), but it is an *instrumental* good in that it is the precondition of being filled.

> **O**nly those who are empty have room to receive what God has to give. Only the poor in spirit have room to receive God's Spirit. Emptiness is blessed only because it is the essential precondition to being filled. Poverty is instrumentally, not intrinsically, good.

It is often difficult for the materially rich to experience profoundly the provision of the God who owns everything. It is sometimes difficult for the smile of God to light up the face of beautiful people. It is often difficult for the brilliant and educationally rich to be filled with the wisdom and discernment of the mind of Christ. It is difficult for those glorying in their own prosperity and accomplishments to exult in the glory and provision of God. If we are full of pride and our own spirit, there is no room for God's Spirit. It is blessed to be poor in spirit if we are sitting at the feet of Jesus in faith; ours is then the kingdom of heaven.

How we become poor. Sometimes we are poor (in wealth, in health, in spirit) because of what others have done. We may be the victims of neglectful parents, abusive spouses, lawyers, drunken drivers, incompetent teachers, exploitive therapists, unethical pastors, embezzling

---

[2]"The objector to poverty of spirit fails to understand the power of emptiness. The power Jesus refers to on the spiritual level is the same power that makes bowls, windows, and rooms useful on the physical level. Fill them up and they become useless; you take way their potentiality, their possibility. That power makes motherhood great on the biological level; it is the empty womb that can generate life." Peter Kreeft, *Back to Virtue* (San Francisco: Ignatius, 1986), p. 105.

accountants or violent hoodlums and thieves. We may be poor in health because of carcinogens dumped into our air, food and water supply by industry. We may be economic victims of racist or unfair employers or landlords. Our spiritual, emotional, relational and physical lives usually bear scars from some of these sources. We are sometimes the victims of what others have done and don't deserve the poverty, pain and havoc that have been brought into our lives.

Why Are We Poor and Needy?
1. We are the victims of others' actions.
2. We suffer from our own bad choices.
3. We choose to renounce some things.

Some of our poverty, however, is of our own making. We have made choices that were unwise or even wicked. Not all of our poverty is the fault of others. Nobody forced us to be lazy or foolish or irresponsible with our money or educational opportunities. Our choices with respect to smoking, drinking, gambling, eating, exercise and sexual practices are usually our own, and some of us are poor because of choices we have made in those areas. We have blown opportunities, ruined relationships, caused scars in others and in ourselves.

Dietrich Bonhoeffer understood the Beatitudes as describing a poverty that results from a third source. This poverty accompanies the disciples in their "leaving all" to follow Jesus. As Bonhoeffer sees it, the Beatitudes describe not only *privation* but *renunciation*—a renunciation of power, experience, knowledge, possessions (the poor in spirit), of peace and prosperity (those who mourn, who bear the world's sorrow), of their rights (the meek), of their own righteousness (hungering for God's righteousness instead), of their dignity and honor (the merciful), of their own goodness (the pure in heart) and of violence (the peacemakers).[3]

Thus, the origins of our poverty and neediness may result from three sources: our victimization by others, our own mistakes and our decision to "leave all" in pursuit of Jesus. Whatever its origins, we need to recognize and acknowledge this poverty as the truth and reality of our life, and then bring it to Jesus. We must refuse to remain defined

---

[3]Dietrich Bonhoefer, *The Cost of Discipleship* (New York: Macmillan, 1959), pp. 117-34.

only by our poverty and victimization, our wickedness and failure. Even the self-emptying poverty of renunciation cannot be the end. We face up to our condition. We recognize it as our truth and reality, but we do not remain there. We bring it in faith to God. We cling to Jesus in our emptiness. And he fills us with his kingly presence. We will not remain poor—but we must begin in poverty. Being poor and needy is not only a good place to start, it's the *only* place where we can start the Christian adventure.

Three practices of poverty. The three practices described at the center of the Sermon on the Mount are, in an important way, the practices that express (and protect) true poverty of spirit. Especially for those of us who are rich in so many ways, these practices are essential to the kind of character formation we need. First of all, we give alms (Mt 6:2-4). We give away materially to those in need, quietly and without fanfare. This intends to help the recipients, of course, but giving away significant amounts of what we own is the surest way of liberating us from our dependence on or attachment to possessions. Giving not just from our excess but from our substance is a crucial exercise.

Second, we pray (Mt 6:5-15). We kneel before God as our Father, glorifying his name, praying for his interests, his kingdom, his will to be done. Then we pray for our daily bread, for forgiveness and a forgiving spirit, and for God's leadership and deliverance in the struggles of life. In prayer we express not only our fullness (of praise and thankfulness), we also express our emptiness. In our era of pride and self-assurance, physically getting on our knees for prayer may be more important than it has ever been.

Third, we fast (Mt 6:16-18). We restrict our food in an exercise of self-denial and self-discipline, humbly, quietly and without fanfare. Most fasting in our day is motivated by vanity and obesity. We would be healthier in spirit and in body if we fasted to the Lord on a more-or-less regular basis. By extension, the other needs and wants of our existence also threaten our spirituality when consumption and indulgence are unrestricted. Is there ever a time when we want something and could acquire it—but choose not to? Some degree of "consumer fasting" would contribute greatly to our spiritual health.

Especially when we are living in a self-indulgent, noisy, distracted era, these spiritual exercises of giving, praying and fasting are crucial necessities if we are to be poor in spirit and receptive to our king. This is where our character renewal as biblical people must begin. Faithful, holy, wise disciples make a habit of being poor in spirit and are disposed to give, pray and fast regularly.

Undoubtedly, we need to cultivate poverty of spirit as individuals alone before God. How much better, nevertheless, to live out such discipleship in a community of the poor in spirit. Would that our churches were poorer in spirit! The world's style of triumphalism, success, strutting and boasting is all too common in our churches. Adding a few "Praise the Lords" to such bravado is hardly the path to true sanctification. Such Laodicean hubris grieves and quenches the Holy Spirit—and it is hardly a welcoming atmosphere for the broken and hurting of our world. Cocky Christianity is an offense to God and a betrayal of the gospel. How much better to be sure our communities take up special collections to give to the poor, to redirect our budgets from our comfort toward meeting others' needs, and to schedule days of prayer and fasting.

Three Paths to Poverty of Spirit
1. alms: giving generously to help others
2. fasting: choosing not to fulfill our appetites
3. prayer: gratitude, humility and submission

A community of fellow-pilgrims who know they are poor and in need of God receives the kingdom of heaven. The kingdom means the rule of God. Into the lives of the poor in spirit, God comes as living Lord and leader. Our lives have the direction and protection of God himself. The gracious God is among us as our king, displacing all the other powers, forces or idols we might earlier have been serving.

Those whose character displays a poverty of spirit toward God will also be transformed in their attitudes and relations to other people. Our own poverty, emptiness, ignorance and need before others enables them to give to us and enables us to receive from them. Not independence and distance but openness, receptivity and interdependence will characterize our mutual relations.[4] The poor in spirit are people who have learned that they don't know everything and don't

---

[4]See Alphonse Maillot, *Les Beatitudes* (Paris: Librairie Protestante, n.d.), pp. 15-17.

have everything. They are humble. They will speak and act, but first they will listen attentively. It becomes woven into their character to be this way. As those who are first of all empty and then filled by God's rule, we need not fear being open before others; the throne of our life has been occupied by God; we have nothing to fear.

Responsibility and Mourning: What We Do with Our Poverty

"Blessed are those who mourn, for they will be comforted." The second virtue of the contemplative life is mourning—a second contradiction and anomaly in our culture of assertive, rugged, impenitent individualists. The Greek word used here is *pentheō*, which connotes "grieving, sorrowing, weeping." The Sermon on the Plain says "Blessed are you who weep now, for you will laugh" (Lk 6:21). Jesus himself wept (Jn 11:35). Peter "went out and wept bitterly" after he denied Christ the third time (Lk 22:62). In the greatest of the penitential psalms, David says, after his sin against Uriah and Bathsheba, "The sacrifice acceptable to God is a broken spirit; a broken and contrite heart, O God, you will not despise" (Ps 51:17).

> **P**overty of Spirit
> 1. open and receptive to God's presence and rule
> 2. open, humble and teachable by other people

The sort of mourning that is blessed is the anguish, the remorse, the grief and the sorrow we feel about the poverty described in the first Beatitude. The Beatitudes, remember, are not a random collection of sayings but a careful progression where each builds on its predecessor. Mourning is partly a sorrowing over the pain, offense and need suffered by others, a "bearing of sorrow" in Bonhoeffer's words. But most of all, it is a mourning of our own condition and that of our Christian community. And while we mourn the ways we have been victimized by others, it is finally a mourning of our own sin and failure. This is the mourning of repentance. "God, be merciful to me, a sinner!" cried out the repentant publican (Lk 18:13).[5] Mourning is our assumption of

---

[5]"He designated not simply all that mourn, but all that do so for sins. . . . They that mourn, mourn for misdoings . . . not only for our own, but also for other men's misdoings." John Chrysostom, *Homily XV on the Gospel of Saint Matthew,* in Nicene and Post-Nicene Fathers, ed. Philip Schaff (Grand Rapids, Mich.: Eerdmans, 1956), 10:93.

appropriate responsibility for our poverty and brokenness.

Laughter, denial and rage. "Woe to you who are laughing now, for you will mourn and weep" (Lk 6:25). One of our obstacles to authentic mourning is the tendency of our culture to trivialize or deny the seriousness of our plight. We drown out reality with distracting entertainment and laugh it up with our associates. A tragic news story is followed immediately by a giggling weather report or a commercial celebrating the affluent life of the beautiful people. Our attention is diverted; our sensitivity is dulled. We postpone our day of reckoning with reality. A second obstacle to mourning is a culture that has a long tradition of repressing feelings of grief and sorrow. This has been especially true of the way boys and men are trained. But blessed are those who do not repress it, who do not bottle up their grief, who do not restrain the passion of their repentance and sorrow. It can be a good thing to cry.

When our culture does permit or encourage us to vent our feelings, it often relates to rage at others who have mistreated us. We are encouraged to play the "blame game" and rage out of our victimhood at the parents, racists, gangs, lawyers, neighbors, children, colleagues, bosses or politicians who have hurt us. Our vocabularies grow rich with terms of invective, cursing, insult and demands for revenge. Television talk shows invest good money to put before audiences the pitiful spectacle of rage and accusation between relatives or former friends. The talk show hosts goad the process on with juicy video clips, mean comments from the studio audience and their own defiant provocations. Radio talk shows, no less, are all too often forums for wild rage, accusation and recrimination. But this is mourning as rage, mourning as public spectacle.

> A character that mourns takes appropriate responsibility for its poverty, need and brokenness—regretting, repenting, sorrowing—instead of trivializing and denying it or raging and blaming others.

Mourning and comfort. The mourning that is blessed by the second Beatitude is not the mourning that stops at self-pity or at victimhood, blame and accusation. Those are ultimately aimed at self-justification. The tears of the salt of the earth and light of the world are the tears of those who recognize and acknowledge their poverty in all its dimensions, who regret it, who take responsibility for it, who confess it and repent of their part in it. They are the tears of those who have come to the cross to see the price of their forgiveness and salvation borne by Jesus, of those will take neither their poverty nor their salvation lightly. They feel it deeply: "Amazing grace, how sweet the sound that saved a wretch like me. I once was lost . . . blind." Paul says "hate what is evil"—don't take it lightly (Rom 12:9).

Only those who mourn will be comforted. Only those who weep will experience the laughter of the Spirit. Think about our ordinary experiences: someone who rages on against others or who persists in pride, self-justification and denial cannot be comforted. Those who mourn adopt the tender, repentant spirit that can be comforted. Jesus refers to the coming Holy Spirit as the "Comforter" (Jn 14:16, 26 KJV). The same Greek word *(paraklētos, parakaleō)* is used for the Holy Spirit and for the comfort promised in the Beatitudes. Those who mourn at the feet of Jesus will receive the Comforter. Certainly the Holy Spirit is given to all who come in poverty and faith to Jesus Christ. But the full power and presence of God's comforting

> **O**nly one who mourns can be comforted. Those who rage, blame and hate are inconsolable—and cannot grow in strong character until they pass through poverty to mourning and then comfort.

Spirit alongside and within us depends on our receptivity and mourning. "Godly grief produces a repentance that leads to salvation and brings no regret, but worldly grief produces death" (2 Cor 7:10).

How we mourn. Character traits come partly through our repeated practices, our habits. We express and cultivate the right kind of mourning, first, by our meditation on the cross of Christ. The cross is not just a symbol to wear as jewelry or a good-luck charm around our neck. It is the central event of all history. Jesus suffered and died for our poverty. I understand my need and mourn it when I understand the cross. It is not so much by looking honestly in the mirror that I am moved to sorrow and repentance; rather, it is by looking at the cross of Christ and seeing myself in its shadow. There is a reason why the trial and crucifixion of Jesus are described at such length in all four Gospels. For the apostles, the cross of Christ is at the center of all theology and practice.

We might study and meditate on the meaning of the cross, for example, by looking at Jesus' "Seven Last Words," which explain its significance. For many of us, music is an important avenue by which God speaks deeply, convictingly, to our soul about our poverty and Christ's sacrifice. It might be the "St. Matthew Passion" of J. S. Bach, a great old hymn of the faith like "When I Survey the Wondrous Cross," a song from the Vineyard or Calvary Chapel, or the soul-stirring power of gospel music. Music sometimes helps communicate truth to our soul.

Second, we express mourning by our rigorous self-examination before God and his Word, by opening our heart to God, by kneeling (both physically and symbolically, individually and in the fellowship of others) in prayers confessing to him our sin and need. Reading the penitential psalms, such as Psalm 51, helps focus our mourning and repentance. Listen to the apostle Paul's wrestling: "I know that nothing good dwells within me, that is, in my flesh. I can will what is right, but I cannot do it. For I do not do the good I want, but the evil I do not want is what I do. . . . Wretched man that I am! Who will rescue me from this body of death? Thanks be to God through Jesus Christ our Lord!" (Rom 7:18-19, 24-25).

Mourning
1. responsibly accept our poverty as our own
2. focus on Jesus, the poor Man of Sorrows
3. prayer yielding poverty and sorrow to God
4. humble confession to those we have hurt

Third, we express our mourning and repentance relationally by making a regular practice of confessing and asking forgiveness of those we have hurt. This is a humbling and difficult thing to do, especially because situations are rarely totally our own fault. Faithful and holy disciples make a habit of humbling themselves in this way. Moreover, we grieve for the suffering and poverty of our world. "The whole creation has been groaning," Paul writes (Rom 8:22). Jesus wept as he looked out on the world and the people. So mourning is not just an individual but a community virtue. It is not merely focused on the poverty of the self but beyond.

While our varied temperaments affect the ways this mourning is experienced and displayed (the number of tears does not necessarily equal the degree of true mourning before God!), none of us can skip over this phase in our character formation. We return to it on a daily basis. And how sweet it is to find a church that grieves and mourns over its sin and the sin of the world. How common it is to find churches that omit prayers of confession, repentance and mourning of this sort. But churches that forget to mourn are churches in denial of the reality of human life and the truth of God's Word. Churches that do not mourn find it easy to accuse but hard to comfort, hard to be merciful. Churches that forget to mourn are churches without the strong presence of the Comforter. Blessed are those who mourn, for they will be comforted.

As in the case of the other virtues of good character, mourning and responsibility affect our relationships with other people, not just with God. Those who mourn may appear weak by today's macho standards. Actually, they are strong—strong enough to face the truth, to accept responsibility for their own part in life's poverty and tragedy, strong enough to be honest and open about their sorrow and regret. The tenderness of those who mourn makes possible a renewal of broken relationships. Rage, blame and self-justification all harden people and situations. Mourning, in this biblical sense, softens and restores people and situations.

Gentleness and Meekness: Learning to Let Go in Freedom

"Blessed are the meek, for they will inherit the earth." But what does this third Beatitude mean by "meekness"? How does this relate to the first two Beatitudes? There are a lot of seminars and books on prayer, on love, on stewardship, on leadership, on evangelism—but not very many on meekness.[6] And yet Jesus said, "Take my yoke upon you, and learn from me; for I am gentle [meek] and humble in heart, and you will find rest for your souls" (Mt 11:29). Jesus was himself meek; he invites us to learn from him, from his relationships with his heavenly Father, with erring Peter and the disciples, pesky outsiders, false accusers at his trial and persecutors at the cross.

Moses was described in Numbers 12:3 as the meekest (or most hum-

---

[6]Judith C. Lechman has written the helpful book *The Spirituality of Gentleness* (San Francisco: Harper & Row, 1987)

ble) man on earth—not our usual image of Israel's great leader! Both
Paul and Peter call us to be meek like Jesus. Meekness/gentleness is
one of the fruits of the Spirit (Gal 5:23). Paul appeals to the Corinthians "by the meekness and gentleness of Christ" (2 Cor 10:1); he
says to restore an erring brother in a spirit of gentleness/meekness (Gal
6:1), to walk worthy of the Lord in meekness (Eph 4:2), and to put on a
heart of meekness (Col 3:12). Peter says to give our apologetic for the
faith to outsiders with spirit of meekness, not contentiousness (1 Pet
3:15-16). Meekness is not an optional extra in Christian life; it is a crucial part of the content of our character.

Meekness means letting go. It is a common misconception that
"meek" means "weak," or still worse, "wimp" or "doormat." But Jesus
did not say "Blessed are the weak" or "Blessed are the wimps"—he said
"Blessed are the meek." And surely our Lord was not weak or wimpy!
He was the strongest and boldest of men. The Greek word is *praÿs*,
used in the New Testament to mean "gentleness, humility, meekness,
mildness." The same word was used in secular discussions, for example, of horses that are tamed, that no longer buck against those who
ride them. I will use the term gentleness interchangeably with meekness.

It is Psalm 37 that helps us understand meekness. The third Beatitude is a quotation from Psalm 37:11: "The meek shall inherit the
land." The context of this statement in the psalm helps us understand
its basic meaning. The first eleven verses of this psalm describe the
negative counterparts to meekness: we are told not to be envious and
not to give in to anger or wrath. And three times we are told "Do not
fret" (Ps 37:1, 7, 8). In each case the problem is one of getting all
worked up about things we cannot control. On the other hand, the
psalm calls us to "trust in the LORD," "dwell in the land," "enjoy safe
pasture," "delight in the LORD," "commit your way to the LORD," "be
still before the LORD," "wait patiently for him," and "hope in the
LORD." Then the climax: "the meek will inherit the land and enjoy
great peace" (Ps 37:1-11 NIV).

What these expressions have in common is the idea of calming
down and joyfully trusting our problems to God instead of fretting
over them. The psalm tells us that if we live this way, the Lord "will

give [us] the desires of [our] heart" and that he "will make [our] righteousness shine like the dawn, the justice of [our] cause like the noonday sun" (Ps 37:4, 6 NIV). If we will give up control, the Lord will take over; we do not even need to buy or conquer the land—we shall "inherit it."

So meekness is not the counterpart to swaggering but to fretting! Naturally we should not be arrogant. But the primary message of the third Beatitude is that we should learn to stop fretting and trying to control everything around us. To be meek means to be able to live "out of control," relying on God's power and control. It means to be gentle and tame, to "let go."

We live in an era of powerful technologies gaining control of the earth. We want to be the masters of space and time. Advertisers try to control our appetites and desires. Scientists try to control outer space. Genetic researchers strive to master all genetic causation. Parents try to control their kids (sometimes even when those kids have turned fifty years old!). Factions sometimes try to control the church. We are trained to work hard to improve our self, to control our life. And few of us can resist the temptation to respond to those who mistreat us, so that we can have the last and loudest word.

Most basic of all, however, and most difficult, is our own self. We often want to take responsibility; we want to correct our mistakes; we want to work our way out of poverty and wipe away our own tears, at least. But as faith positions us before God, we cannot alleviate our real poverty or comfort our mourning. This is what the sequence of the first three Beatitudes teaches us. Meekness recognizes this and gives up. Then God can fully take over. And only then are we finally ready to become activists who "hunger and thirst for righteousness" (the fourth Beatitude). It is no accident that later in Psalm 37 we are told, "The righteous shall inherit the land, and live in it forever" (Ps 37:29). We must learn meekness first; then, and only then, we are prepared to rise up in the land with a passionate hunger for righteousness.

Meekness
1. gentle and "tame"—letting go, no more fretting
2. not trying to fill our own poverty and emptiness
3. not trying to comfort our mourning all alone
4. giving up control and resting in freedom

The rewards of letting go. We must learn to let go—to be meek and gentle—because only then are we able to see God's control of our lives and our world. Why will the meek inherit the earth? Because *they are the only ones God can trust* to care for his earth! If you are not meek, you will try to take over even God's territory. From Psalm 37 we learn the tactics for achieving true meekness: trust, delight, enjoy, be still, wait, hope *in the Lord.* Meekness and gentleness are not letting go into the void—but into the hands of God. That makes all the difference.

In practice, we all face situations we wish we could control at home, at work, in the church, in politics. We are tempted to fret and even get riled up and angry. We may need to let go of our ambition (even if we always thought of it as ambition to do some great thing for God). We may need to let go of our ministry or business (even if we were trying to control it only for what we thought was God's greater glory). We might need to let go of our children (even though we only want so desperately to guide them into what is best for them). In these and other situations, we need as biblical people to seek after true meekness, to pray that God will calm our spirits, help us let go, and release in us a deep joy and confidence that he is in control. Meekness is based on confidence in the God to whom we are attached by grace and faith. It comes from strength not from weakness. Meekness flows from courage and confidence, not from fear and timidity.

Meekly, gently "letting go" is based on confidence in God's care. We do not let ourselves (or others) go into the void, but to Jesus.

There is no better example of the meekness we seek than that given by our Lord. He had the power to come down from the cross but yielded his life according to God's will. He could have called down legions of angels to slay his enemies, but he didn't. "Christ also suffered for you, leaving you an example, so that you should follow in his steps. 'He committed no sin, and no deceit was found in his mouth.' When he was abused, he did not return abuse; when he suffered he did not threaten; but he entrusted himself to the one who judges justly" (1 Pet 2:21-23). In so doing, Jesus conquered sin and death and "inherited" the universe as King of kings and Lord of lords.

In many respects, this third virtue is the hardest of them all. It goes against our nature, our social training, our culture, our sense of justice, even against our survival instincts. It is a singular mark of true holiness, purified from all competitiveness and vindictiveness, distinctive and separate from the ways of the world. Meekness, letting go, letting God handle things, is extraordinarily difficult to practice when we suffer unjustly—or when we are mourning some poverty we have caused. Yet there are times when we have no other choice; we are powerless, and it is either fret—or give it to God. Perhaps even more difficult is meekness when we do have a measure of control: letting go of our kids or career, for example.

Our communities of faith are gymnasiums for practicing meekness. Over and over we are tempted to seize control for the cause of truth (not just for our own ambition!). Meekness is an issue in our relations one with another. It is also an issue in our corporate stance toward God and toward our neighborhood and world. Few church-growth strategists, and fewer still "Christian" political organizers, seem aware that there can be, and will be, no faithful growth or activism without our beginning in a posture of genuine meekness and gentleness at the foundation of all we do.

Meekness and gentleness are character traits we practice before God. But they also mark our character in its relationships with others. The meek and gentle person does not need to be in control of everything at every moment but can leave things in God's hands—and in others' hands. If we must hang on to our control, if we can't let people and situations be free, we are blocked in the development of good Christian character. We cannot salt the earth or light the world. We cannot be blessed.

> **P**overty/openness and mourning/responsibility are very, very difficult virtues in our era. Meekness—letting go—may be the most difficult of all in our aggressive, controlling culture of power.

The Virtues and Habits of the Servant
In the first three Beatitudes, then, we have an account of the virtues of the contemplative life of faithful, holy, wise disciples. With God's help we cultivate openness and poverty of spirit, then responsibility and

mourning, then meekness and gentleness. This kind of character receives the soul-restoring blessing of God. Jesus Christ enters immediately as our heavenly king, we are comforted by the Holy Spirit, and God gives us his earth as the theater of our life with him. These three initial virtues are the traits of the *contemplative* life because they have less to do with action than with attitude. They are a profound reorientation of our perspective and our stance toward ourselves and toward God. They are fundamental traits of character for those in the role of servant. Our role is not just that of disciple but that of servant.

Humble servants of God. The biblical concept of *humble servanthood* builds on poverty, mourning, and meekness. "Humility" means to be "low" or "lowly"—the opposite of pride, arrogance and self-assertion. "He has told you, O mortal, what is good; and what does the LORD require of you but to do justice, and to love kindness, and to walk humbly with your God?" (Mic 6:8). "Humble yourselves before the Lord, and he will exalt you" (Jas 4:10). "God opposes the proud, but gives grace to the humble" (1 Pet 5:5). Poverty, mourning and meekness are the ways of the humble.

Our Lord stressed the importance of humility: "All who exalt themselves will be humbled, and those who humble themselves will be exalted" (Lk 14:11). Childlike humility is essential even to enter God's kingdom: "Truly I tell you, unless you change and become like children, you will never enter the kingdom of heaven. Whoever becomes humble like this child is the greatest in the kingdom of heaven" (Mt 18:2-4). Jesus practiced what he preached. "Let the same mind be in you that was in Christ Jesus, who . . . emptied himself, taking the form of a slave . . . he humbled himself" (Phil 2:5-8).

"Submission" is an important aspect of this humble servanthood. The word (Greek *hypotassō*) literally means "rank yourself under," or "take the lower rank." "Subordination" is a better, more precise translation. Biblical people are to take the subordinate rank, to voluntarily become servants.[7] Jesus taught his followers that they are to serve.

---

[7]John Howard Yoder, *The Politics of Jesus* (Grand Rapids, Mich.: Eerdmans, 1972), pp. 163-92. Yoder has a magnificent discussion of voluntary "revolutionary subordination" in the Christian life.

"Who is greater, the one who is at the table or the one who serves? Is it not the one at the table? But I am among you as one who serves" (Lk 22:27). Jesus demonstrated this servanthood by washing the feet of his disciples—and instructed his disciples to do likewise (Jn 13).

To be a humble servant requires a certain attitude toward God: he is our Master and Leader. Our attitude toward our self is that we are no better than anyone else. Like everyone else, we begin poor and whatever we have is the gift of God, not a tribute to our own superiority. Our attitude to others is that they are loved by God (no matter how unlovable to us), and we are ready to serve them—not out of compulsion but in free obedience to Christ. Think of what this would mean for the way work gets done, decisions are made and leadership positions are assigned in our churches. What if we all were committed to humble servanthood (as we should be)? What if we saw this constellation of character traits (poverty, mourning, meekness) as a prerequisite for church leadership?

Ready for the world. Our character should not change when we turn our attention from God to our church or our neighborhood. We stay "in character" and willingly assume a humble servant position in relation to governing authorities, business managers, in fact, to everyone (1 Pet 2; Eph 5:21). Christians who find themselves in roles with authority over others (in business, politics, education) are not exempt; they humbly serve those they lead. Essentially, Jesus said, "Among the nations the rulers lord it over others. But among you it shall not be so. Among you the servant of all is the leader and the leader is the servant" (Lk 22:25-26).

Even when we are surrounded by hostility and threats, remember that Jesus sends us out as "sheep into the midst of wolves" (Mt 10:16). "It is the Lamb of God, Jesus Christ, who takes away the sins of the world. . . . In the world everyone wants to be a 'wolf,' and no one is called to play the part of a 'sheep.' Yet the world cannot *live* without this living witness of sacrifice. That is why it is essential that Christians should be very careful not to be 'wolves' in the spiritual sense—that is, people who try to dominate others."[8]

---

[8]Jacques Ellul, *The Presence of the Kingdom* (New York: Seabury, 1967), pp. 10-11.

No one who truly draws near to Jesus Christ in faithful discipleship will go away arrogant and full of pride. The world may encourage us to swagger and boast, but Jesus remakes us as humble servants. In a world of noise and chatter, we will listen. In a world of self-assertion, we will humbly volunteer to serve. In a world of takers, we will give. In a world of pain and suffering, we will come alongside with quiet compassion. Truly biblical people are far from perfect, but they seek to listen to others, to invest some quality time quietly hearing the cry and concern of a neighbor or colleague. Biblical people are receptive, willing to learn from all others, willing to be served and to serve. They are prepared to weep with those who weep. We are not just the talkers; we are the listeners. Biblical people know how to observe sabbath—and bring sabbath to others. They understand ceasing as well as striving.

Remember again that we are talking about character, about the ongoing, daily orientation and disposition of our lives, the inclination of our hearts and minds, the habits of our daily life. It is not something we live out in one context but not others. Rather, it is what we wish to be at every moment in every situation. There is no progress on building good character until we absorb these initial traits of the life of faith. Faithful, holy and wise disciples must become open, responsible and gentle servants. Our world cannot be salted and lighted—and we cannot be blessed—if we skip over this stage on life's way.

There are many models for what a church, a community of faith, should be. Some see the church as a temple, others as an entertainment center, a classroom, a support or therapy group, a business, a hospital or a gym. What about the church as a community of humble servants of God and our world? Who is promoting this model today? What authors, seminars and consultants are pushing this concept? It will be hard for individual disciples to be fully reshaped as humble servants so long as the communities in which they worship don't treat it as an important matter. And it will be impossible for us to be faithful or effective "activists for righteousness" if we don't begin here.

For Reflection or Discussion

1. What have been your experiences with "poverty of spirit" and "mourning"? Can you share an example of someone you have known (or known

about) who was a good model of poverty/openness and mourning/responsibility?

2. Do you agree with the author that meekness/gentleness (in the Psalm 37 sense of not fretting but "letting go" and giving up control) may be the most difficult of the eight Beatitudes to practice in our culture? Why or why not?

3. How have alms giving, prayer, fasting and music played a part in your life and affected your character?

4. What can be done to help our churches move closer to the model of "a community of humble servants"?

Eight

RIGHTEOUS,
JUST & MERCIFUL

The Leader

*I*f we want to cultivate the good character offered to us by God in Jesus Christ, the strategy we must follow will be quite different from any other possibility. It is a pattern that can be pursued in the midst of the inner city, the suburbs or out in the country. It can be pursued by high school dropouts as well as well as by the degree laden. God will invade wherever he is invited, and this invasion starts a revolution in our character.

When God invades, we are "conceived of the Holy Spirit" and "born again" to a new life. We emerge from the womb as "faithful and holy disciples," attached to Jesus Christ in faith—and thereby made holy in distinction from the world around us, gaining a new kind of wisdom each day we grow. We are nurtured in the cradle of poverty, mourning and meekness, emerging from this cradle as humble servants.

Birth and infancy, no matter how sweet and endearing, are not, however, the *goal* of the new life. The main substance of the Christian life is not the birth experience. Renunciation and contemplation are not our goal; they are the *way* to our goal. We must, therefore, get out of the cradle and grow up into the mature, active life. To shift the metaphor for a moment, the design and quality of the foundation determine to a great extent the possibilities of the building, but the foundation is not the building.

The building, the substance and heart of the *active* Christian life, is *righteousness*. God's people "will be called oaks of righteousness. . . . I the LORD love justice. . . the Lord GOD will cause righteousness and praise to spring up before all the nations" (Is 61:3, 8, 11). Jesus taught, "Strive first for the kingdom of God and his righteousness" (Mt 6:33). Paul urged Christians to present their bodies to God as "instruments of righteousness"; "The kingdom of God is . . . righteousness and peace and joy in the Holy Spirit" (Rom 6:13; 14:17).

Unfortunately, "there is no one who is righteous, not even one" (Rom 3:10). "All our righteous deeds are like a filthy cloth" (Is 64:6). However, "the righteousness of God has been disclosed, . . . the righteousness of God through faith in Jesus Christ for all who believe" (Rom 3:21-22). We are given "the free gift of righteousness" (Rom 5:17). God forgives us and has "clothed us" in his righteousness (Is 61:10).

We do not seek for righteousness in order to earn our way into God's graces; that could never work. We are first forgiven and accepted freely in his grace and mercy and then *given* righteousness as a gift from God. Nevertheless, we need to "unwrap" and "open" God's gift of righteousness. We must integrate this gift into our lives and not leave it on the shelf. The thrust of the fourth Beatitude is that a good character hungers and thirsts for this gift, to possess it, understand it and to weave it into the tapestry of daily life.

He Leads Me in Paths of Righteousness

Recall again the pattern of Psalm 23: (1) the LORD becomes my shepherd; (2) he makes me lie down in green pastures and restores my soul; and (3) he leads me in paths of righteousness. The Beatitudes teach the same pattern: (1) disciples come to Jesus in faith; (2) they are called to poverty, mourning and meekness; and (3) they are called to hunger and thirst for righteousness. We are called to "walk in righteousness"—but we cannot truly recognize, understand or apply God's righteousness until we are first emptied of all our own competing ideas and loyalties; then God can fill us with his perspective.

The fourth through eighth Beatitudes are the virtues of the active life of the disciple. This sequence begins and ends in *righteousness*: "hungering and thirsting" for it (the fourth Beatitude) and being "persecuted" for it (the eighth Beatitude). Within this "righteousness package" we learn that righteousness must be accompanied by mercifulness (the fifth Beatitude) and purity of heart (the sixth Beatitude), culminating in peacemaking (the seventh Beatitude). In this chapter we examine righteousness and its intimate companion virtue, mercy, as these help us define our role as active leaders in the world.

The Hunger for Righteousness and Justice

Our situation with respect to the hunger for justice and righteousness is quite different from what we observed in the preceding chapter. Few people sing the praises of being humble, poor in spirit and meek. Multitudes, on the other hand, cry out for justice and fairness. In a remarkable way, a young child asserts claims for justice very soon after learning to speak. "It's not fair! Johnny took my crayon!" "Why did you give her more ice cream than me? That's not fair!" Long before their first lesson on ethics or justice, children have a hunger and thirst for righteousness of some sort.

At the other end of the spectrum, consider even the most cynical, jaded, anarchistic philosopher, who speaks and writes that "there are no moral standards" and "your ideas of right and wrong are nothing but an expression of your likes and dislikes." But when this philosopher's lover or companion is unfaithful, when someone breaks into his house, assaults him and trashes his prize possessions, when another scholar plagiarizes his ideas and takes credit for them, suddenly we hear an anguished cry for justice! We humans disagree on the meaning of justice, but we cannot live without treating it as a reality to be pursued. Everybody hungers, on occasion, for righteousness.

What is righteousness and justice?[1] In our present-day context, jus-

---

[1]On justice see Mary Ann Glendon, *Rights Talk: The Impoverishment of Political Discourse* (New York: Free Press, 1991); Karen Lebacqz, *Six Theories of Justice* (Minneapolis: Augsburg, 1986); Alasdair MacIntyre, *Whose Justice? Which Ration-*

tice is mostly about defining and protecting individual rights. "Fairness" is probably the main synonym today. Justice and fairness mean that people get what they deserve or what is due to them (equal pay for equal work, punishment that fits the crime, etc.). From the Bill of Rights onward, such a rights orientation to justice has dominated our discussions. Many people are hungry for their rights today. Frankly, many of them ought to be!

Don't women have a right not to be sexually harassed in workplaces? Don't Christians and Muslims deserve the same rights as feminists, Nietzscheans, Marxists, Freudians and Kantians to advocate peacefully their viewpoints in public universities? Don't cancer victims have a right not to be cancelled by their health insurers (to whom they have heretofore faithfully paid their premiums before getting sick)? Don't Palestinians have a right to their land? And so on.

Rights are a very important part of justice and righteousness, but we can hardly be satisfied with narrow notions of individual *rights* that fail to explore the *responsibilities* that attend such rights.[2] Nor can we accept any bill of individual rights that fails to articulate a broader sense of community rights, the rights of future generations or distant peoples.

Justice today often means *nothing but* this demand for personal rights (a never-ceasing, growing list). How do we figure out the list? Who counts as a "human" with rights? Can majorities exclude minorities in a democratic vote on rights? Not too long ago women, ethnic minorities and the propertyless had few or no rights. Today we debate the rights of trees, children, illegal aliens and the unborn. How do we protect rights? What do we do when rights come into conflict (e.g., one person's right to free speech vs. another's right to privacy)?

---

ality? (South Bend, Ind.: University of Notre Dame Press, 1988); and James P. Sterba, *Justice: Alternative Political Perspectives* (Belmont, Calif.: Wadsworth, 1992).

[2]"Excuse me, but you are asking for justice, aren't you? How can you limit justice to what is coming to you? Must you not also consider what you owe to others? The beam of the scale of justice is a rigid thing. . . . And you will pass under this beam, and you will be weighed against this standard. Are you so certain, dear angel, that you are able to pay your debt?" Jacques Ellul, "We Don't Want Charity, We Want Justice!" in *A Critique of the New Commonplaces* (New York: Knopf, 1968), p. 292.

Rights are important, but they cannot be the whole or even the center of the justice and righteousness for which we hunger and will be satisfied.

For most ancient philosophers, justice was not just about personal rights and duties but was the overarching virtue of the whole person and the whole community.[3] It meant, in a broad sense, whatever is right and just and fair, a situation or condition where harmony, order and happiness could reign. For Plato, "justice in the soul" exists when each part of the human person (the reason, the "spirited part," the appetites) is in its proper place, performing its proper function. "Justice in the social order" exists when each person or class in society (slaves, laboring classes, guardians, intellectuals) is in its proper place, fulfilling the role for which nature has fitted it, each person rendering to society what they should, each person receiving what is due them.

Justice today often means nothing but the demand for personal rights—with little thought for the rights of others (the poor, future generations, distant peoples, God), or the duties and responsibilities that must accompany all rights. A very thin brew compared to biblical justice.

Within this broad, inclusive conception of the domain of justice, Aristotle and others tried to map out the details and distinctions (for example, between economic, distributive justice and criminal, retributive justice). But one of the great arguments from the classical and biblical side is that there is a grand unity and inclusivity to justice and righteousness. Our English terminology of "righteousness" and "justice" often misleads us. Our habit is to think that "righteousness" refers to a personal virtue and "justice" to a social or political one. "Righteousness" has to do with sex and lies; "justice" has to do with the distribution of wealth and the quality of our laws.

The Greek philosophers and New Testament writers used *one* word (*dikaiosynē*) to refer to both arenas. It is wrong-headed to think that we could achieve personal righteousness while treating the poor

---

[3]See Plato *The Republic* bks. 1, 4, 8, 9; and Aristotle *Nicomachean Ethics* bk. 5. Of course, justice was a hotly debated subject, not easily resolved. *The Republic* is a dialogue in which different views are represented and debated.

unfairly, or that we serve as genuine heralds of justice in the political or civil rights arenas while betraying our family commitments, or that my personal rights matter while social justice does not.

In addition to the *content* and *meaning*, we must also examine the *grounding* and *justification* that gives force and authority to a given view of justice and righteousness. For many philosophers this grounding or justification was thought to be nature (often understood in a very broad sense, i.e., not just the nature we encounter with our five senses but "reality," the "universe"). Something called "natural law," "natural rights" or "natural justice" exists. Nature decides our roles, responsibilities, duties and rights. We figure out these lessons of nature through the exercise of our reason.

> The biblical and classical authors did not view justice as a social virtue separate from righteousness as a personal virtue. We need to recover their unified conception.

But it is difficult to agree on what nature and reason say about justice and righteousness. Some have a "harmony" model of nature, but others (e.g., Hobbes, Darwin, Nietzsche) read nature as implying an ethics of power and struggle establishing the rule of the stronger. Reason and nature do not yield ethical agreement among their most ardent philosophical proponents. Nature is flawed, and our perceptions of nature are hazy. Reason leads people into debate and disagreement at least as often as out of it.

In discussions since the Enlightenment, the grounding of justice has usually been shifted from nature to society. We have to rely on community or political authority. For some, that meant *rex lex*—the king makes the law (and justice), but increasingly in the modern world, we have preferred a more democratic approach. Laws, rights and justice are grounded in a social compact or contract, a political agreement. It is the government (and behind it, the people) that decides what our rights will be and how they will be interpreted. This can be dangerous, of course, for our social and political compacts are also flawed by human weakness and perversity.[4]

Just as there is value and truth in seeing justice/righteousness *both*

---

[4]See Stanley Hauerwas, "The Politics of Justice: Why Justice Is a Bad Idea for Christians," in *After Christendom* (Nashville: Abingdon, 1991), pp. 45-68.

as an affair of individual rights *and* as a grand, broad-ranging affair of
all that is right and good and leads to personal and social harmony—so
too there is value in a conception of justice that *both* tries to make
sense of nature (reality, the world, my self) as we understand it *and*
sustains our social and political agreement. These justice options are
not so much wrong as inadequate. They need to be subordinated to
something better.

Biblical righteousness and justice. Our usual, popular image of religiously based "righteousness" is uptight, straight-laced Puritans living
austere, joyless lives of renunciation and self-discipline, with a critical,
killjoy stance toward others. "Self-righteousness" is a criticism, not a
compliment, often directed at Christians. Many people with these mis-
conceptions or bad experiences will not think that biblical Christian
justice is the improved version for which we hunger!

The biblical vocabulary suggests something much richer than these
popular images and phrases. Most basically, biblical terms like "just,
justice, right and righteousness" have the root meaning of "being lined
up straight"—like "justified type" on a page, where the letters are lined
up straight with each other. But what is the standard by which we
decide this rightness, justice or straightness?

The biblical terms *righteousness/justice* (Hebrew *tsedeq,* Greek
dikaiosynē) refer fundamentally to an attribute of God's character;
righteous judgment (Hebrew *mishpat,* Greek *krisis*) refers to God's
will and decision. God is completely right, just and fair in his goodness.
"The LORD is righteous; he loves righteous deeds" (Ps 11:7). God
"speaks," "judges" and "acts" righteously (Ps 119:160, 164; Is 45:19;
1 Pet 2:23; Rev 19:2).[5]

God's justice is knowable through his words and acts in human history. "The will of God in the manifestation of justice is therefore no
rigid framework wherein we can arrange our concepts. Nor is it a kind
of principle from which we can deduce a system. . . . God's righteous-

---

[5]For good discussions of biblical justice and righteousness, see Stephen C. Mott, *Bib-
lical Faith and Social Change* (New York: Oxford, 1982); and Christopher J. H.
Wright, *An Eye for An Eye: The Place of Old Testament Ethics Today* (Downers
Grove, Ill.: InterVarsity Press, 1983).

ness . . . is only found in the act of judgment. We cannot know either its essence or its form apart from the present and concrete act of God, which is judgment. . . . Only in judgment do we grasp justice."[6] The content of the justice and righteousness for which we hunger can, thus, never be detached from the living God and a quest to know and understand God's will and decision about what is right and just or wrong and unjust.

At the center of this revelation of justice stands Jesus. "Surely this was a righteous man," said the centurion at the death of Jesus (Lk 23:47 NIV). "We have an advocate . . . Jesus Christ the righteous" (1 Jn 2:1). In him, the justice of God meets the injustice of humanity. "All the characteristics of God's righteousness are united and embodied in the life, the death and the resurrection of Jesus Christ. Jesus Christ has become the righteousness of God. There can be no justice whatsoever, even relative, outside Jesus Christ. . . . Jesus Christ as the righteousness of God exercises this justice. One could say that his whole life is this exercise."[7]

So the *content* of God's justice and righteousness is as broad as the content of God's character. The *agenda* of justice is the agenda of God. God's justice agenda *includes* a concern for individual rights, especially those of the poor and downtrodden. It includes a grand vision of social and personal harmony. The *grounding* and *justification* of this justice is in the character and authority of God; it is known through the revelation of God, above all in Jesus Christ.

Content/Scope	Based on	Known by
1. individual rights	social compact	reason/choice
2. order/harmony	nature/reality	reason
3. life in totality	God's character	revelation

Figure 8.1. Three justice/righteousness options

God is the Creator of the world, of all reality and of the individual person. We must expect that the justice that God reveals will make

---

[6]Jacques Ellul, *The Theological Foundation of Law* (New York: Seabury, 1969), p. 46.

[7]Ibid., p. 42.

sense of what we learn from nature, reality and reason. The latter cannot be read accurately without God's clear revelation in Jesus Christ, but, with the latter, the former should make sense. Since God has created us for cohumanity and for freedom together, it also makes sense to think that the justice of God will be the very best guidance for our social and political agreements on civil justice.

A biblical righteousness/justice is not first of all human-centered but God-centered. It is not narrowly or statically rights-oriented but is dynamic and embraces the whole of God's character and the whole of our life. God's call to be righteous and just is a call to conform to his standard of righteous thought and action. It means to hunger to know, understand and apply what God is, says and does. To be righteous means to find out what God thinks, what God's standards are, how God has judged and acted.[8]

The Menu That Satisfies Our Hunger

The fourth Beatitude is about *hungering* and *thirsting* as a character trait or virtue. This means cultivating the taste, the appetite and the desire for something. That something is God's *righteousness* and *justice*. I want to pursue this metaphor with a discussion of the menu at God's table, or café of righteousness. It is in studying this menu and in developing a taste for these items so that we regularly want more of them, and increasingly dine on them, that our character will be refashioned. How do we acquire a taste for something? Sometimes we are driven to it by our deep need for something—anything!—that will satisfy us and keep us alive. Sometimes we are drawn to it by sampling it and discovering how good it is. Both paths are relevant to our hunger for God's righteousness.

Simply getting hungry and thirsty is not the whole story, of course. We must *act* on our hunger. "Justice is realized above all in an external

---

[8]"What sort of righteousness? . . . The whole of virtue . . . godliness . . . the whole practical wisdom of the soul." Chrysostom contrasts this hunger for righteousness with the evil of covetousness, a hungering for "gaining, and compassing ourselves with more and more" in an unsatisfiable quest. John Chrysostom, *Homily XV on the Gospel of Saint Matthew*, in Nicene and Post-Nicene Fathers, ed. Philip Schaff (Grand Rapids, Mich.: Eerdmans, 1956), 10:94-95.

act . . . every external act belongs to the field of justice. Whatever external act a person performs, it is either just or unjust. . . . Wherever justice in the full sense is done, the external act is an expression of an inner assent."[9] In its fullest sense then, righteousness/justice is exhibited in acts that conform to the character of God, and with which our mind and heart are in agreement. But the lesson of virtue ethics (and of Scripture) is that our habits and desires, our character, must be reshaped if we want the right actions to occur. Just actions depend on a character that habitually hungers for God's justice.

How shall we describe the righteousness/justice menu for which we should hunger? As indicated above, righteousness is an account of the character of God—rather broad and inclusive, not easy to summarize! And yet we have some great summaries in the Bible. I want to think of it in terms of ten items. The Ten Commands occupy a very

> Hunger is not a virtue if there is no food available or if all that is available is poisonous. When there is tasty, nutritious food available, hunger is a virtue that focuses our attention, turns and mobilizes us toward that food.

special place as the covenant between God and the people, carried in the Ark of the Covenant.[10] "If we diligently observe this entire commandment before the LORD our God, as he has commanded us, we will be in the right," said Moses in reference both to the *shema* and the Ten Commandments (Deut 6:25). The Ten Commandments are a ten-fold description of what is "right," and that is righteousness and justice.

Think about the Ten Commandments as you look at the menu in figure 8.2.

This is a rich and holistic agenda that covers all of life's concerns. It is more than enough to challenge us for a lifetime and yet simple enough

---

[9]Josef Pieper, *The Four Cardinal Virtues* (South Bend, Ind.: University of Notre Dame Press, 1966), pp. 60-63.

[10]In part two of my introduction to Christian ethics, *Doing Right,* the Ten Commandments and the double Love Commandment will supply the framework for an ethic of principles and practices. The character virtue of hungering and thirsting for this righteousness is basic and essential, but in *Doing Right* we will take a much longer, deeper look at what this righteousness and justice means for the dilemmas of our time.

Café Righteousness

—Menu—
Our Motto: Satisfaction guaranteed to those who dine here

First Courses

1. *God!* all of God, all yours, no competition, nobody but God
2. *Living God!* the real, living God; no substitutes,
images, or dead idols

Second Courses

3. *Conversation with God!* the real thing where you call out God's
name and he answers—no silence, no vain or insulting talk
4. *Rest & Work with God!* creative, liberating, purposeful work—
and great weekends together

Third Course

5. *Honoring Parents!* appreciative, respectful, creative caring for
the agents God has used to bring life and grace to you

Fourth Courses

6. *Protecting Life!* caring for life, making peace, avoiding death and
violence in act, word, and thought
7. *Protecting Relationships!* building flourishing, faithful
marriages and friendships, preventing betrayal and breakdown
8. *Protecting Property!* caring for the earth, promoting just
distribution and safekeeping of our material infrastructure
9. *Protecting Truth!* helping the whole truth be told in loving,
helpful ways, unmasking lies and deception that
threaten well-being

Fifth Course

10. *Heart Healthy!* attitude check—wanting the best for others,
overcoming envy, undermining covetousness and bad attitudes

Figure 8.2

to be a practical guide for all ages and circumstances. I will only make
some brief comments about how these ten items relate to our character formation.

"You shall have no other gods before me." The first commandment
is the foundation and theme of the whole list. It is because of who
God is that murder or theft or covetousness is wrong. It is by being in
relation to God that we will have both the wisdom and the strength to
keep the other commandments. The fundamental theme of this command is that God invites us into an exclusive relationship with him.
He will be our God, with nothing allowed to separate us from him. A
good character is one that develops a taste for God, an unquenchable
desire to know God better and then live in unbroken relationship
with him, refusing all other rival objects of worship and ultimate loyalty. If we don't resolve this issue of who our God is, nothing else can
be resolved.

"You shall not make for yourself any graven image." The second
command specifically tells us never to replace the living God with a
dead or fixed image. That was the basic problem of idolatry in the Old
Testament: not just an image representing some rival god, but any
fixed image representing the Lord God of Israel was wrong! Why?
Because God is alive, speaking, listening, acting, relating to his people
and his world. The command urges a character that hungers to know
God in a living, vital, growing way. Command one is about exclusivity;
command two is about vitality.

"You shall not misuse the name of the Lord." In biblical terms a person's name represents his or her character; calling out the name ini-
tiates a relationship and a conversation. To use the name without
intending to initiate a relationship or conversation is profane, disrespectful and relationship destroying. A good character develops a hunger to call out the Name and have another conversation with God.
Conversation with God leads to life and growth and light.

"Remember the sabbath day; work six days." In this double command we are invited to set aside focused, sabbath rest to celebrate and
be renewed *with* God—and we are called to work six days *for* God,
according to God's own pattern of creation. A good character hungers
to understand, experience and promote this way of resting and working in the world. This is a major agenda item!

"Honor your father and mother." In the fifth command we are told
to care for the father and mother God has given us. A good character

hungers to understand this—how to care for and respect our parents in today's world, how to deal with the hard cases of abusive or neglectful parents, and how to honor those who actually did serve as God's agents in caring for us as though we were their children.

"You shall not murder." A good character hungers and thirsts to know how God wants us to overcome the hateful violence and revenge that ravages our world. We hunger to know what to do about guns, missiles, diplomacy, violent movies and games, child and spouse abuse, and abortion. We hunger to know how to act positively to protect life and health.

"You shall not commit adultery." We hunger to know how to build good, life-enhancing, stable marriages and protect them from sexual and emotional betrayal. On a broader level, we hunger to know how to build and protect covenanted friendships, so urgently needed in our era.

"You shall not steal." We hunger to know how to overcome the causes of poverty and the motivations to steal that afflict not only hoodlums on the street but corporate thieves and political crooks. We hunger to understand better what is God's property and how to be faithful and generous stewards.

"You shall not bear false witness." A good character hungers to be honest and tell the truth. We hunger to know how to protect the truth in a world of lies, deception, propaganda and half-truths. We hunger to know how to find the truth in rapidly growing mountains of data that overwhelm us.

"You shall not covet." Finally, a good character hungers to be free of obsessing over what properly belongs to others, whether a spouse, a home or anything else. We hunger to have a healthy heart that hungers for God but is not hungering for what it should not. We hunger to know how to have such healthy attitudes in a world of total advertising that perfects its tactics for enflaming people's acquisitive desire and sense of entitlement.

God's righteous character is our model. The Ten Commandments instruct God's people about righteousness. It is the agenda, the menu for the people. But it is crucial to note that this is a tenfold description of what God is like. Hungering for righteousness is not just hungering to do what God commands but hungering to know God himself! Thus it is God who above all (1) maintains a unique, exclusive place for each of us and will not allow anyone to come between him and us, (2) always treats us as living persons, never substituting some fixed image of us, (3) always knows our name and speaks to us with respect for who we are, (4) works hard and faithfully for us and takes quality time to be with us, (5) honors and cares for our parents, (6) protects our life, (7) protects our relationships ("what God has joined together . . ."), (8) protects our property and gives us our daily bread, (9) always tells us and others the truth, and (10) always wills our best.

> The Ten Commandments are not just instructions for human righteousness—they are an account of God's own righteous character.

The community of the hungry. As a menu, the preceding looks interesting; as an agenda or assignment, it is a bit daunting—especially in our hectic, stressful world. It is important to remember, first, that our basic theme is very short and simple: hunger and thirst to know and experience God's righteousness. When ten items seem overwhelming, return to the one summary and simplify your focus.

Second, all of this is an exercise for communities, not isolated individuals. The Beatitudes were taught to a small band of disciples as a project to work on together. The Ten Commandments were given to the congregation, not to an isolated Moses or Miriam to pursue. It is a terrible mistake to pursue these hungers all on your own. Find a community. Join a small group! Build a friendship! Then carve out some time to pray together and to talk about what these things mean—what kind of people God wants us to become.

Filled and satisfied? The Beatitude promises that those who hunger for righteousness will be filled and satisfied. "How blessed you are" if at the core of your life you have a deep appetite for righteousness! *This* is an appetite that will be satisfied by the goodness of God. The Ten Commandments promise similar rewards: "Do what is right and good in the sight of the LORD, so that it may go well with you" (Deut 6:18).

Part of what is implied here is that it is a mistake to put any other hunger at the center of life. To do so might plant poisonous weeds in the soil of our existence. A hunger for power, money, fame or pleasure, for example, could never be satisfied and would lead to misery. But the point is also that this hunger for righteousness really is the key to satisfaction in life. At the end of our life, if we have spent our efforts hungering for God's righteousness and justice, we can look back with a sense of satisfaction. To pursue God's righteousness is to live. Anything less is not only unworthy or possibly dangerous, it is fundamentally boring by comparison! To hunger for God's righteousness is an unending, richly satisfying adventure.

Earlier I argued that the ancient philosophers were not all wrong to look for a justice that fits the reality of our universe and our humanity. And I argued that modern philosophers were not all wrong to look for a justice that is embraced by a social agreement or compact. The movie *Babette's Feast* showed in a powerful way how a great feast of the right stuff, served with love, can overcome barriers and create community. I believe that the menu at God's Café Righteousness has the power to do the same. It is the agenda that accurately addresses our human reality, its challenges and potentials. And it is an adventure that can unite people, drawing them out of narrowness, provincialism, self-interest and fear. This is an immensely satisfying menu for which to hunger.

Mercifulness: The Imperfect World

Righteousness/justice is the great master theme of our active life in the world. But there can be no perfect justice in human affairs. Even in its narrow sense of rights, conflicts occur and something has to give. Rights are violated and often a fair restitution cannot be made. We are finite, error-prone creatures who make mistakes. We are also sin-prone creatures who sometimes choose what is wrong. When those wronged demand justice, they often mean a harsh, vengeful penalty. Those who wrong others often engage in avoidance, denial and self-justification. In this atmosphere, "Blessed are the merciful, for they will receive mercy." The fifth Beatitude sounds soft and weak to some, hopelessly idealistic to others.

Even Aristotle, however, argued that the virtue of justice must be accompanied by the virtue of equity, which allows us to finesse the interpretation and application of justice. Our rules of justice simply cannot cover all circumstances. In the larger, more robust biblical notion, justice is always accompanied by mercy. The fourth Beatitude must be accompanied by the fifth.

Old Testament scholar James Muilenburg describes the relationship of justice and righteousness to compassion and mercy this way:

> As Israel's King, the Lord is also Judge. As sovereign over her existence, he determines what is right and what is wrong. His will is the supreme issue for her life, exalted above the wills of human judges and leaders. But more than that, while his function is to maintain justice, to uphold the right, to preserve the peace and well-being of the community, it is not his punitive judgment that is central in the legal contexts but rather his desire to protect the right and establish it, to help and save Israel, to come to the rescue of those who have no voice in court. Therefore, as Judge he is the Helper and Savior and Deliverer and Redeemer of his people.[11]

Justice is not an abstract set of standards but an account of the character of the living God who wishes to save us and bring us life. There is no justice without mercy. "Gracious is the LORD, and righteous; our God is merciful" (Ps 116:5).

God's mercy is his "bowels" of compassion (Hebrew, *racham, rachamin*) and his "lovingkindness" (Hebrew, *hesed*). "His mercy endures forever" is a recurring chant in the Old Testament (e.g., Ps 136; NRSV "steadfast love"). The same one who is led in God's "paths of righteousness" says "surely goodness and mercy shall follow me all the days of my life" (Ps 23:6) "What does the LORD require of you but to do justice, and to love kindness, and to walk humbly with your God?" (Mic 6:8).

At the cross of Christ, the righteousness and mercy of God are united. God's perfect justice is satisfied and his perfect mercy extended. What Jesus exemplified at the cross, he taught by following the fourth with the fifth Beatitude. Mercy follows hard on the heels of

---

[11]James Muilenburg, *The Way of Israel: Biblical Faith and Ethics* (New York: Harper Torchbooks, 1961), p. 37.

justice. The New Testament word for mercy (Greek *eleos*) means both *pardon* for one who has done wrong and *kindness* to one in need of help. Biblical mercy is not based on what one deserves. It flows from the character and love of God. The people of God pass it on out of obedience and gratitude to God and out of compassion for their neighbor. Obedience to God's command ("Be merciful") *drives* us to mercy; compassion for our neighbor *draws* us to mercy. Mercy is expressed in words and deeds: we tell offenders that they are forgiven and we offer help to those who do not deserve it.

Mercy perfects justice and righteousness. Mercy is a perfection and completion of justice. Where the Sermon on the Mount says, "Be perfect, therefore, as your heavenly Father is perfect" (Mt 5:48), the parallel text of the Sermon on the Plain says, "Be merciful just as your Father is merciful" (Lk 6:36). We live in a vengeful era. Movies with revenge themes (the bloodier, the more popular) propagandize us. Most of us are ready enough to ask for (even "beg for") mercy when we need it. We have a much harder time extending it to others. But "never avenge yourselves, but leave room for the wrath of God; for it is written, 'Vengeance is mine, I will repay, says the Lord.' No, 'if your enemies are hungry, feed them; if they are thirsty, give them something to drink; for by doing this you will heap burning coals on their heads.' Do not be overcome by evil, but overcome evil with good" (Rom 12:19-21).

A**t the cross of Jesus Christ, God's righteousness and mercy were, each and together, fully carried out. Any disciple who "takes up the cross and follows Jesus" must make this his or her guiding model of justice—and mercy.**

Justice must be pronounced, but its application must be tempered by mercy. This is why we pray, "Forgive us our sins as we forgive those who have sinned against us." Receiving forgiveness is something we all need from God and from others, but it is inextricably linked with our extending forgiveness to others, which will always be necessary in this broken world. To have mercy and to forgive is not to deny or ignore the offense, it is to face up to it squarely, and then to choose to let go of our demand that the scales be completely balanced. There is a cosmic sense in which our practice of being merciful prepares us to receive God's mercy. There is a human sense in which being merciful to others inclines others to be merciful to us. How merciful are others likely to be to us if they see us refuse mercy to the needy and offensive in our lives?

Peter Kreeft gives a great description of mercy:

> Mercy goes beyond reason (how could a computer understand it?), beyond justice, beyond right, beyond law. Where justice says "punish," mercy says "forgive." Where justice says "this is a debt," mercy says not that there is no debt but to dismiss the debt. To say there is no debt would be a lie since justice speaks the truth, and even mercy cannot contradict the truth, but mercy can say "dismiss the debt." . . . A frequent mistake about mercy, one which hides its mystery, is to believe that it is a mere subjective attitude. . . . But real mercy is more objectively real and more costly than that. It forgives debts that are objectively real, not subjectively imagined, debts that must be paid.[12]

Justice and righteousness must never be sold out or minimized. We are not to practice denial and sweep injustice under the carpet. We must hunger and thirst for righteousness and take a stand for justice in economics, politics, racial relations, marital disputes and international conflicts. But having started with justice, we must press for the mercy characteristic of God and appropriate to the particular reality of the situation. We cannot completely balance the scales of justice for those enslaved, abused or dispossessed in the past. We cannot undo many injuries or take back many words. We must approach the righteousness challenge with a character habituated to justice and mercy together, not just to a ruthless justice owing more to Dirty Harry than to the God of Jesus Christ.

Biblical people are neither cold-hearted conservatives nor soft-headed liberals. Sometimes our churches have seemed to give up completely on the discipline of righteousness. Other times we have seemed to stand for righteousness (with excommunications and shunning) and forgotten the mercy that must accompany it. A hard-nosed rhetoric of righteousness only reinforces pride and division. It deters the hurting, needy and guilty from coming to the community of Christ. Righteousness without mercy leads only to judgment and death, but mercy without righteousness sells out the high calling of God for some insipid

---

[12]Peter Kreeft, *Back to Virtue* (San Francisco: Ignatius, 1986), p. 113.

lower standard. They must remain together, in the order of the Beatitudes.

Who will represent this character in our angry, divided, contentious world today? Jesus wishes to shape biblical people into righteous activists, people hungry to pursue God's justice in the world, people whose interpretation and application of that justice is always tempered by mercy. This is the salt of the earth and the light of the world.

The Virtues and Habits of a Leader

John Naisbitt, author of the best-selling *Megatrends*, once defined leadership as "finding a parade and getting in front of it." That, however, is not leadership but opportunism. Jacques Ellul, a much wiser guide, used to say that we should never underestimate the potential of a small group of people who are resolutely joined together around a truth. That, in my opinion, is much closer to an acceptable concept of leadership. Naisbitt's "leader" is actually a *follower* of his "megatrends," not a leader or "trendsetter."

Mercy Must
Follow Justice
1. God always includes mercy in justice.
2. Perfect justice is impossible in life.
3. Be clear and honest about what justice/righteousness deserves.
4. Give pardon to the guilty.
5. Show kindness to the needy.

We believe that the righteousness of God is the truth that sets people free. Never in history have we so badly needed people of good character to step out in leadership—of businesses, neighborhoods, families, clubs, churches and political movements. We are living in an era of massive conformity—not one of creative, redemptive leadership. The prospects are not good for the future if better leaders do not arise.

Perhaps twenty or so men and women signed on as *disciples* in Jesus' original band, and this soon became seventy or a hundred. In a few years they led a revolution that changed history. Their objective was not so much to change history as to be faithful to the truth, to live faithfully in the world in a community of God's followers. Disciples of Jesus learn soon that loving and serving God and our neighbor is what it's all about. *Disciples* are shaped into humble *servants*. That move goes against our cultural and natural grain. It is a bit of a shock to be reshaped, reeducated as a disciple into a servant!

The next step is, if anything, even more shocking and surprising. *Servants* become *leaders*. There is no other way to lead in God's church and God's world; one *must* become a *servant leader* and renounce *domination leadership* forever. The leader is the servant of all; the servant is the true leader (Lk 22:24-30; Jn 13:1-17). Our church and world have never in history needed this approach more. Instead of hungering for power, we need people who will hunger for God's righteousness and justice. That is the key to good leadership.

For Reflection or Discussion

1. What are the instances of unrighteousness and injustice today that trouble you most? How are these concerns of yours grounded in Jesus and Scripture?
2. Can you think of a person or an event that shows the hunger for righteousness and justice in a way we should emulate? Describe him/her/it.
3. Are there any actions that we simply should not ever forgive? Why? Do you think this is God's conclusion also?
4. What can our churches and Christian communities do to better exemplify the right combination of righteousness and mercy?
5. Describe a good leader you have seen or known. What made this leadership great? Did servanthood and righteousness have anything to do with it?

Nine

LOVING, SACRIFICIAL & GENUINE

The Peacemaker

*T*he Beatitudes reach a culmination with "Blessed are the peacemakers, for they will be called the children of God."[1] It is in
making peace that we are most recognizably the children of
God. There was peace in God's original creation, and we are headed for
peace in God's eternal kingdom. Jesus is the Prince of Peace. What is
this peace? Why does it seem so far away? What should we do to be
faithful peacemakers today? What does it mean to have a character
that is oriented to peacemaking today?

Peace Is the Goal

In the sixties and seventies we talked about this a lot. Peace symbols
and peace marches were everywhere. People hitchhiked and picked up

---

[1]I want to discuss this peace goal first and then go back and show why "purity of
heart" (the sixth Beatitude) is a prerequisite to peacemaking.

hitchhikers without worrying about being attacked. There was a wide-spread spirit of sharing. Compared with our meaner-spirited contemporary times, the sixties and seventies sometimes have a certain nostalgic appeal!

The sixties and seventies were by no means a utopia for peace and freedom. We had (you may have forgotten) a Filthy Speech Movement, as well as the better-known Free Speech Movement. We had dope freaks as well as Jesus freaks. We had lots of hypocrisy to go with the idealism. High aspirations for peace, community sharing and simplicity were awakened, but it all disappeared before long because it was naive and unrooted. At best, we could say that the good seed of peace was sown among weeds, which eventually choked it, or on unfertile, stony ground, where a little drought killed it off.

So we will not get the peace we want and need by going back to the sixties model, but we had better look for peace somewhere! As we begin the third millennium on our calendar, there is conflict and violence in every part of the globe: Hutus and Tutsis, Pakistanis and Indians, Russians and Chechnyans, Iraqis and Kurds, Palestinians and Israelis, Irish Protestants and Catholics, Indonesians and East Timorese, Serbs and anyone near them—everywhere we look around the world, death and violence flare up with appalling frequency. This is a world of jihad, desert storms, bullies, tough guys, assassinations, terrorism, hostile takeovers, brutal competition, pit bull dogs, AK-47s, threats and counterthreats. In such a world, peace and love sound like foolishness and weakness, like sentimentality and pipe dreams.

In America we kill our unborn, abuse our children, batter our spouses, mail bombs to our enemies, and shoot some innocent bystanders as we drive by. This is the era of gang violence, gangsta rap, office and school rampages, and citizen militias—with Charlton Heston and the National Rifle Association leading the crusade to ensure that all Americans have the personal right to their own military assault arsenal. Cowardly provocateurs on the airwaves and in movie studios build audiences and profits by pandering to anger, hatred, vengeance and bloodshed. (Their appeals to free speech make as much sense as free speech for fools who cry "fire" in crowded theatres.) And while we can attach male faces to most of the above, the feminist movement, which could have stood for peace and for life, is knee-deep in the blood of the unborn, sacrificed for the personal convenience of pro-choice women (and their irresponsible male sperm-donors).

Our era is appallingly decadent and violent. More weapons, more vengeance, will not stem this tide. Just the opposite. We desperately need a new and better approach to peacemaking. Do you believe it?

Christians bear a heavy load of responsibility for this situation. The traitors who wrap themselves in the American flag, buy a gun and join the hysterical throngs dashing to the right are contributing only negatively to our crisis. The apathetic majority has simply disappeared from public responsibility. For many of them, Christianity is personal therapy in a hundred different fashions, none of which have any relevance to the peacemaking challenge in society.

Christians are present, but not as salt and light. Our character has been shaped by something other than God. We are nowhere near being a "city set on a hill" showing another way, speaking another message. We have slipped off the hill and merged, inconspicuously, into the masses below. But a world without light and an earth without salt are doomed to decay and rot. That is why we are responsible. No matter what our palace polltakers say, the overall impact of American Christianity on the injustice and violence that beset us today approaches zero.

> W e Christians are responsible not just for what we do but for what we don't do. When we fail to enter the world as faithful "salt" and "light"— and terrible things happen out there —we are deeply (not totally) responsible.

There are personal and congregational exceptions, but the overall picture is bleak indeed.

For anyone who cares at all about the biblical message, peace and peacemaking assume a very high degree of importance. In a violent ancient world, Israel's God is the God of peace; its Messiah will be the "Prince of Peace" (Is 9:6). Our well-known "benediction" concludes: "The LORD lift up his countenance upon you, and give you peace" (Num 6:26). God urges his people to "seek the peace and prosperity of the city to which I have carried you in exile" (Jer 29:7 NIV). The people of God look forward with hope to the day of peace when swords will be beaten into plowshares and war will be studied no more (Is 2:4).

Jesus says "Peace I leave with you; my peace I give to you," "I have said this to you, so that in me you may have peace" (Jn 14:27; 16:33). The Christian gospel is the "gospel of peace" (Acts 10:36; Eph 6:15). God the Father is the God of peace, Jesus brings "the peace of Christ," and the Holy Spirit produces the fruit of peace (1 Thess 5:23; Col 3:15; Gal 5:22). The normal New Testament salutation is "Grace and peace to you"—just as the standard Hebrew salutation is "shalom."

What is peace? For many, peace is simply the absence of war and conflict. Peace means being left alone, undisturbed. It means tranquility and quietness. Peace is the removal of threats. Of course, even this thin or minimal peace has its merits. Philosophers can pace and philosophize; artists can paint; entrepreneurs can start businesses; the people are free to do what they wish without fear of danger. The biblical concept of peace, however, is much richer than this. The Hebrew word for peace, *shalom*, refers not just to a cessation of strife but a

> "**T**hin," minimal peace is the absence of overt conflict. "Thick," rich, biblical shalom peace is, in addition, a reconciled, restored relational context in which people can flourish together pursuing life, love and righteousness.

state of health, completeness, harmony, safety, security, prosperity and well-being. The New Testament Greek term, *eirēnē*, means harmony and *shalom* in relationships, replacing strife and division with the fullness of life together.

Christians are explicitly called to make peace in three arenas: with God, among Christians, and with all people—even their enemies. Peace is always the gift of God, but the gift launches an adventure in which the recipients play an active part. The first task is personal and "vertical"—to enter fully into personal peace with God. The foundational gift is: "Since we are justified by faith, we have peace with God through our Lord Jesus Christ" (Rom 5:1). The personal peacemaking quest is: "In everything by prayer and supplication with thanksgiving let your requests be made known to God. And the peace of God, which surpasses all understanding, will guard your hearts and your minds in Christ Jesus" (Phil 4:6-7). "Let the peace of Christ rule in your hearts" (Col 3:15).

Cultivating this first aspect of the peacemaking virtue helps us to be centered in peace within ourselves, accepting ourselves as God accepts us—loved, valued, accepted and completely forgiven. We need peace in our emotional life, overcoming anxiety, fretfulness and compulsiveness. We are revisiting here those first movements of "having our soul restored," cultivating meekness, letting go and giving ourselves to God. God fills our receptive, gentle hearts with his peaceful, strong presence.[2]

Peacemakers also help others toward this peace with God in their "ministry of reconciliation" (2 Cor 5:18-19). The first arena and foundational work of peacemaking concerns this "vertical" relationship with God. Reconciliation (Greek, *katallagē*) means a complete change and a restoration of a broken relationship. We were at enmity against God; we can be reconciled and at peace. We want a habit of drawing people toward the good news that God is for us and wishes to have us in his family in unbreakable solidarity and communion. We must not allow others to define themselves as beyond the love and grace of God, but rather gently and firmly insist that God knows and loves them as they are.

Our second peacemaking arena is "horizontal" reconciliation in the community of faith. "You who once were far off have been brought near by the blood of Christ. For he is our peace. . . . He has . . . reconcil[ed] both groups to God in one body through the cross, thus putting to death that hostility through it. So he came and proclaimed peace to you who were far off and peace to those who were near" (Eph 2:13-17). This horizontal peace is also fundamentally the gift and work of God, but still we are challenged to make "every effort to maintain the unity of the Spirit in the bond of peace" (Eph 4:3). "Let us then pursue what makes for peace and for mutual upbuilding" (Rom 14:19).

Even in our little homogeneous churches we are too often divided. We must not overlook the importance of working for peace within our present enclaves. This means calming passions, mediating disputes, drawing foes together in a prayerful, shared commitment to reconciliation. Peacemaking means helping some to listen more openly and

---

[2]"We are not at peace with others because we are not at peace with ourselves, and we are not at peace with ourselves because we are not at peace with God." Thomas Merton, cited in Peter Kreeft, *Back to Virtue* (San Francisco: Ignatius, 1986), p. 146.

attentively, and others to speak openly and calmly, helping each to understand the other. Peacemaking can be hard, frustrating work, but allowing antagonism and alienation to persist is worse.

In the New Testament era, the greatest division and conflict in the church was between Jew and Gentile. Nothing is clearer than that Jesus Christ insisted on uniting in peace those two deeply alienated groups. In our own era, the scandal of racial division in the church is one of our most terrible failures. Our society is still too divided and alienated racially; our Christian communities too often mirror this separation. Martin Luther King Jr. observed that eleven o'clock Sunday morning is the most segregated hour in the American week. Think of the powerful witness to our world a racially reconciled church would have. But will we seek it?

> If Paul were writing his letters in America today I believe he would write as much about reconciliation between our ethnic groups as he did about Jew and Gentile back then. Racial/ethnic tensions and walls are the most tragic wound in today's church. Jesus must be weeping.

If we want to develop a biblical character, we must make reconciliation and peacemaking a core virtue. We must breech all the lines of division, not just race but economic class, gender, age, nationality and cultural preference. We cannot just do something symbolic once in a great while; we must be habituated to daily prayer and work for such reconciliation and peace.[3] Jesus went to the cross to make us one in him. We must take up the cross and cross the street at least! The hour is late, and we are mostly sitting on our hands. John Chrysostom described peacemakers as those who "set at one again others, who are at strife. . . . This became the work of the Only Begotten, to unite the divided, and to reconcile the alienated."[4]

---

[3]"The 'peacemakers' . . . are not simply those who bring peace between two conflicting parties, but those actively at work making peace, bringing about wholeness and well-being, among the alienated. . . . The peacemakers . . . are engaged in expressing to others what they themselves have come to experience in Jesus' ministry." Robert Guelich, *The Sermon on the Mount* (Dallas: Word, 1982), p. 107.

[4]John Chrysostom, *Homily XV on the Gospel of Saint Matthew*, in Nicene and Post-Nicene Fathers, ed. Philip Schaff (Grand Rapids, Mich.: Eerdmans, 1956), 10:94-95.

In a third arena, we must be peacemakers among all people. "If it is possible, so far as it depends on you, live peaceably with all" (Rom 12:18). We must refuse to tolerate, much less cause, alienation between ourselves and our neighbors and colleagues. The only scandal and offense we should cause is that of the cross. We must resist and overcome divisions and hostilities, salting and lighting our world with reconciliation. Peacemakers reject the demonization of others and insist on representing and welcoming them with respect.

The great test of our peacemaking is when we are persecuted or when we see others being persecuted and want to protect them. Dietrich Bonhoeffer, who knew about this firsthand in Nazi Germany, wrote: "Nowhere will that peace be more manifest than where they meet the wicked in peace and are ready to suffer at their hands. The peacemakers will carry the cross with their Lord, for it was on the cross that peace was made."[5] Eventually Bonhoeffer participated in the German resistance, which later attempted to assassinate Hitler. For this and other "crimes" he was executed on April 9, 1945. At the very least, his story should teach us to be activists and peacemakers well before such desperate situations develop and harden.

Peacemaking
1. calming anger, comforting the injured
2. reducing/ eliminating conflict, strife, violence
3. promoting *shalom*, harmony, flourishing in a common life together
4. promoting reconciliation/peace with God
5. promoting reconciliation/peace in church
6. promoting reconciliation/peace in world

At all three of these levels (the self before God, the community of faith, and the world that God has created), we want to have peacemaking as a character trait, as a capability, power, disposition and inclination. We want to have the habit of nurturing reconciliation on the basis of righteousness and mercy, not on the basis of a cheap "peace at any price" that papers over deeper problems. In a world quick to accuse and divide, we want to reconcile and unify. In a world of tribalism and self-assertion, we want to promote a healthy diversity in unity. In a world of conflict, we want to promote

---

[5]Dietrich Bonhoeffer, *The Cost of Discipleship* (New York: Macmillan, 1963), p. 126-27.

cooperation. In a world of competition we want to promote teamwork.

Peace is the future promised and guaranteed by God. Swords will be beaten into plowshares, the wolf will eat with the lamb, and war will be studied no more. It is the characteristic of the coming age, but we are called to bear witness to it and live it out as much as possible, even now (Rom 13:11-14).

Beyond Righteousness to a Durable, Robust Peace

There is a bumper sticker that says, "If you want peace, work for justice." There is a lot of truth to this. The order of the Beatitudes confirms that righteousness comes before peacemaking. In Paul's great summary statement, the kingdom of God is "righteousness" and "peace," in that order (Rom 14:17). "The effect of righteousness will be peace, and the result of righteousness, quietness and trust forever" (Is 32:17). "Righteousness and peace will kiss each other" (Ps 85:10).

We desperately need peace, but "peace at any price" is fleeting and illusory. In politics and marriage, in business competition and athletic contests, there is no peace without justice. There can be no peace where wickedness, unrighteousness and injustice dwell (Is 48:22).

Any peace not based on justice is a cheap and fleeting illusion; if you want peace, fight for justice. Any justice that remains harsh, unbending and accusing, and doesn't proceed to mercy and then to peacemaking, is a fraud that has nothing to do with God's justice.

Unrighteousness and injustice produce and maintain division, strife, pain and grievance. This is why no peace will be achieved until we face the righteousness issue. In political, national, ethnic and international relations it is always extraordinarily difficult to make peace. But it is utterly impossible unless there is a foundation of justice. So too with marital discord: no peace happens by papering over justice issues. Peace is very difficult to restore after the assaults of injustice and unrighteousness. It can be done—but only on the basis of justice.

The peace that God makes possible is more than just the cessation of war or the absence of injustice. Biblical peace is not just a kind of détente. Christ's love builds on righteousness to produce peace in the rich sense of *shalom* and healthiness, and in the sense of *harmony*.[6] Righteousness and justice have a robust, positive content, as we saw in the previous chapter. Because of this, a peace built on righteousness participates in this menu. We must also understand that when we use the term *reconciliation,* we refer to something greater and more positive than mere forgiveness or an agreement to let bygones be bygones. One person can forgive, but it takes two to be reconciled. Reconciliation means concretely beginning to establish a positive, common link once again after it has been broken.

Consider an analogy from choral music: unrighteousness might be thought of as everyone doing their own thing—singing whatever and however they wish. Righteousness is correctly (in tune, on key, neither flat nor sharp) singing the notes as written by the composer and assigned to you. This is the first requirement in any musical group: sing accurately your assigned notes. Nevertheless, a performance might still be terrible, even with everyone singing on key. Even if we sing the correct notes, we might sing them too loud or soft, too fast or slow, too wrapped up in our own part.

Peace, then, is when we all sing the right notes (righteousness) in harmony with each other's voices (peace). Peace requires righteousness, but it is communitarian, not individualistic. God's righteousness is manifold: there are many notes in our complex score (not any note will do, but still manifold and rich). The goal is not sameness but harmony, not uniformity but unity. This is the peace we seek for ourselves, our community and our world. Demonstrating such peace in our character and community is the salt and light our violent world so desperately needs.

Peacemaking Requires Genuineness and Purity of Heart
The Beatitudes teach us, however, that justice and righteousness are

---

[6]"Shalom is intertwined with justice. In shalom, each person enjoys justice, enjoys his or her rights. There is no shalom without justice. But shalom goes beyond justice. Shalom is the human being dwelling at peace in all his or her relationships: with God, with self, with fellows, with nature. . . . But the peace which is shalom is not merely the absence of hostility, not merely being in right relationship. Shalom at its highest is *enjoyment* in one's relationships." Nicholas Wolterstorff, *Until Justice and Peace Embrace* (Grand Rapids, Mich.: Eerdmans, 1983), p. 69.

not the only foundation of peace; they are absolutely essential but not sufficient. As we have seen earlier, the different sort of peacemaker we need, holier and wiser than usual, begins not with justice and righteousness but with openness, gentleness, a willingness to relinquish control and to serve. This peacemaker listens with an open mind and heart before discerning what justice calls for in the situation. The peacemaker proposes the most just resolution possible under the circumstances and then urges appropriate mercy and forgiveness, since perfect justice is impossible to achieve in this world.

The sixth Beatitude calls us to cultivate *purity of heart* as a further essential accompaniment of righteousness and mercy. "Blessed are the pure in heart, for they will see God." Like mercy, purity of heart is not an admired or easily acquired trait in our era. Moral decadence and pollution are part of the problem, as noted earlier in studying holiness. But purity of heart is also made difficult by our environment of fear and suspicion. We are inclined to be guarded. All of us have had experiences of trying to be open and honest—and being misunderstood or attacked because of it. We instinctively protect ourselves and keep our real opinions and feelings inside. We hide our own hearts—and we believe others are doing the same.

Purity of heart does not mean gullibility and naiveté, but it also goes against the other extreme, the epidemic of suspicion and cynicism. On the broader terrain of our history, Marx taught us to suspect (indeed, to assume) a class-interested economic motive behind whatever anyone says or does. Freud taught us to suspect/assume a deep psychosexual motive underneath all overt behavior. And Nietzsche taught us to assume a will to power driving people's speech and action, even if they are teaching meekness and forgiveness![7] While these masters of suspicion still influence our culture, we now also have feminist

---

[7]Jacques Ellul, *Hope in Time of Abandonment* (New York: Seabury, 1973). "We have learned no longer to place our confidence in anything, no longer to have faith in anyone, no longer to believe in a person's word, nor in a sentiment, no longer to accept the lasting quality of a relationship, no longer to believe that it could be authentic or truly representative of the person. We have learned that every good feeling merely expresses some self-satisfaction or some hypocrisy, that all virtue is a lie, that all morality is false, that all devotion is vain or a sham, that all speech hides the truth. We have learned that only the lie is true" (p. 50).

suspicion, racial suspicion, anti-Washington suspicion, antiliberal suspicion and religious suspicions of various kinds. In each case, what someone says or does is rejected and reinterpreted from the ideological perspective held by the accuser.

Much of this suspicion is well-founded because of the hypocrisy that is its counterpart. Politicians routinely employ human relations techniques to discover what words and ideas to use with different groups of potential voters, hiding their real positions in the process. Plagiarism, cheating and false representations surround us. Advertisers do their best to hide their real motives (sales results) and the weaknesses or dangers of their products and foist on us their propaganda of how our lives will be better if we buy from them. It is no wonder that we become a little guarded and wary, but it is too bad when we fall all the way into cynicism and suspicion.

The good character we are seeking to build requires a much different approach in which genuineness, purity of heart and integrity play an essential role. "Who shall ascend the hill of the LORD? And who shall stand in his holy place? Those who have clean hands and pure hearts, who do not lift up their souls to what is false, and do not swear deceitfully. They will receive blessing from the LORD" (Ps 24:3-5). "Create in me a clean heart, O God, and put a new and right spirit within me" (Ps 51:10). In faith we are invited to draw near to God, with a "true heart," "with our hearts sprinkled clean from an evil conscience and our bodies washed with pure water" (Heb 10:22). "Cleanse your hands, you sinners, and purify your hearts, you double-minded" (Jas 4:8).

The Greek word for this purity is *katheros,* which is used in the New Testament for physical, religious and moral cleanness, and freedom from stains, blemishes and contamination. Jesus stressed that purity of heart was more important and fundamental than external ritual cleanliness: "Woe to you, scribes and Pharisees, hypocrites! For you clean the outside of the cup and of the plate, but inside they are full of greed and self-indulgence. You blind Pharisee! First clean the inside of the cup, so that the outside also may become clean" (Mt 23:25-26). Purity of heart is the interior side of holiness. Our interior and exterior should correspond with each other.

Only God can make us clean and pure, and give us a new heart. Nevertheless, we are called to assist God in maintaining the purity that already he has given to us. Purity of heart requires some "garbage disposal." It means identifying and getting rid of the thoughts, attitudes, motives and feelings we harbor that are not righteous, not shaped by the mind of Christ. It means recognizing and abandoning all suspicious, calculating and cynical attitudes toward others.

Single-minded integrity. Purity of heart means an undivided commitment to righteousness and mercy. As we saw earlier with respect to faith and holiness, it is primarily our pursuit of God that separates us from the world. So too, it is by giving our heart in passionate love to God that purity is best achieved. "Purity of heart is to will one thing," wrote Søren Kierkegaard. "That one thing is God who is the Good."[8] "The psychology implied in this Beatitude is Hebrew rather than Greek. In classical Greek philosophy, head rules heart, reason rules will. In Scripture it is reversed. The heart of man is not the head but the heart, the prefunctional root of all psychic functions, including reason, understanding, wisdom. 'Keep your heart with all diligence, for out of it spring the issues of life,' says Solomon (Prov 4:23)."[9] Purity of heart means to be single-minded, sincere, transparent and without guile before God.

Purity of heart means making a habit of *integrity* in place of *hypocrisy*. Integrity means there is an equivalence between what is in our heart and what we display in our words and deeds.[10] We harbor no hidden motives or agendas. We cultivate simplicity, purity and transparency. John Chrysostom said the pure in heart are "not conscious to themselves of any evil."[11]

Purity of heart does not mean recklessly, indiscriminately, blabbing all our opinions and thoughts to everyone. There are things to guard in our hearts. Rather, it means quietly searching and cleansing our heart

---

[8]Søren Kierkegaard, *Purity of Heart Is to Will One Thing* (New York: Harper Torchbooks, 1956).

[9]Peter Kreeft, *Back to Virtue* (San Francisco: Ignatius, 1986), p. 175.

[10]See Stephen L. Carter, *Integrity* (New York: BasicBooks, 1996), on integrity as a crucial "pre-political" virtue.

[11]Chrysostom, *Homily XV*, p. 94.

to make sure our interior life and thought correspond, without hypocrisy, to our exterior life, to our speech and our acts. It means not harboring different motives than those we avow as we work for righteousness, mercy and peace. When we say "This is the truth," or "I forgive you," that is precisely what we mean in our heart; we are not holding back or "just saying it."

Speaking and listening. Purity of heart is important both for our own communication and action, and for our interpretation of others. While it is true that people often do have hidden motives, consistent and epidemic suspicion is a recipe for the total breakdown of communication and social cohesion in our society. It is the way out of the lazy and fearful. We must refuse to automatically, stereotypically attribute economic, sexual or power motives to everyone.

Purity of heart unclouds our vision so that we can clearly see God and his righteousness, mercy and peace. Purity of heart is usually, eventually, detectable by others; duplicity, hypocrisy, suspicion and hidden agendas will undo our best efforts for righteousness, mercy and peace.

Purity of heart means listening, asking clarifying questions and giving the benefit of the doubt to those we hear. We put the best construction, the best interpretation, on what we hear, not dismissing it in some paranoid suspicion. We should not be naive, but we have to take some risks.

The virtue and habit of purity of heart has results. First, it enables us to "see God." Purity of heart helps clarify our vision of the righteousness and mercy of God, unclouded by self-interest, class bias, paranoid fears or other factors. It is not to the brilliant mind, or to the aged or experienced, or to male or female, but to those who are pure in heart that God reveals himself. There can be no authentic righteousness/justice without *mercy*—and now we know there can be no righteousness/justice/mercy without *purity of heart*.

Second, purity of heart enables us to be more effective peacemakers. Often, people can detect the fact that we have hidden motives or thoughts or that we are not being straight with them. Duplicity and hypocrisy are the sure road to the undoing of our best efforts on behalf of righteousness and mercy. We want purity of heart so that our mercy is genuine and not mere condescension or manipulation. Furthermore, it is so difficult—and yet so essential—for peacemakers to establish a reputation for genuineness and integrity. If we can really have purity of heart as a virtue, an ongoing trait of character, avoiding personal hypocrisy and rejecting suspicion of others, we will have many opportunities to serve as mediators and reconcilers.

Purity of Heart
1. holiness in one's interior life
2. genuineness, integrity, consistency, no hypocrisy or conflict between what we think, say, and do
3. no cynicism and suspicion of others that refuses to believe or accept what they say or do at face value

We (and our communities) must practice genuineness, and welcome it in others. We must not punish people for saying what is truly on their minds—or for demurring from some opinion or action that would violate their heart. If we sing "Just as I am, without one plea" to others, let us welcome people just as they are. Let us do what we say and mean what we say and do. Maintaining a pure heart means risking that we will be victimized by someone's rejection or hidden agenda. But as an old Quaker said to a worldly realist, "You've chosen to be the last one to do the right; I've a mind to be the first and set the rest an example."

Love Makes Peace

Part of the reason why peace is so elusive is because righteousness, mercy and purity of heart are so rare. But peace is also elusive because *love* is so uncommon. Despite the frequency of love jargon in popular music and culture, many of us are too busy for genuine love! Our relationships tend to be functional, technical, short-term and utilitarian—and that's not love. People need warmth, acceptance, caring, community, friends and intimacy. We fail in ways that require forgiveness, help and correction. We become alienated and estranged from others in ways that only love can overcome. Only love, the true article, can meet these needs.

In our world, peacemaking is often viewed as hardheaded negotiation. Love is hardly considered because it is considered as mere sentimentality, desire and nice feelings. "I love you" usually means "I desire you" or "I enjoy you." Even this reduction is often further narrowed to a merely physical or sexual level. This kind of "love" has a place in human life, but it is not the hearty stuff that makes for peace. Sentimentalism will not bring peace to Serbia, Palestine, East Timor, Ireland or the other hot spots mentioned above.

Along with faith and hope, love is one of the three great "theological virtues." Like righteousness/justice, love is a grand, comprehensive concept that can refer to the whole of goodness and virtue. It is especially close to the fifth, seventh and eighth Beatitudes (mercy, peacemaking, bearing up under persecution). Peacemaking without love will fail; peacemaking is love in action.

No one can dispute how persistent and central love is in the Bible. In the Old Testament, biblical people recited daily the *shema:* "Hear, O Israel: The LORD is our God, the LORD alone. You shall love the LORD your God with all your heart, and with all your soul, and with all your might" (Deut 6:4-5). In the New Testament, Jesus calls this the greatest commandment in the law and the prophets (Mt 22:34-40; Mk 12:28-34) and also the summation of the gospel of eternal life (Lk 10:25-28).[12] Love is a major theme in the teaching of Jesus.

God loves us and wishes to elicit our love in return. "Whoever does not love does not know God, for God is love. God's love was revealed among us in this way: God sent his only Son into the world so that we might live through him" (1 Jn 4:8-9). God's love is not just a feeling and desire he has for us, it is his action in reaching out to us. In his love, he solves our righteousness problem with justice and mercy at his own expense. His heart is pure and unchanging in his will to have us in his family.

Who and where do we love? Our answer sounds a lot like the earlier section on peacemaking and reconciliation. Loving God comes first. John says, "Whoever does not love, does not know God." When we begin to comprehend the love of God, we cannot help but begin to love him. A shared love of God enables communities of faith to be communities of peace.

---

[12]Victor Paul Furnish, *The Love Command in the New Testament* (Nashville: Abingdon, 1972).

Second, as Jesus famously said, "Love one another. Just as I have loved you, you also should love one another. By this everyone will know that you are my disciples, if you have love for one another" (Jn 13:34-35). Francis Schaeffer used to say that this is the fundamental "mark of the Christian." Paul writes that love is the "more excellent way," the foundational "fruit of spirit," and we should "live in love, as Christ loved us and gave himself up for us" (1 Cor 12:31; Gal 5:22; Eph 5:1-2). The letter to the Hebrews says to "provoke one another to love" (Heb 10:24). Peter says that Christians must above all "love one another deeply from the heart" (1 Pet 1:22).

John says over and over that we must love one another, for "God is love." "Those who say 'I love God,' and hate their brothers or sisters, are liars; for those who do not love a brother or sister whom they have seen, cannot love God whom they have not seen. The commandment we have from him is this: those who love God must love their brothers and sisters also" (1 Jn 4:8, 20-21).

Third, we are called to love our neighbors. To the command to "Love the Lord your God," Jesus added "You shall love your neighbor as yourself" from the Holiness Code (Lev 19:18). Together, he said, this summarizes the law and the prophets (Mt 22:34-40; Mk 12:28-34; Lk 10:25-28). Paul also emphasizes that we should "owe no one anything except to love one another; for the one who loves another has fulfilled the law" (Rom 13:8; Gal 5:13-14). James says that to love our neighbors is to fulfill the "royal law" (Jas 2:8).

In the Sermon on the Mount, Jesus says that love applies even to our enemies and those who mistreat us. "You have heard that it was said, 'You shall love your neighbor and hate your enemy.' But I say to you, Love your enemies and pray for those who persecute you, so that you may be children of your Father in heaven; for he makes his sun rise on the evil and on the good, and sends rain on the righteous and on the unrighteous. For if you love those who love you, what reward do you have? Do not even the tax collectors do the same? And if you greet only your brothers and sisters, what more are you doing than others? Do not even the Gentiles do the same? Be perfect, therefore, as your heavenly Father is perfect" (Mt 5:43-48).

The cross and the table. In our study of character virtues, we need to think about two basic forms of love.[13] The first of these is *sacrificial love.*[14] This is related to the mercifulness of the fifth Beatitude and the courageous persistence under persecution of the eighth Beatitude. John writes about this kind of love: "We know love by this, that he laid down his life for us—and we ought to lay down our lives for one another" (1 Jn 3:16). "In this is love, not that we loved God but that he loved us and sent his Son to be the atoning sacrifice for our sins" (1 Jn 4:10).

This first form of love is expressed in the cross, in sacrifice. "Cross love" is an altruistic "gift love." The love of the cross acts in personal sacrifice for the good of the other. The love of the cross means giving the gift of mercy and forgiveness, even when it is undeserved. It means going the extra mile and serving the other, putting the other's needs first. Cross love is sacrificial servanthood. Husbands, for example, ought to love their wives, Paul says, "as Christ loved the church and gave himself for her" (Eph 5:25). The symbol for this first form of love is the cross.

Cross love is related to *kindness.* The "loving kindness of God our Savior appeared" (Tit 3:4). In the ages to come God will "show the immeasurable riches of his grace in kindness toward us in Christ Jesus" (Eph 2:7). Think of Jesus with children, with the sick, poor, outcast and lost; this was the kindest man on earth. We, too, must "put on" kindness (Col 3:12).

The second form of love is *friendship, brotherly and sisterly love.* The apostle Paul writes, "Love one another with mutual affection" (Rom 12:10). Where cross-love is altruistic and sacrificial, and may or

---

[13]On love see: Gene Outka, *Agape: An Ethical Analysis* (New Haven, Conn.: Yale University Press, 1972); Gilbert Meilaender, *Friendship: A Study in Theological Ethics* (South Bend, Ind.: University of Notre Dame Press, 1981); Søren Kierkegaard, *Works of Love* (New York: Harper Torchbooks, 1962); and C. S. Lewis, *The Four Loves* (New York: Harcourt Brace Jovanovich, 1960).

[14]Greek scholars point out that *agapē* and *philia* are not used with clear, consistent, distinct meanings in the New Testament—we have to understand their connotations in specific contexts, and their usages overlap. For that reason I will use the terms "sacrificial love" and "cross love" for the first form of love and "mutual love" and "table love" for the second. "Erotic love" (based on the Greek word *eros*) has a place in the Bible (e.g., Song of Songs) but is distinct from the *agapē/philia* meanings.

may not be reciprocated, friendship is the kind of love that is shared and exchanged. It is the love that characterizes peace. The great symbol for such love is the table where people enjoy a feast with each other. Communion tables in churches symbolize this love and friendship into which Christ has brought us.

Our goal is the friendship, camaraderie, mutuality, shalom and celebration of "table love." Our path to that goal will necessarily include "cross love"—forgiveness and sacrifice. We will never get to the table except by way of the cross.

Peacemaking is the activity of bringing people, formerly estranged, into this sort of feasting and friendship at table. The coming kingdom of God is described in symbolic terms as a great "marriage supper of the Lamb"—a great feast to which all people and nations are invited (Rev 19:9). Heaven is *not* depicted as a place where we will all hang on crosses for each other (eternally engaging in sacrificial love). Mutual love is not *second-best* love but is, in fact, the ultimate form. It is a mistake to exalt the sacrificial love of the cross in a way that somehow deprecates the love of the table.

Unless we are truly pathological, we want this friendship, this love of the table. Doesn't everyone crave the peaceful fellowship of friends—in marriage, in relationships with colleagues, family members, neighbors, nations? The biblical message affirms this as a basic human need and desire, going back to our creation in cohumanity where it is "not good for one to dwell alone." The problem is how to get there from here, how to get to the table of friendship in our relationships.

Therapy and counseling might help. Better communication will help. But we know that in every case, justice will need to be at the foundation. We can not fellowship in peace at our tables with the unresolved bitterness and hurt of injustice. Nor can we achieve true friendship and peace without adding mercy (sacrifice, forgiveness, the love of the cross) to justice. We cannot get to the table except by way of the cross; the feast is the goal—but the cross is the way.

Cross love, in practice, means going out of our way, humbly serving the interests of peace, working for the good of enemies as well as friends. It may cost us weariness, time, extra effort, misunderstanding, rejection and unjust suffering. Cross love means extending forgiveness even when forgiveness is not reciprocated. Cross love leads us to pray

for enemies and to listen to their pain and anger. Cross love is sacrific-
ing ourselves for others. It is *necessary* for peace and reconciliation to
happen in our broken world; it is *possible* because we are attached in
faith to Jesus Christ who made peace by suffering on the cross for us.
The power of his resurrection life in us makes it possible for us to follow in his footsteps.

Peacemakers always have in mind to "bring people to the table"—
not the negotiation table but the feasting table. And while "table love"
is a metaphor, actually physically eating with oth-
ers is an important concrete action. Do we want
racial reconciliation? It's a start to invite people of
other races to eat with you. Truth and justice
issues must be faced, but even as we work on
those, we should try to find ways of beginning to
live out the peace that is our ultimate goal. Our
tables (and lifestyles) too often exclude, when
they could include.

Cross love was not a virtue in Greek ethics, nor
has it been in most cultures, ancient or modern.
Table love and friendship have been praised by
many (Aristotle wrote one of history's greatest
essays on friendship, *philia,* in his *Nicomachean
Ethics*)—but they escape us unless we seek this peace table by way of
the cross. All of this has largely been forgotten or misunderstood even
by Christians, who often seem to prefer to be tough, powerful and
intimidating.

Love
1. sacrificial, cross
love: extends help to
those in need, for-
giveness to guilty—
even if they will not
or can not recipro-
cate.
2. friendship, table
love: draws people
together in mutual
conversation, tasks,
celebration—recip-
rocated not from
duty but from joy.

The Virtues and Habits of the Peacemaker

Without peacemakers our society will continue to live in an environment of growing fear and death with the strong preying upon the weak.
Our world desperately needs, and God passionately calls us to, another
way: the way of love and peacemaking. This is not some naive, do-
gooder, pie-in-the-sky rhetoric but the realism of the cross and resurrection. We do not want more people who react with a swift, vengeful
instinct when their toes are stepped on, or their car is cut off on the
highway, or their possessions are stolen.

As we now review and summarize the peacemaker's character and strategy, think about these five examples: a marriage on the rocks, an adult child alienated from a parent, tension and fear haunting the relations of two different ethnic groups living near each other, a church about to have an angry split, Palestinians and Israelis trying to get along in peace after fifty years of violence and injustice. Let me be bold and brash: the only truly viable strategy for peacemaking is the following, as specified in the Beatitudes.

---

1. holiness: because of faithful commitment to God, the peacemaker refuses to be owned by any party or interest
2. openness: the peacemaker doesn't know everything and is open to listen and learn; poverty/weakness are acknowledged
3. responsibility/mourning: the peacemaker is not superior but empathizes with those who suffer or are responsible
4. gentleness: the peacemaker doesn't try to control everything; things are kept fluid and free
5. justice: the truth is put on the table as fully and openly as possible; actions and responsibilities are named and fair compensations and responses identified
6. mercy: some injustices cannot be righted at all; most cannot be perfectly corrected; forgiveness and mercy are needed
7. genuineness: no suspicions or hidden, unstated feelings or agendas are allowed
8. reconciliation/peacemaking: agree on specific, concrete, positive activities together that evidence a good-faith relationship that moves positively beyond the past

---

Figure 9.1. The character and strategy of a peacemaker

My argument is that this strategy for peace and reconciliation must be followed in *any* situation of conflict and alienation. There can be no peace without a degree of humility and openness. If any of the parties (including the mediator) feels or comes across as though they know everything, no progress can occur. Progress also requires the stages of mourning/responsibility/empathy and gentleness/freedom. Justice and truth issues must be acknowledged, even if the opponents can't agree on all the precise details (but they must have *some* agreement on the justice issues or no progress can be made). The need for forgiveness and mercy and for integrity is clear, I think, from the discussion in this chapter. We won't achieve durable, meaningful peace in any serious conflict without this strategy. Good character is character that has this

conflict without this strategy. Good character is character that has this strategy not as an external set of principles but as an internalized set of ongoing habits and traits.

For Reflection or Discussion

1. Have you ever been in a situation where peace was difficult to come by and you needed to act as a peacemaker? What did you do? Did it work? Why or why not?
2. Have you known someone whose purity of heart and integrity were especially obvious and praiseworthy? Was this person also good at peacemaking and reconciliation as far as you know? Do you agree that there is a connection?
3. How have you been the recipient of the sacrificial love of the cross from someone else? How about the friendship love of the table? How have you tried to give the two loves to others?
4. How can our churches better teach and practice love, peacemaking and reconciliation—in both our community life together and in our relations with the world?
5. Discuss each of the five problem cases at the end of this chapter. Is this really a workable, realistic approach to resolving marital conflicts? International relations? Ethnic conflicts? Church and family breakdowns?

Ten

HOPEFUL, COURAGEOUS & JOYFUL

The Ambassador

*O*ne of the best things about the Christian way of life is its utter realism. Our vision is set on the loftiest and most attractive ideals imaginable—and we actually taste their accomplishment from time to time. But Jesus and Scripture never pretend that life in this world will not be rough. "In the world you face persecution" (Jn 16:33). We must be prepared to build good character and community in the midst of a broken and difficult world.

When the Going Gets Tough

The "active life," described by the virtues of the Beatitudes, begins in hungering for righteousness and culminates in peacemaking. One more virtue must be added: *persevering in righteousness in the face of persecution*. We hunger and we push for a peace built on righteousness—but even if we run into great resistance, even if we fail to achieve our goal, we do not quit. We do not abandon the righteousness agenda even if persecution arises.

"Blessed are those who are persecuted for righteousness' sake, for theirs is the kingdom of heaven." In an elaboration of this eighth Beatitude, Jesus goes on to say, "Blessed are you when people revile you . . . and utter all kinds of evil against you falsely on my account. Rejoice and be glad, for your reward is great in heaven, for in the same way they persecuted the prophets who were before you" (Mt 5:10-12).

The character of this opposition is "persecution," being "reviled" and "falsely" spoken against with "all kinds of evil." The reason (excuse!) for these attacks is our "righteousness" and Jesus Christ ("on my account"). Those who undergo these trials should "rejoice and be glad" because they are blessed with (1) the kingdom of heaven now, and (2) a reward in the future. Pursuing God's righteousness is worth it, even if we are persecuted. Why? First, it is when the going gets tough like this that we experience God's presence and rule (the kingdom of heaven) most fully and intimately.[1] In Psalm 23 the language about God is third person ("he leads me," etc.) until the going gets tough. In the valley of the shadow of death and in the presence of enemies the language for God shifts to second person ("you are with me," etc.). The heat of trial collapses the distance from "he" to "you."[2]

A second reason not to bail out when the going gets tough is that it is deeply satisfying to know that someone is helped by our efforts, however painful. Hanging in there with righteousness is a crucial component in bringing salt and light to the earth. It is easier to take those hits knowing that it is, in the broader scheme of things, helping somebody. Third, we know that God is pleased, and that matters. All of us would gladly suffer to protect our kids and loved ones and their interests.

---

[1]In the final chapter we will look more fully at "character on trial," what causes testing and how to respond.

[2]By now it should be no surprise to find that in Psalm 23 after the "paths of righteousness" we may come to the "valley of the shadow of death" and find ourselves in the "presence of my enemies." My intention in alluding to Psalm 23 from time to time is to demonstrate that the character described in the Beatitudes is consistent with what God reveals in the Old Testament. While there are rich and intriguing (sometimes puzzling!) variations in biblical teaching, I maintain that there are fundamental ethical themes that cut across the whole canon of Scripture and that this is because there is one God behind it all addressing what is, after all, one humanity.

Why? That's love! It is blessed and meaningful and satisfying to sacrifice for someone you love and who you know will appreciate what you have done. Fourth, it is gratifying to stick with our team. Much of the time we are persecuted, there are others beside us, suffering the same thing—or praying for us in solidarity. It is not good to dwell alone—or to abandon our team when the going gets tough. It is good to remain in solidarity with not only our contemporaries but with the prophets, apostles and martyrs before us.

We need to be sure, of course, that our persecution is not the result of our own blunders and offenses. "Let none of you suffer as a murderer, a thief, a criminal, or even as a mischief maker" (1 Pet 4:15). If we suffer persecution, let it be "for doing what is right," if we are reviled, let it be "for the name of Christ" (1 Pet 3:14; 4:14). If we give offense, let it be the "offense of the cross" (Gal 5:11). If we are regarded as fools, let it be because of the "foolishness" of the gospel of the crucified (1 Cor 1:21-25).

Let us be brutally honest: sometimes Christians have been rejected and persecuted because they have come across as arrogant know-it-alls, witnesses who don't know how to listen, evangelists interested only in showing others that they are wrong and that we possess all truth. We have spoken too confidently about things we didn't fully understand. We have spoken of the love of God without demonstrating its reality. Sometimes Christian students have thought they were victims of anti-Christian prejudice—when the problem was that their work was substandard and their advocacy was offensive. Sometimes Christian musicians have cried "persecution" when their music didn't get airplay—but the real reason was that it was not good music.

> Not all persecution of Christians is because of faithfulness or righteousness; some of it is because of Christian arrogance, offensiveness, mediocrity and ignorance.

Still, some persecution and opposition is part of the Christian experience. If we never experience it in *any* form, it is probably because we are in some way unfaithful to Jesus' calling in the world. Why is this so? Think about school kids who work hard and succeed in their studies—only to be ridiculed by lazy, ignorant, goof-off students. They are persecuted because they awaken a bad conscience among the lazy. The presence of goodness convicts the consciences of those who do evil; the practice of righteousness reminds the unjust and wicked of their true condition. This is the reason why the Prince of Peace and Righteousness was crucified, and this is the reason why his followers will also have to bear the cross.

Persecution for Righteousness
1. on account of Jesus and righteousness
2. not for our own sins, weaknesses, failures
3. our Lord comes close to help and guide
4. we stay linked to our team, past and present
5. we rejoice in the promise of future victory

The fact is that some Christian professors *have* been discriminated against or persecuted for their faith. Some Christian students have been ridiculed by teachers for their convictions. Some deserving employees have been passed over for promotions because they would not compromise their Christian character. Christians who would not compromise have lost elections.

Among the most painful and frustrating cases of persecution are instances when allegedly *Christian* leaders—even bishops in the church—have ridiculed, marginalized, persecuted and treated with contempt those who were seeking to be faithful to the gospel. Friendly fire (getting shot by your own troops) is often the worst form of persecution.

Courage and Patience Under Fire

Courage and patience are lauded often throughout the Bible as desirable character traits. The eighth Beatitude assumes them but does not name them explicitly. It takes both courage and patience to continue when persecuted for righteousness sake. For Plato and the ancient Greek philosophers, courage was one of the four cardinal virtues along with justice, wisdom and self-control. Courage (fortitude, bravery) meant literally the "readiness to fall in battle," the determination rooted in the "spirited part" of human nature to fight on despite opposition.[3] For Aristotle, the virtue of courage is the mean between cowardice (the vice of deficiency) and recklessness (the vice of excess). For Plato and Aristotle, one becomes courageous by over-

---

[3]See Josef Pieper, *The Four Cardinal Virtues* (South Bend, Ind.: University of Notre Dame Press, 1966), pp. 117-41.

coming the instinct to flee when threatened and, instead, obeying the voice of reason about what is right. By repeatedly doing courageous things we gain the habit and build the capacity for courage.

Biblical courage is distinct from classical courage in at least two ways. First, it is inextricably bound up with the presence of the Lord. "Be strong and courageous; do not be frightened or dismayed, for the LORD your God is with you wherever you go" (Josh 1:9; see also Deut 31:6). Courage comes not from an innate power within us but from God's presence and strength. Second, biblical courage is future oriented. Courage is inspired by hope and confidence about the future, not merely by stoical compliance with the abstract requirements of reason, truth, and justice.

> **G**od gives us courage—the capacity to say yes and persist in doing the right thing even when it hurts, we are exhausted, and everything inside us says, "Quit now!" Self-control is its partner—the capacity to say no and decline to do the wrong thing even when we want it so bad it hurts, and everything inside us says, "Grab it now!"

True courage is *patient* and *persevering*—it is not just an occasional heroic moment. Patience is a "fruit of the Spirit" (Gal 5:22). It literally means "longsuffering" (Greek *makrothymia*) and "abiding under" (Greek *hypomonē*). As longsuffering, patience means restraining one's wrath, holding off on judgment, tolerantly putting up with imperfect people and with our disappointments and lack of immediate fulfillment. In the Old Testament, Job is a model of such longsuffering patience. Longsuffering patience is the capacity to continue to absorb the negative (suffering, persecution, hardship) in light of the promise of what is ahead. Jesus Christ is longsuffering in delaying his return, not wishing that any should perish (2 Pet 3).

Patience as "abiding under" means persistently continuing to do the good. Jesus displayed this characteristic when he "for the sake of the joy that was set before him endured the cross" (Heb 12:2). The eighth Beatitude calls us to courageously persevere in the positive agenda, continuing to pursue righteousness and peace even in the face of opposition or in the absence of apparent progress or success.

We live in a soft and impatient era. We want what we want now, if not sooner! Deferred gratification is not a popular concept. We wish to be free from pain. The pain threshold in advanced technologically developed societies is certainly much lower than elsewhere on the globe or at other moments in history. Rather than being longsuffering, we incline toward griping or immediate vengeance; rather than persisting patiently in doing good, we give up and quit. The good biblical character we are trying to build is of another type: courageous, patient, persevering, longsuffering and tenacious.

Hopeful in the Midst of Difficulty

Earlier we looked at two of Paul's famous "theological virtues," faith and love. Faith draws us near to the living Christ who, though unseen, is present with us; we become disciples through faith. Love relates us not only to God but also to our neighbor in sacrificial efforts to bring about reconciliation, peace and life. Hope, the third theological virtue, links us to God's future, to the coming kingdom of God. Hope is also the most subjective of the three virtues. It is something we guard in our heart as our orientation to what is not yet, to our expectation of what is coming.

Courage
1. bravery, fortitude, "readiness to fall in battle"
2. neither cowardice nor recklessness
3. comes from the presence of the Lord with us
4. strengthened by confidence in the future outcome
5. longsuffering patience continues to absorb negative
6. persevering patience continues to do positive

The Beatitudes teach us to live in expectation.[4] The second through seventh Beatitudes promise their blessings in a future tense: You *will* be comforted, inherit the earth, be filled, receive mercy, see God, and be called the children of God. The eighth Beatitude ends with "Rejoice and be glad for great is your reward in heaven." While these Beatitudes' promises are often experienced in

---

[4]"Hope is believing in the beatitudes in spite of appearances. Happy are those who weep—how foolish that is, for those who weep are unhappy and promising them consolation is a sorry jest. In any case Jesus says that they are happy now, already, at the present time. The one who weeps is happy now. This beatitude is true only because it is a word which God himself pronounces over the one who weeps. Hope teaches us to accept as true what God says and to regard as untrue what the evidence of the senses affirms. It is the direct opposite of what Eve does when she accepts the evidence of the fruit which she is offered." Jacques Ellul, *The Ethics of Freedom* (Grand Rapids, Mich.: Eerdmans, 1976), pp. 18-19.

part in this life, their complete fulfillment lies in the future. God's kingdom is partially here and partially deferred to the future.

A life with hope is a rare phenomenon in our world. To be sure, there are many who put their hopes in technology and science, or in one or another movement, candidate or guru. For large numbers of people, though, life has very little hope. Many feel like the Psalmist, overwhelmed, with no way out: "My days pass away like smoke. . . . My heart is stricken and withered like grass. . . . I lie awake. . . . mingle tears with my drink" (Ps 102:3, 4, 7, 9). What can we say to our neighbors who feel such despair? What can we offer to a world drowning out its hopelessness with noisy, frantic, desperate diversions of all kinds? Compulsive overeating, alcohol and drug addiction, obsessive workaholism, mad quests for fame, for power and financial success—these are signs of despair, not hope. The offices of our psychologists and therapists are thriving on an epidemic of hopelessness.

Of course, hopelessness is not just an issue in personal life and social relationships. The magnitude of the global problems of hunger and disease, of violent political conflict and terrorism, and of environmental degradation are truly depressing if you take a serious look around the world. How can we ever overcome these problems in any significant way? For some of us, most encounters with television and popular culture are equally depressing. The mediocrity of our Christian witness offers some further cause for hopelessness.

It might be even worse than all of this. In his provocative and powerful book *Hope in Time of Abandonment,* Jacques Ellul suggests that our age is like that time feared by the prophets, when God turns away from the world.[5] We are experiencing the silence of God because of our refusal of his Word and our preference for the idols of our age.

The most difficult challenge to hope is when we undergo sustained opposition and unfair persecution—even though we are trying our best to do the right thing and contribute to peace. It is well and good to say "be of good courage" and "be patient" in these times, but in a very

---

[5]Jacques Ellul, *Hope in Time of Abandonment* (New York: Seabury Press, 1973). Ellul is not saying that individuals do not experience God today but that God seems silent and absent from the broader culture and its institutions.

basic way we must be able to hope in order to keep going. Hopefulness
is an essential aspect of the eighth Beatitude.

What is hope? Hope, in its most general sense, is a positive attitude
or disposition toward the future. Broadly defined, hope includes our
wishes, dreams and fantasies, whether well grounded or not. In biblical
terms, hope is "confident expectation" in God
(Greek *elpis, elpizō*). Christian hope is distinctive,
first of all, in its confidence.[6] Biblical hope is not a
wish or a dream but a confident expectation. Now
this helps get through the hard times!

> Hope is the "future tense" of faith. It is hope's confident expectation that makes it possible to have courage and patience during times of persecution.

The second distinctive is its object: Christian
hope is placed in God—not in science, technology,
evolution, progress, human nature, the nation or
anything else. Biblical hope is about what God will
do both in our own human experience next week
or next year and at the end of my life and the end of human history.

Both the Old and New Testaments often exhibit a strong sense of
historical expectation, whether in hope of a bright future (the promises
of God) or in dread of coming judgment (the warnings of God). For
example, compliance with the Ten Commandments is urged partly in
the confident hope that "it will go well with you and you will live long
in the land." The prophets, as expected, look to the future (e.g., Is
65:17-25; Jer 33:1-9; Mal 4). The psalmist says "I wait for the LORD . . .
and in his word I hope; . . . O Israel, hope in the LORD! For with the
LORD there is steadfast love, and with him is great power to redeem"
(Ps 130:5, 7). Hebrew time is linear, moving forward; it is not an end-
lessly repeated cycle.

The coming kingdom of God, including Jesus' own promise to
return, looms large in the Gospels (Mt 24; Jn 14:1-4). Peter and Paul

---

[6]"Faith binds man to Christ. Hope sets this faith open to the comprehensive future
of Christ. Hope is therefore the inseparable companion of faith. . . . Hope is nothing
else than the expectation of those things which faith has believed to have been
truly promised by God. . . . Without faith's knowledge of Christ, hope becomes a
utopia and remains hanging in the air. But without hope, faith falls to pieces,
becomes a fainthearted and ultimately a dead faith. It is through faith that a man
finds the path of true life, but it is only hope that keeps him on that path." Jürgen
Moltmann, *Theology of Hope* (New York: Harper & Row, 1967), p. 20.

gave a full and comprehensive articulation of the theology and ethics of hope. God has caused us to be born again to a "living hope through the resurrection of Jesus Christ from the dead." God "raised him from the dead and gave him glory, so that your faith and hope are set on God" (1 Pet 1:3, 21). In these phrases the apostle Peter shows that the basis of Christian hope is the fact of the resurrection of Jesus Christ. If Jesus' crucifixion on Friday was followed by his resurrection on Easter Sunday, then all things are truly possible. To the extent that we are attached to Jesus Christ, we will expect that an "Easter" lies ahead at the end of our own history. Christians bear witness also to innumerable experiences of God's renewing intervention in daily life.

If the resurrection of Jesus is the basis, the ultimate *goal* of Christian hope is the return of Christ. "Set all your hope on the grace that Jesus Christ will bring you when he is revealed" (1 Pet 1:13). All of our little microhopes are caught up in the great macrohope of the Second Coming of Jesus Christ. Because of Easter we know that at the end of our life, after the final step on our road, the living Jesus Christ will greet us with his amazing grace. Paul describes it in similar fashion to Titus: we wait for the "blessed hope"—the "manifestation of the glory of our great God and Savior, Jesus Christ" (Tit 2:13). The return of Christ means judgment as well as reward, destruction of evil as well as re-creation of the heavens and the earth, but this evokes not terror but hope because the Christ who will return is the same gracious Savior who has forgiven all our offenses.

Think about this image: hope means that on this road you are travelling you confidently expect that the living, resurrected Jesus stands up ahead. To be even more precise, Jesus is coming toward us on the road we travel. Because Jesus is up ahead, we can take the next step in confidence, our energy is renewed, and we know we will make it. If we collapse and don't make it to him, he will nevertheless come to where we fall. Courage and patience under persecution become possible with an outlook like this.

Christians must remember their faithful predecessors who dared to question the slavery system in the eighteenth and nineteenth centuries. Slavery had been taken for granted as a global institution from time immemorial. Bible verses were quoted to support it; well-known religious leaders joined in the justification of the enslavement of other human beings. Economic realism and popular common sense argued that the abolitionists could not succeed. Without slavery the economy would collapse. Other nations would have slaves and those who didn't would then be vulnerable and at a disadvantage. But abolitionist Christians insisted, against all odds and despite all persecution, on being faithful and righteous. They knew that in the coming kingdom of God, there would be no slavery. They clung to the absurd hope that God would honor their efforts and be up ahead on their road. They were right, and slavery was nearly wiped from the face of the earth. God can bring hope into the most intransigent, hopeless situation.

In our own day the Berlin Wall and the iron curtain looked permanent. Small bands of Christians in Eastern Europe faithfully prayed and worked in hope—and, largely because of this, an unthinkable, mostly peaceful revolution swept communist totalitarian military rule away. Since Jesus Christ has defeated death, he can defeat nuclear holocaust and environmental disaster. AIDS might be overcome. The gospel may be preached in Tiananmen Square some day. You might be reconciled to your parents or children. Love might bloom again in your marriage. You might be set free at last from your codependence or addiction. You may find true love at last. You might be healed. Joy might return to your sad and depressed soul.

> Anybody who really believes that Jesus rose from the dead can have hope in the bleakest of circumstances and hardest of times.

A Christian remembers that first Easter and has hope. There is no depression as hopeless as death itself, no financial stress as intransigent as the grave, no alienation from friends or family as severe as the separation that death brings, no social problem so radical and extreme as death and the grave. Our Lord has conquered the great and final foe through his cross and resurrection. We can be hopeful even in the midst of tribulation and persecution.

How hope works. As a virtue, hope restructures our character in that (1) our value and worth ultimately rest on God's choice to receive us into his family, not on any other basis; our life is valuable and of serious, ultimate concern to God. And (2) we do not need to fix everything now, or satisfy every need now; we can be more patient because we know that fulfillment and restoration are a definite part of our future with Christ.[7] We "hold fast to the confession of our hope without wavering, for he who has promised is faithful" (Heb 10:23).

Hope works in at least three ways. First, hope *liberates.* Christian hope *relativizes* this world and this present history because we know that absolute justice and peace can only occur with the return of Christ. This liberates us in the present from idolatrous, perfectionist, utopian schemes and the absolutizing of positions, parties, nations or ideologies. Perfection comes only at the end. Thus, we can avoid taking our projects or ourselves *too* seriously.

Hope leads to an ethics of freedom. "Freedom is the ethical expression of the person who hopes. Hope is the relation with God of the person liberated by God."[8] Hope frees us in the present by binding us to the end. "Freedom is created by God for man and in man. If hope is the response of man to God's love and grace, freedom is the response of God to man's hope, giving man the possibility of living out hope concretely and effectively in daily life. . . . There is thus a strict reciprocity between hope and freedom. God loves, man hopes, and God makes free."[9]

Second, hope *motivates* our ethical behavior. "Hope . . . brings with it . . . the relativizing of all things *and* a total seriousness applied to the relative. . . . The absolute of God does indeed relativize everything but God's Word tells us to take absolutely seriously this relative, which he himself took seriously enough to give us his Son."[10] If our hope is genuine, we must take seriously the promise that Christ is returning, bringing his rewards with him (Rev 22:12). "We will all stand before the judgment seat of God" and "be accountable to God" for our life (Rom 14:10, 12).

Motivated by hope (rather than dread), the servants of the coming Lord want to act in ways that will deserve a "Well done, good and faithful servant!" (Mt 25:23 NIV). We ought to be "leading lives of holi-

---

[7]This reminds us of the third Beatitude: meekness, gentleness and the capacity to let go.

[8]Ellul, *Hope in Time,* p. 239.

[9]Ellul, *Ethics of Freedom,* p. 13

[10]Ellul, *Hope in Time,* p. 242

ness and godliness, waiting for and hastening the coming of the day of
God" (2 Pet 3:11-12). "All who have this hope in him purify themselves" (1 Jn 3:3). Thus, while Christian hope relativizes the present, far from producing apathy, it
motivates and gives absolute seriousness to that
relative.

> We have an
> ethics of hope in that
> we are to act as
> people of the coming
> day, even though it is
> still night. The future
> day shapes our
> values, virtues and
> actions today. That's
> revolutionary.

Third, hope *guides* ethical behavior; it provides a distinct content to Christian character
and action in the present. "The night is far gone;
the day is near. . . . Let us live . . . as in the day"
(Rom 13:12-13). The Holy Spirit who guides us is
the down payment or pledge of our future inherit-
ance (Eph 1:13-14). None of this must lead to perfectionist or utopian
misunderstandings. This present era remains fallen and only the
return of Christ will resolve the problem of the world as a whole.

Nevertheless, it is our future hope that guides our present, particular action. We are not called upon to purge, reform and manage the
world as a whole. We are called to find ways of acting as faithful signs of
God's promised future. It is this eschatological orientation that made
Jesus' life so singular and unique. It is this ethic of hope that will ren-
der Christian presence distinctive as true salt and light in our earth.[11]
The ethical question is "How can we, in our character and action, as
individuals and in social groups, creatively demonstrate and faithfully
promote today the glorious reality of Christ's coming kingdom of truth,
love, justice and peace?"

Paul advised Titus that we should say no to ungodliness and strive to
"live self-controlled, upright and godly lives in this present age, while
we wait for the blessed hope" (Tit 2:12-13 NIV). Learning to say no to
the lies and unrighteousness of our culture, learning how to say no to
that voice telling us to give up and avoid the persecution—this is a crucial act of hope as well as of courage. Learning to say yes to a godly way
of life—this is also a crucial act empowered by the blessed hope. Lacking this twofold approach, we cannot persist in faithfulness through
persecution.

---

[11]This theme parallels the discussion of holiness earlier in chapter six.

As Jürgen Moltmann describes it, "The hope of the gospel has a polemic and liberating relation, not only to the religions and ideologies of men, but still more to the factual, practical life of men and to the relationships in which this life is lived. . . . In practical opposition to things as they are, and in creative reshaping of them, Christian hope calls them in question and thus serves the things that are to come. With its face toward the expected new situation, it leaves the existing situation behind and seeks for opportunities of bringing history into ever better correspondence to the promised future."[12]

Hope
1. confident expectation, not just a wish or dream
2. based on Jesus' resurrection from dead
3. oriented toward Jesus' coming again
4. frees us: relativizes human history in light of the end
5. motivates us: accountability, reward, judgment
6. guides us: show future reality and goodness now

Joy: The Interior of Hope

At the end of the Beatitudes, Jesus says "rejoice and be glad"—even in the face of persecution. Hope can produce true joy in our lives. Joy is the fruit of the life of hope and of the refusal to be defined psychologically or emotionally by immediate circumstances. Joy was characteristic of Jesus and was his gift to his followers. "I have said these things to you so that my joy may be in you, and that your joy may be complete" (Jn 15:11). While it is a present experience, joy is always eschatologically oriented. Jesus "for the sake of the joy that was set before him endured the cross" (Heb 12:2). The Bible is full of references to joy, delight, bliss, exultation and merrymaking. The inner joy of the disciple and the joyful festival of the community of faith are not just recommendations but commands: "Rejoice in the Lord always; again I will say, Rejoice" (Phil 4:4).

Joy (Greek *chara*) is the mirth, the smile, the lightness and release of the spirit within us that emerges when we are able (1) to see with gratitude the good that is present (the glass is half full!) and (2) to let go of the challenges we cannot meet and the problems we cannot fix (the glass is half empty). Hope yields joy because today's partial good

---

[12]Moltmann, *Theology of Hope,* p. 330.

can be seen not as a disappointment but as a promise and a deposit on its future fulfillment. Karl Barth has said that joy is both "anticipatory" and also "gratitude for an effected fulfillment."[13] We rejoice in the appearance of the promise. We rejoice that we are not expected to fix everything. We are freed from our despair and frustration. Our hearts sing in gratitude.

Stanley Hauerwas writes that joy

> is a present disposition that pervades our whole life. It is the presupposition of all the virtues. . . . Joy thus becomes the disposition born of a hope based on our sense that it cannot be our task to transform the violence of this world into God's peace, for in fact that has been done through the cross and resurrection of Jesus. Our joy is the simple willingness to live with the assurance of God's redemption. . . . The joy we receive as Christians is not that of a passing occasion. Rather it is a joy that derives from finding our true home among a people who carry the words and skills of God's kingdom of peace. . . . Joy thus comes to us as a gift that ironically provides us with the confidence in ourselves which makes possible our living of God's peace as a present reality."[14]

Paul's great text says that the kingdom of God is "righteousness and peace and joy in the Holy Spirit" (Rom 14:17). Joy is the third essential thing in this summary of the life that pleases God and our neighbors. Our hunger for righteousness and our peacemaking have too often been accompanied by the long, sad face, the angry denunciation, and a holier-than-thou, sanctimonious spirituality. The Bible doesn't know this grumpy righteousness: "Rejoice in the LORD, O you righteous" (Ps 33:1).

There is a sense in which righteousness orients us to God in faith, peace orients us to our neighbor in love, and joy in the Holy Spirit orients our self in hope. Joy is the playful, grateful, inner sense of God's Spirit inside of us and of God's control outside of us. It is that deep mirth that bubbles up as we see everything in the light of eternity and thus do not take others or ourselves *too* seriously. "May the God of

---

[13]For a marvelous discussion of joy in the Christian life, see Karl Barth, *Church Dogmatics* III /4, trans. G. W. Bromiley (Edinburgh: T & T Clark, 1961), pp. 374-85.

[14]Stanley Hauerwas, *The Peaceable Kingdom* (South Bend, Ind.: University of Notre Dame Press, 1983), p. 147.

hope fill you with all joy and peace in believing, so that you may
abound in hope by the power of the Holy Spirit"
(Rom 15:13).

There has been a temptation in Christianity
from time to time to make personal joy the most
important thing, perhaps even the *only* thing in the
Christian life. Some Christians hop around end-
lessly from church to church, trying to get their
own joy satisfied. Joy is crucial, but it is still third
on Paul's list and must follow righteousness and
peace. If we make our own joy the most important
thing, we may find righteousness imperiled and
peace threatened. In the Beatitudes joy is *part* of the call to persevere
in righteousness under persecution—it is not lifted out as a separate
item. Joy is not just "happiness" in the contemporary sense of a fleeting emotional high. Joy is *deep* and never the mere product of present
good circumstances but always connected somehow to hope in God's
future.

> **J**oy
> 1. mirth, gladness,
> lightness of being,
> humor
> 2. deeper than cir-
> cumstantial happi-
> ness
> 3. follows, not pre-
> cedes, righteous-
> ness
> 4. intimately related
> to hope

The Virtues and Habits of the Ambassador

The disciple is shaped into a servant. Only a disciple/servant can
become a leader and then succeed as a peacemaker. The fifth role we
need to look at is that of an ambassador. It is when the disciple/servant/
leader/peacemaker is faced with rejection, failure and persecution that
it is most important to remember that "this world is not my home"; we
are ambassadors on assignment to represent another world.

The *primary* citizenship (politically, culturally or otherwise) of a
Christian can *never* be American, Brazilian, Kenyan, Swedish, Korean
or the like. We live in these countries as *ambassadors* from another
country. Our primary citizenship is with another people, the kingdom
of God (many of whom, of course, are with us in our "host" country;
our "embassy" sometimes has a large staff).

Christians are called to be the representatives of another way of
life in the world. The language of the Bible is very clear. Our "citizenship is in heaven" (Phil 3:20). Biblical people of old "confessed that
they were strangers and foreigners on the earth, for people who speak

in this way make it clear that they are seeking a homeland. . . . They

> **A**s "strangers and pilgrims" we feel our separateness, our alien, sojourning, nonconformist position not of this world.
>
> As "ambassadors" we feel our call to enter fully into this world as ambassadors, envoys, and representatives of another kingdom.

desire a better country, that is, a heavenly one. Therefore God is not ashamed to be called their God; indeed, he has prepared a city for them" (Heb 11:13-16). We have here no "lasting city" but are "looking for the city that is to come" (Heb 13:14). From this perspective, we are "strangers and pilgrims" in the world (1 Pet 2:11 KJV). We are a "chosen race" and a "holy nation" (1 Pet 2:9). Christians share a very distinctive, unusual, transnational, transcultural identity in the world.

When the Lord speaks to Solomon and says, "If my people who are called by my name humble themselves, pray, seek my face, and turn from their wicked ways, then I will hear from heaven, and will forgive their sin and heal their land" (2 Chron 7:14)—this is not a prophetic reference (or promise) to the United States (or any other member of the United Nations). It is a promise to the people of God, originally to Israel, now to the community of faith, the church in every land. To apply this to the United States is offensive both to non-Christian U.S. citizens and to other nations outside the United States of America. It distracts us from the burning need to apply this text to the church today. It is the *church* that is "God's people, called by his name."

Our calling is not to "baptize" the United States into a Christian nation, nor is it merely to slip quietly through this world into the next. We are to bear witness to the next world, to live out the life of the next world, even in the present. We are to act as ambassadors of the city to come, in the world that now is. Here is Paul's language: "From now on, therefore, we regard no one from a human point of view. . . . If anyone is in Christ, there is a new creation: everything old has passed away; see, everything has become new! . . . So we are ambassadors for Christ, since God is making his appeal through us" (2 Cor 5:16-20).

We represent God's kingdom as its ambassadors. We are called not to flee the world but to be *in* the heart of the world as Jesus was. We are called to be *not of* the character of the world, just as Jesus was not

(Jn 17:14-18). As Paul says, we are not to be conformed to this age but rather "transformed" by the renewal of our mind; we are representatives of the "coming age" (Rom 12:1-2; 13:11-14).

No ambassador will be worth anything if he or she does not learn the language and customs of the people. No ambassador is effective who stays in the diplomatic compound and refuses to mix with the people. No ambassador will be successful who only talks of the home country and never shows any interest in the joys and trials, the needs and opportunities of the country of residence. "Seek the welfare of the city where I have sent you into exile, and pray to the LORD on its behalf, for in its welfare you will find your welfare" (Jer 29:7). As "strangers and pilgrims" we are not of the world, but as "ambassadors" we are plunged into the world with an important role to play.

Jacques Ellul's graphic description of our situation is worth quoting at length:

> The Christian belongs to two cities. He is in the world, and he has a social life. He is the citizen of a nation; he has a place in a family; he has a situation, and must work to earn money; the setting of his life is the same as that of other men; he lives with them; he shares with them the same nature and the same conditions. All that he does in the world, he ought to do seriously, because he is bound up with the life of other people. . . . On the other hand, he cannot wholly belong to this world. For him this world can only be a "tabernacle," in which he is a "stranger and a pilgrim." For him it is a temporary situation, although extremely important, because he belongs to another City. He derives his thought from another source. He has another Master.
>
> All this should be understood in the most strictly material sense: living in this world, he belongs to another: like a man from one nation who resides in another nation. A Chinese residing in France, thinks in his own terms, in his own tradition; he has his own criterion of judgment and of action; he is really a stranger and a foreigner; he is also a citizen of another State, and his loyalty is given to this State, and not to the country in which he is living. It is the same with the Christian, he is the citizen of another Kingdom, and it is thence that he derives his way of thinking, judging, and feeling. His heart and his thought are elsewhere. He is the subject of another State, he is the Ambassador of this State upon earth, that is to say, he ought to present the demands of his Master,

he establishes a relation between the two, but he cannot take the side of the world. He stands up for the interests of his Master, as an ambassador champions the interests of his country.[15]

The kingdom of Jesus Christ to which we belong, and which we represent, exists now, even though it is hidden and contested. It is only in the future (and God alone knows when) that this kingdom will reign in universal peace. We are not to be persecuted in our pilgrimage and ambassadorship for any eccentricity cultivated for its own sake. Rather, if we are persecuted, it must be because the world finds that it cannot tolerate the goodness and righteousness of God as a witness in its presence.

Think about how foreign embassies are sometimes the objects of hostility by people in the host country. Often these hostilities are based in the mistakes and injustices of the past. The kingdom of God is the kingdom of truth, justice, righteousness and peace. Unfortunately, Christians have often made mistakes in the past and betrayed the character of the kingdom of God. We are the cause of much of the hostility against our ambassadorship. But not all of it. There is an irreducible conflict between the Spirit of God's kingdom and the demonic side of any given earthly political entity. If you are an ambassador for Christ, you will on occasion feel the heat of that conflict. But as John Chrysostom said, "On the one hand, if we live in wickedness, though there be none to speak ill of us, we shall be the most wretched of all men; on the other hand, if we apply ourselves to virtue, though the whole world speak evil of us, at that very time we shall be more enviable than any."[16]

So in this hurting, needy, violent world, our calling is not to escape but to invade, not as the domineering lords of the earth but as the hopeful and joyful ambassadors of Jesus Christ and the coming city of

---

[15]Jacques Ellul, *The Presence of the Kingdom* (New York: Seabury, 1967), pp. 44-45.

[16]John Chrysostom, *Homily XV on the Gospel of Saint Matthew*, in Nicene and Post-Nicene Fathers, ed. Philip Schaff (Grand Rapids, Mich.: Eerdmans, 1956), 10:99. Most of the time, he says, we shall be admired for our virtue. But even if we are faced by an enemy or persecutor, like Nebuchadnezzar with the three Hebrew children thrown in the furnace, our persecutors will often be compelled to change and praise God.

God. The irony is that if we try to save our life, we will lose it; in losing our life, we will find it. To have a strong personal identity, to know unmistakably that I am valuable and unique, to have a strong future hope—this is God's will for each of us. It is not by fleeing the world but by loving our neighbors as God loves them, that meaning and self-worth arise. It is wise and proven counsel to advise those who feel that their life is meaningless that they should go do something to help someone else. We were not made to live for our self alone but for God and for others. Our task is not to turn inward or escape but to gladly take on our roles as hopeful, joyful ambassadors.

Persecution will afflict us from time to time for we live in a broken, fallen world. We will fall short of our goals and make mistakes. *Normally*, however, we will not experience persecution but rather approval. The one who serves Christ with righteousness, peace, and joy is "acceptable to God and has human approval," Paul says (Rom 14:17-18). Reflect for a moment on the kind of people that result: people with deep and thoughtful convictions about righteousness, truth and the will of God—regarding all aspects of life. But these people know how to forgive and extend mercy; they have integrity and bring reconciliation. They can peacefully share these convictions with those having different views about such justice issues. They learn to hold and articulate their convictions in a way that respects others, builds them up and preserves the peace. In addition, they are joyful, not grim-faced, grudging or negative.

People of this type are in short supply. When they can be found, people like this are almost always appreciated and listened to not only by their fellow-Christians but also by their neighbors and colleagues. They make great ambassadors. How successful would ambassadors be if they only brought a severe, divisive message of righteous condemnation or an arrogant "we know how to do it better in our home country" attitude?

For Reflection or Discussion

1. Have you ever been persecuted "for righteousness' sake"? or "on account of Jesus"? or because of your own mistake? How did you handle it?

2. Describe an example of courage and patience you have admired. What do you think are the best ways to teach our children courage and patience?
3. How have hope and joy been a part of your life experience? Have you ever seen sorrow and hopelessness converted into joy? How does this transition happen?
4. What can we do in our churches to help Christians more readily and effectively take on the role of ambassadors for Christ?

Part Three

TEST

Eleven

———

GOOD CHARACTER
ON TRIAL

We have considered why good character is so important, how to build it, and what makes up its content. What happens if we decide not to pursue this character-building agenda? What if we do nothing? Someone once said that all that is necessary for evil to triumph is for good people to do nothing. If we do nothing about building good character, we will inevitably be trapped in some second-rate substitute identity. Here are five troubling examples.

If We Do Not Build Good Character
First is the "accommodationist Christian"—the great enemy alternative to the faithful, holy and wise disciple. This character is inclined to conform to the world. Perhaps this manifests itself in an unreflective nostalgia for the Ozzie and Harriet fifties. Or perhaps the temptation is today's "political correctness" (whether measured by the Left or the Right). Still others uncritically pursue a sexual, political or economic agenda originating in our culture. When church-planting strategies are

driven mainly by market research techniques, when pastoral fitness is measured primarily by psychological testing, and when worship is shaped primarily by popular taste, these are signs of impotence and a lack of biblical character. Of course we should learn from our culture, but we must not let the world set the agenda and direction for our character or community. In times past, this accommodation was called worldliness—conformity to the latest fashions in thinking, spending and acting.

Second is the "arrogant Christian"—the enemy alternative to the open, responsible, gentle servant. The dominant character trait is pride. Arrogance might be manifested in our self-congratulation about our attendance, buildings or wealth. We might be arrogant about our knowledge, thinking that we know everything and have nothing to learn from others. Arrogant Christians are great at talking, poor at listening. Our service to others can be limited to condescending, token gestures that reinforce our sense of superiority. Arrogance is usually accompanied by narrowness. Our pride in what we have blinds us to what we lack.

Third is the "apathetic Christian"—the enemy alternative to the just and merciful leader. Apathetic Christians lack the passion and commitment to fully develop their life with Christ. They are lazy, distracted and disobedient to God. Knowing the truth, they fail to pursue it fully or act on it. When polls show that Christian attitude and behavior is almost indistinguishable from the surrounding society, this is not just due to accommodation but to apathy. Apathetic Christians can display vast energy in their careers but lethargy in their faith. We are alarmed by babies that do not grow and develop on schedule. We seek to help kids who are dropouts. But some are just as developmentally bad off in the Christian life. Christian character has to do with growth, life, vitality and engagement.

Fourth is the "antagonistic Christian"—the enemy alternative to the loving peacemaker. Negativity, denunciation and a mean-spirited antagonism dominate the believer's character. Certainly there is a prophetic edge to a biblical identity. However, the Christian voice in recent politics is so often angry, divisive, punitive, reactionary and disrespectful. Few things ought to shame us more than the mean-spirited, cheap shots directed at American political leaders—even when those leaders are unapologetic believers in Jesus, working in incredibly difficult positions. Yet they are vilified not just by the ignorant, talk-show-manipulated masses but by "Christian leaders"! Antagonistic Christians are a divisive force in the church and in the world. They undermine the witness of the reconciling, liberating Gospel in the world. Criticizing, condemning and accusing others is not the sort of character to which God calls us.

Fifth is the "after-life Christian"—the enemy alternative to the hopeful ambassador. This character is preoccupied with the *inner-life* and the *after-life*. Certainly these are important biblical concerns, but we must not allow our fear of, or distaste for, the world—or our longing for the life to come—to undermine our calling to be present as God's ambassadors in this world. The Bible rarely if ever discusses either the inner-life or the after-life without probing its implications for our total character and life in this world where we are placed. We must not retreat into a spiritual fortress or hothouse, or run away from the threats on our streets, our schools, our neighborhoods, our world.

If we do not become	We may end up as
1. faithful, holy disciples	1. accommodated conformists
2. humble servants	2. arrogant know-it-alls
3. righteous, merciful leaders	3. apathetic do-nothings
4. loving peacemakers	4. divisive antagonists
5. hopeful ambassadors	5. selfish escapists

Of course, these five negative character types are generalizations and caricatures into which few if any people fit exactly. In reality each of our lives consists of some success and some failure. But if we do not consciously pursue good character, the result will not be *neutral* but *negative*.

The Vices We Must Avoid

Our problems are not over even if we do commit ourselves to building a good and godly character. We saw in the previous chapter that persecution for righteousness is a part of Christian experience, almost by definition. Every moment in life cannot be like resting in "green pas-

tures" and by "quiet waters." Every day cannot be experienced as lop-
ing victoriously along "paths of righteousness." As Psalm 23 indicates,
we will also find ourselves in the "valley of the shadow of death" and in
the "presence of our enemies." Our world is a place of failure, weakness, strife and conflict. Even in our most sacred environs, the church
and the family, the good that we seek is often tested and tried. The
shadow of death—death in relationships, death to dreams, physical
death—cannot wholly be escaped.

Earlier we noted that the biblical way is to "overcome evil with
good" and that in the original creation, God identified the good—and
prohibited eating from the tree of the knowledge of good and evil. Our
primary concern in this book is to explore the good. In fact, it is ironic
that there are more vices than virtues listed in Scripture and that so
much of its moral teaching, notably the Ten Commandments, is presented in negative form ("you shall not"). I also mentioned earlier that
experts in counterfeit money focus most of their study on authentic
bills and coins, not on counterfeits. Still, they take a look once in a
while at some of the tricky and deceitful counterfeits that some try to
pass into circulation.

Why does the Bible present some of the moral life in negative
terms? One answer is that the fundamental master theme of Christian
life and ethics is to live out our love in freedom, not in compliance with
detailed laws and rules. The rules and laws that exist in negative form
are warning signs of potential slave masters waiting to take us captive
and end our freedom. "You shall not steal," for example, is a sign
posted to warn us not to lose our freedom by giving ourselves over to
possessions. Remember that negative warning sign and then go out and
be free in how you deal with things. Jacques Ellul has said that the first
act of freedom is to say no. That helps make sense of the negative form
of some biblical moral instruction.

What is evil? Ancient and medieval thinkers often described evil
as a failure, flaw or incompleteness in the good. Evil does not have a
specific weight of its own but requires the good as a kind of host. In
this sense, even Satan was created good but has become evil as a
fallen angel, and the "principalities and powers" are demonic fallen
angels. Sin is "falling short" of the glory of God—not just a specific

mad spiritual virus. However we wish to deal with evil as a theological and philosophical problem, we are always left with it as an ethical problem![1]

It is common sense to think that the opposite of every virtue must be a vice. Aristotle believed that every true character virtue has *two* vices related to it; every virtue is a mean between two extremes: a vice of excess and a vice of deficiency. Thus, courage is the mean between recklessness and cowardice; self-control is the mean between self-indulgence and self-denial. He counseled that we should be especially careful about the vice that we find more attractive.

During the Middle Ages it was common to summarize "seven deadly sins" as counterparts to the seven great virtues (justice, prudence, courage, temperance, faith, hope and love). Pride, envy, and anger were seen as the vices of "perverted love." Sloth was the vice of defective or deficient love. Avarice, gluttony and lust were the vices of excessive love (for possessions, food and sex, respectively).[2]

> The Seven Deadly Sins: pride, envy, anger, sloth, avarice, gluttony, lust

The Bible itself has many accounts of the vices. The Proverbs warn against dishonesty, lust, greed and laziness. Jesus and the prophets inveigh against pride, hypocrisy, greed, violence and so forth. Paul's list of the fruit of the Spirit (the virtues) follows an even longer list of the "works of the flesh" (the vices): "fornication, impurity, licentiousness, idolatry, sorcery, enmities, strife, jealousy, anger, quarrels, dissensions, factions, envy, drunkenness, carousing, and things like that" (Gal 5:19-21).[3] Victor Paul Furnish comments about Paul's vice lists, "It is noteworthy that these lists . . . are heavily weighted with 'social vices,' vices which disrupt the life of the commu-

---

[1]On the problem of evil, see Augustine *The City of God* 11.22; Ted Peters, *Sin: Radical Evil in Soul and Society* (Grand Rapids, Mich.: Eerdmans, 1994); Cornelius Plantinga, *Not the Way It's Supposed to Be: A Breviary of Sin* (Grand Rapids, Mich.: Eerdmans, 1995).

[2]Peter Kreeft describes the seven deadly sins in *Back to Virtue* (San Francisco: Ignatius, 1986), pp. 92ff.

[3]Other vice lists are given in Matthew (15:19), Romans (1:28-32; 13:13), 1 Corinthians (5:9-11; 6:9-10), 2 Corinthians (12:20-21), 1 Timothy (1:9-10), 2 Timothy (3:2-8), Titus (3:3) and Revelation (21:8).

nity. . . . Paul's vice lists, unlike those of the Hellenistic world in general which emphasized 'personal' vices, are particularly formed for the life of the community."[4] In our pursuit of good character and community, it is worth our while to pay attention to these catalogs of vices to avoid. Many Christians have been good at remembering that murder, adultery and theft are vices; we have not remembered as well that "anger, quarrels, dissension and factions" are part of the same foul list.

> **T**he Works of the Flesh: fornication, impurity, licentiousness, idolatry, sorcery, enmities, strife, jealousy, anger, quarrels, dissension, factions, envy, drunkenness, carousing

The Enemies We Must Fight

What is behind these vices anyway? Is there some more basic force or power we must fight against? We want to be sure that in our combat we fight against the true foes of God's goodness, not anything else. Our world is prone to "demonize" one thing or another. We do not want to be blind to our real enemies.

Let me be clear at the outset that *God* is not the source of our vices or our trials. "No one, when tempted, should say, 'I am being tempted by God'; for God cannot be tempted by evil and he himself tempts no one" (Jas 1:13). Jesus was "led up by the Spirit into the wilderness" (certainly it is God who *allows* trials to occur), but then he was "tempted by the devil" (not by God) (Mt 4:1). Where do these trials come from? What is the nature of this evil that confronts us and tests our character and community?

We are not robots or machines but the free creation of God, who has made us with certain basic appetites, desires and needs. God has placed us in a world of vast challenges, opportunities and possibilities. We find ourselves in conflict with our own desires, with things outside ourselves, with the world, with other people, even with spiritual forces and the devil himself.

One way to summarize our enemies is to warn about the world, the flesh and the devil. While God (and his people) love the world in an important sense, we are also told "Do not love the world or the things

---

[4]Victor Paul Furnish, *Theology and Ethics in Paul* (Nashville: Abingdon, 1968), p. 84.

in the world . . . for all that is in the world—the desire of the flesh, the desire of the eyes, the pride in riches—comes not from the Father but from the world. And the world and its desire are passing away, but those who do the will of God live forever" (1 Jn 2:15-17).

The problem, addressed by John, is attachment to the old world, the passing age of the "night," in its alienation from God and its corruption and rebellion. The problem is desire, lust or love for the old order. And what is called "the world" in a large sense is called the "flesh" on a personal level. The old world is at war with God on a cosmic level—the old flesh is at war with the spirit on a personal level. "World" and "flesh" are not to be understood in a woodenly material way. In other texts we are told that "God so loved the world" and that the "body is a temple of the Holy Spirit within you . . . therefore glorify God in your body" (1 Cor 6:19-20). Jesus was resurrected in a body (not as a flesh-denying spiritual force). Our future redemption will be bodily as well as spiritual. The trial of our character and community has to do with the nature and object of our love. The temptation is to love the old self and the earthly city in its rebellious autonomy and pride.

The "works of the flesh" include envy and jealousy—not just fornication and drunkenness—spiritual attitudes as well as bodily acts. The problem of the "world" and the "flesh" turns out, at bottom, to be a spiritual problem. "Our struggle is not against enemies of blood and flesh, but against the rulers, against the authorities, against the cosmic powers of this present darkness, against the spiritual forces of evil in the heavenly places" (Eph 6:12). Jesus at the cross "disarmed the rulers and authorities and made a public example of them, triumphing over them" (Col 2:15). Nevertheless, the battles continue even though the outcome of the war has already been decided.

Careful! The *world* is a multifaceted term in Scripture. God loves the world and so should we. The world that we must not love is all aspects of the world that are in rebellion against God.

The *flesh* does not mean the "body" in Scripture—the flesh we must fight against is any sinful desires and habits that were part of our old life before meeting Jesus. It's not all physical.

Although this language of principalities and powers is broad and seems to encompass all forms of evil and darkness that beset us, there is a special significance to what we might call structural or institutional

evil. "The powers seem to be able to transform a natural, social, intellectual, or economic reality into a force which man has no ability
either to resist or control. This force ejects man from his divinely given
position as governor of creation. It gives life and autonomy to institutions and structures. It attacks man both inwardly and outwardly."[5]
John Howard Yoder suggests that "we have here an inclusive vision of
religious structures . . . intellectual structures ('ologies and 'isms),
moral structures (codes and customs), political structures (the tyrant,
the market, the school, the courts, race, and nation)."[6]

The trial of our character and community originates in part from
our conflicts with these principalities and powers. Our foe is not
merely personal (though many of our trials seem to come from persons); there is such a thing as corporate, structural and institutional
evil. Our foe is not merely human or natural (though it is often that);
there is a supernatural force and power behind evil. These principalities and powers lie behind the disintegration of the good world God
created into the fallen "world" we must not love; they lie behind the
fall of the good life of man and woman into the "flesh" that must be
overcome. We are engaged in a cosmic battle, whose outcome is the
victory assured by Christ, but whose daily skirmishes continue.

As God is the fountainhead of all good, so it is Satan, the devil, who
is the fountainhead of all vice and evil, all temptation to love the flesh
and the world in the wrong way. "Put on the whole armor of God, so
that you may be able to stand against the wiles of the devil" (Eph 6:11).
Both "Satan" (from the Hebrew *satan*) and "devil" (from the Greek
diabolos) mean the same thing: an "accuser" who hurls a charge at
someone (Rev 12:7-12). His accusations are false, for Satan is a liar,
and the father of lies (Jn 8:44). He divides people from God and from
each other.[7] We do not need to visit a "Satanist" cult to get a first-hand
glimpse of the devil at work; all we have to do is observe the demonic
power of accusation and division in our midst.

---

[5]Jacques Ellul, *The Ethics of Freedom* (Grand Rapids, Mich.: Eerdmans, 1976), pp.
152-53.
[6]John Howard Yoder, *The Politics of Jesus* (Grand Rapids, Mich.: Eerdmans, 1972),
p. 145.
[7]Dietrich Bonhoeffer, *Life Together* (London: SCM, 1954), has a powerful discussion
of the way "accusation" destroys our community.

The devil acts as a "roaring lion" sometimes, overpowering in his assaults. He slithers in quietly as a "serpent" on other occasions. He comes as an "angel of light," but he is really the "prince of darkness." He has been defeated at the cross, but he is still the "god of this world," who has "blinded the minds of the unbelievers" (2 Cor 4:4). He acts with his legions as an unseen demonic force, bringing trial and temptation into the lives of biblical people and all others. Possession and destruction, addiction and folly, are in his wake. He can operate in mysterious, supernatural ways—but he can just as easily work in ordinary ways, as the principalities and powers capture our institutions and nations, or enslave us through our money or our drugs.

> We don't have to visit a Satanist meeting to see the devil and his demons at work. The essential, main activity of Satan/devil is accusation, falsehood and division. Wherever that threefold combination is visible, Satan is laughing with glee at his success.

But we are told to "resist the devil and he will flee from you" (Jas 4:7). There is no better way to prepare for the trial of our character and community than to cling in faith to Jesus Christ. We must claim the victory of his cross, pray for God's protection, and fight (with our fellow soldiers at our side). In fact, it is always best to think of our trials as combat against Satan and his hosts—and to view people as his unwitting minions. The fact that the devil attacks through people does not define their essence but their problem. It is their Creator who defines their essence.

The Tests We Must Undergo

The story of the temptation of Jesus gives us a specific account of the trial (not just the enemy behind it) of our character. Jesus was baptized (just like his people), and then he was tempted by the devil (just like his people).[8] The three temptations of Christ are the paradigm of our character test. "The three temptations are the sum of the temptations that man can encounter. In them Jesus faces all the possibilities of temptation. His later temptations . . . are simply variations on those that he undergoes here." At the same time, "if we can assimilate all human temptations to these three temptations of Jesus, we certainly

---

[8] Matthew 3:13—4:11; Luke 3:21-23; 4:1-15.

have to realize that our temptations are infinitely less total, complete, and radical. They correspond far less to what Jesus is than to what we are."[9]

Major Enemies of Good Character
1. the "flesh": unredeemed, selfish, appetite-driven
2. the "world": evil systems, structures, practices
3. the demonic: principalities and powers in revolt
4. Satan/devil: the accuser, liar and divider

It is only after overcoming these three major tests that "Jesus, filled with the power of the Spirit, returned to Galilee, and a report about him spread through all the surrounding country. He began to teach in their synagogues and was praised by everyone" (Lk 4:14-15). So with us: our character, our life and ministry, can only proceed in the power of the Spirit when we have come to terms successfully with these three challenges.

The self and its appetites. The first trial of our character has to do with how we relate to our self and how we satisfy its needs and desires. The Spirit led Jesus "into the wilderness to be tempted by the devil. He fasted forty days and forty nights, and afterwards he was famished. The tempter came and said to him, 'If you are the Son of God, command these stones to become loaves of bread.' But he answered, 'It is written: "One does not live by bread alone but by every word that comes from the mouth of God." ' " (Mt 4:1-4, citing Deut 8:3).

God has created us with certain personal appetites, desires and needs—and he has created wonderful gifts to satisfy those desires and needs. In Jesus' case, he was hungry and alone. Jesus needed food—and the satisfaction of our hunger by bread (or other food) is one of God's greatest gifts to us. God wills our life. This trial is not about a choice between dying of starvation and a sin of eating to live. God does not will our death but our life. What is at issue is *how* we satisfy our appetite, *how* we seek our life and bread when we are hungry and in need. This first trial is especially acute when we are isolated and alone, as Jesus was in the wilderness.

Satan urges us to seek bread alone—bread disconnected from anything except our own personal appetite. "You are hungry: satisfy yourself! You need it, you deserve it, it is in your power to meet your

---

[9]Ellul, *Ethics*, pp. 52, 59

needs!" And what is depicted here in terms of hunger and food is equally true for our other needs such as sex, clothing, shelter, health, beauty, pleasure, work, possessions and rest. The world screams at our hungry souls and bodies: "satisfy your needs, reach out and take that fruit, buy that house, that car, get that woman or man!"

Jesus overcomes this trial by affirming a different way of satisfying our needs: not "bread alone" but bread in the context of "every word from God." Jesus was "led into the wilderness" by God's Spirit—he will also satisfy his hunger and eat his bread only in the

> The test of our self and its appetites is most intense and acute when we are all alone and we have gone without being satisfied for a while. If that is your situation, be careful!

texture of a life under God's word and Spirit. The satisfaction of our personal needs and desires must take place within the pattern given by the whole word of God. It is by bringing our poverty to Jesus that we will be filled. It is by hungering and thirsting after his righteousness that we will be satisfied.

The challenge is not to become a monk or hermit or ascetic fleeing our appetites. Rather, it is to locate the satisfaction of our desires and needs within the wholeness of a life lived in obedience to God's Spirit and word. Jesus did in fact miraculously make bread (and wine) for the hungry. That is not the issue. If we do not learn to deal with food—and sex, and material possessions, and other needs and desires—in this way, we will never know the excitement and power of having a character under the power of God's spirit.

This is always the first trial, the first challenge to Christian character. We make the commitment to God. Our heart is his. We come to him in faithful discipleship. But then later, away from the community of faith, alone in the wilderness, our self and its appetites rises up. What will we do? Will we remain faithful and holy? Will we try to satisfy our own poverty and hunger in our own way?

Using God or loving God. The second great trial of our character has to do with how we relate to God. "Then the devil took him to the holy city and placed him on the pinnacle of the temple" (Mt 4:5). Our trials are not just in the wilderness, they come in the holy city, at the temple—in the church, in Christian organizations, in good Christian

life. And the devil said, " 'If you are the Son of God, throw yourself
down; for it is written, "He will command his
angels concerning you," and "On their hands they
will bear you up, so that you will not dash your
foot against a stone." ' Jesus said to him, 'Again it
is written, "Do not put the Lord your God to the
test" ' " (Mt 4:6-7, citing Deut 6:16).

The test of our
relationship to God
is most intense and
acute not alone in
the wilderness but
in our religious
community. If you
find yourself using
God or lured by
others to recklessly
put God to the test,
instead of simply
loving him—the
devil is after you. If
you are now on any
kind of pinnacle in
your church, be
careful!

If our first trial has to do with our relationship
to our self and its needs—the second concerns
our relationship with God. This is the spiritual
trial. The temptation is to use God, trying to
manipulate him, trying to force him to act in
response to our whim and our recklessness. It is
also the temptation to misuse the word of God.
Scripture is quoted here, by the tempter, with an
appearance of respect for its authority—but it is
being taken out of context, manipulated and used
for a selfish purpose.

We don't need to be starving by ourselves in the wilderness to be on
trial. We might be in a conversation quoting Scripture in an elder's
meeting at the church. We might be tempted to manipulate God, all the
time disguised with the phrases and cadences of piety and Holy Scripture! What we must do is to love, trust, follow and obey the Lord our
God. If this is the case, and then if God leads us to do so, we will in fact
be enabled to walk on the water or dive off temples. God will miraculously quiet the storm. He will intervene in mighty ways in our life.

We are surrounded today, on the one hand, by the scoffers of the
world who want to dare us and provoke us to prove our relationship to
God by some fool act of testing God. On the other hand, there are
some Christian leaders urging us to adopt a view of God that if we just
do x, y or z, God will automatically make us healthy and wealthy. But
"Do not put the Lord your God to the test!" It is the devil who tries to
get us to distort our relationship with God in this way. This is again a
temptation to abandon the relationship of faith and holiness. It is a
temptation to stand arrogantly before God instead of assuming the posture of his humble servants. It is a temptation to fashion our own

understanding of God's righteous will instead of submitting to the true righteousness of God.

If we don't learn to relate to the living God in trust, faith, obedience and love, if we tempt God, manipulate him, misquote Scripture in support of personal self-serving projects, if we tempt him, we will never build the good character God offers us. Our ministry and life will be barren of God's Spirit. Will we cling to God in faith and love, with all of its surprises—or will we use and manipulate God as a function of our own agendas? Shall we cling to God's living person or reduce God to an impersonal machine or force at our disposal? This is the second great trial of our character.

The power and glory of the world. The third trial of our character concerns our relationships with other people. "Again, the devil took him to a very high mountain and showed him all the kingdoms of the world and their splendor; and he said to him, 'All these I will give you, if you will fall down and worship me.' Jesus said to him, 'Away with you, Satan! for it is written "Worship the Lord your God, and serve only him." ' " (Mt 4:8-10; citing Deut 6:13).

This third trial is about the temptation to acquire power over people, groups and institutions ("the kingdoms of the world and their splendor") by means of worshiping and bowing down to Satan. "Worshiping and bowing down" in the Bible is not just a matter of a brief ritual but of the orientation of our life. "Present your bodies as a living sacrifice, holy and acceptable to God, which is your spiritual worship" (Rom 12:1-2). Worshiping Satan means presenting ourselves to him for his use, in his spirit, with his tactics, for his purposes. Satan, the devil, is the divider, the deceiver, the liar and the accuser.

The third temptation is to acquire social, economic or political power and glory by giving our lives and our careers to the spirit and style of the devil. Instead of being faithful and holy disciples we are unfaithful and

The test of our relationship to the world around us is most intense and acute when we are on any "high mountain" where we can see how beautiful, desirable and accessible it all is. If you are in a position to see all that economic potential, all that political clout, all that cultural fame and adulation, be careful! The devil will offer it to you in his own way: lies, division, accusation, as a pathway to power. Don't take it. Bow down to God alone.

accommodated to the pattern of the world. Instead of humble servant-hood we display the arrogance of power. Instead of righteous, merciful leadership we engage in the injustice of the devil. Instead of loving peacemaking we seek conquest. Instead of joyful and hopeful ambassadorship we adopt the cynical acquisitiveness of the world around us.

Consider the scurrilous, negative political campaigns for candidates and ballot initiatives that we have come to expect in America. Consider the brutal competition and deceptive advertising of many businesses. Consider the lies and deception of the entertainment industry. Consider the disgraceful state of journalism today, where any falsehood or innuendo that will sell gets published immediately. Consider the epidemic of cheating and plagiarism in the world of education and certification.

Jesus calls us to worship the Lord God and serve him only. If we go to our offices worshiping and serving the Lord alone, we will be bowing down to the Lord of truth, compassion, fairness, justice, righteousness, servanthood and peace. If social, political or economic power are then given to us, we will accept them in humility as stewards of God's possessions. The fact is that, as Jesus would later say, all power *is* his, in heaven and on earth. The third trial is not the temptation to power per se; it is the temptation to seek power over others through the tactics of Satan. And while this temptation is especially acute in the corridors of the financial district and in capitol buildings—it rears its head also in all interpersonal relations, in marriages, parenting, church leadership and on faculties of schools at all levels. The trial occurs whenever we are on any "high mountain" in life, where we can look out on the various "kingdoms of the world."

Our character will not be tested and tried, we will not be ready for life, work and ministry with Jesus until we come to terms directly with this third great problem. Rather than worshiping God, loving our neighbor and letting power and glory take care of them-

The Three Tests of Character
1. the self and its appetites: follow my desires autonomously—or locate within broader purposes of God?
2. the world's kingdoms: seek their power and glory by the devil's way—or serve God and let everything else follow?
3. God: use and manipulate God for own interests—or love and worship him?

selves, we are tempted to take a shortcut to glory and power through Satan's dubious means. This is the third trial of our character.

Has God really spoken? Running through these three temptations of Jesus is a reminder of the first great temptation in human history. "From the time of Adam's expulsion from paradise every man is born with this question, which Satan has put in Adam's heart. That is the first question of all flesh: 'Has God really said?' "[10] Adam and Eve were created to live in open communion with God. God's word created them. His word sustained their life and guided them. The devil slipped into their good and innocent world and brought about their downfall by putting into question the word of God. When they listened to this big question, it was only a small step to the devil's next word: God is wrong; you will not surely die if you do what you want.

In Jesus' second temptation, the devil misuses Scripture, twisting the meaning of God's word. In all three responses, Jesus quotes from God's word (Deuteronomy in this case), which decides the issue for goodness. Our search for good character and community, and now our response to the trial of that character, must be grounded in and shaped by God's word, which means Jesus Christ and Scripture. This book has been filled with quotations from Scripture. You may ask whether so much was necessary, whether the study could not have proceeded with a little less Bible. The answer is an unequivocal no. We cannot build good character or good community without the Bible, the Word of God, as our ever-present authority and guide. To take another route and let moral philosophy or psychology guide our reflections is to choose to build our character on the sand. Great will be our fall when the storms and trials arrive.

Passing Our Character Tests
Developing our personal character, and that of our communities, is not without its challenges and problems. In our broken world we will face trials of various kinds. These trials can make us or break us. While we seek God's character *formation*, there will also be forces acting for its

---

[10]Dietrich Bonhoeffer, *Creation and Fall: Temptation* (New York: Macmillan, 1959), p. 102.

de-formation. Our Lord has prepared us to expect these tests. "In the world you face persecution. But take courage; I have conquered the world!" (Jn 16:33). Jesus modeled as well as taught the appropriate response to trials. Jesus was made "like his brothers and sisters in every respect" and because "he himself was tested by what he suffered, he is able to help those who are being tested" (Heb 2:17-18). Jesus himself can "sympathize with our weaknesses" because he "in every respect has been tested as we are, yet without sin" (Heb 4:15). Our Lord knows what we face.

Jesus taught us to pray "lead us not into temptation, but deliver us from the evil one" (Mt 6:13 NIV). "Temptation" in the Bible means a "testing," a "trial" or a "proof." "Keep awake and pray that you may not come into the time of trial" (Mk 14:38). We pray that we will not be led into temptation and trial, but they cannot always be avoided. When they arrive, we can overcome, and God can bring good out of our experience. Jesus says "Blessed are those who are persecuted" because they can experience the kingdom of heaven now and will receive a reward for their faithfulness in the future.

James says that "whenever you face trials of any kind, consider it nothing but joy, because you know that the testing of your faith produces endurance; and let endurance have its full effect, so that you may be mature and complete, lacking in nothing. . . . Blessed is anyone who endures temptation. Such a one has stood the test and will receive the crown of life that the Lord has promised to those who love him" (Jas 1:2-4, 12).

We watch and pray that we will be able to avoid the trial of our character. But when it cannot be avoided, we pray for God's strength and help. We "run with perseverance," surrounded by a great cloud of witnesses, remembering the prophets and faithful who have gone before us, "looking to Jesus the pioneer and perfector of our faith" (Heb 12:1-2). We remember, "No testing has overtaken you that is not common to everyone. God is faithful, and he will not let you be tested beyond your strength, but with the testing he will also provide the way out so that you may be able to endure it" (1 Cor 10:13).

We not only face the trial of our personal character but the trial of our community life as well. Some of our most difficult experiences in life are the conflicts, struggles, failures and weaknesses in our churches and Christian organizations. The history of the church is, sadly, a history with many struggles and conflicts that ended in division. Often it has been a history of persecution as well—"Christians to the lions" has a familiar ring to it. Israel was enslaved in Egypt, attacked by the Philistines and hauled off into captivity by Babylon. The New Testament church was persecuted regularly, and we often read of enemies and false teachers who test it from within.

Strength through trials. The trial of our character is no fun, but we need to think of it as an opportunity for growth and strength, not just as a negative scourge to be borne patiently. Remember these parallels: we cannot build physical strength unless we push against weights or exert ourselves walking up a hill. We cannot acquire intellectual strength unless our critics push against us with their arguments, and we learn to respond. A child cannot develop its personality unless its parents push against it with boundaries and guidelines. So too, we cannot develop strength in our character without obstacles and the engagement of various trials.

The Bible often uses athletic and military metaphors (running a race, wrestling, putting on armor and weapons) to describe this aspect of Christian life and growth (1 Cor 9:24-27; Eph 6:10-17; 2 Tim 2:3-5; Heb 12:1-13). God allows us to encounter trials as a father disciplines his child. Trials can build holiness and righteousness, endurance and maturity. Our trials can deepen our spiritual life, focus our priorities and drive us closer to our Lord. There can be a personal payoff.

In our communities (friendship, household, church), trials and troubles can either shatter us or strengthen us. The intense persecution of the church in China under communist rule produced a vast network of strong, house churches. Cases of persecution of Christian high-school students have sometimes led to revival on campuses as faithful young men and women stand up for Christ. Financial trials have sometimes caused Christian communities to pray more and to refocus their priorities.

Twenty-five years ago I began attending a church that seemed unbelievably full of grace and truth. Their mutual love and care for each other, and their welcoming outreach into the community to the most diverse crowd imaginable, was astonishing. I had never experienced anything like this, and for the next two years (until I moved to another part of the country) I thought I was in a little corner of heaven. What explained this phenomenon? I learned later that six months before I had arrived a devastating scandal had come to light, involving two of the five leaders of the church. Failure, pain and anguish drove the church en masse to its knees in repentance. With their pride crucified, they drew together humbly before God, and the power of the Holy Spirit swept through this fellowship for the next few years. Trials can either shatter or build our communities of faith.

Our personal and community trials can be helpful or redemptive for others outside of our circles as well. Our participation in the struggle makes us better able to sympathize and empathize with others, better able to come alongside the hurting in our world. Our willingness to accept suffering sometimes shames and convicts our oppressors into their own conversion or growth. Sometimes it arrests or breaks the cycle of violence in our world and bears witness to another way.

Finally, our trials can also bring glory to God. Our suffering for Christ is a personal offering of worship to God, a "filling up the sufferings of Christ," a bearing of the cross. Just as it brings honor to a coach for a team not to give up against overwhelming opposition, not to quit when it seems like they are going to lose big, and their body and mind are crying out for rest—so too, on the greatest playing field of all, it glorifies God when his people bear up under trials.

Who are you anyway? At the bottom of all of our trials and challenges is the question of our identity. It is the character question. In two of Jesus' three temptations the devil's opening line was "if you are the Son of God." Satan was challenging Jesus' identity, challenging whether he really was the Son of God. "If you're the Son of God . . . prove it this way!"

Jesus refused to allow that challenge to sidetrack or mislead him; he knew who he was. God had said at Jesus' baptism, just before the temptations, "This is my Son, the Beloved, with whom I am well pleased," and that was sufficient. Jesus received his identity and self-understanding from God. He did not let the enemy redefine him. Jesus *acted* as the Son of God, loved and liked by God his Father. He did not try to prove it or even argue it; he acted it out by quoting from the family writings, maintaining the family character, following in the family spirit.

Many of our problems today arise, or become overwhelming, because we do not remember—or know, or believe—who we are. Therapists' and counselors' offices are jammed with people of all ages, searching for their true identity. Not just young people but middle-aged and older types are often confused and throw everything overboard as they embark on a journey to "find themselves." One of the reasons for the popularity of bumper stickers, buttons and T-shirts (announcing our political positions, musical and sports loyalties, and so on), is that we are trying to borrow some identity.

The most basic, fundamental question in the tests and trials of human life is "Who are you?" Many people today have never figured that out and are lost.

God's answer, if we accept it, is "You are my son/daughter, whom I love, and whom I like." Believe that, and you have crossed from death and confusion to life and an adventure in meaning.

Everything in good character is built on that foundation.

We are the sons and daughters of God. God loves us. God likes us. In his amazing grace he has chosen us for his family. Without that bottom-line identity, our deep hunger for acceptance and approval will seek to be satisfied by responding to other masters. This is also why we need to carry out our Christian adventure in fellowship with other men and women who love God, who know God's word, who are filled with God's Spirit. They can help us hear God's voice to us, reminding us who we are.

Each of the trials of our character and community is embedded in the most basic question of all: Who are we? What is our character? Where is our community? Do we really believe that we are God's sons and daughters whom he loves and whom he likes? Are we (warts and all) the body of Christ, the holy nation, the community of God's presence? Will we accept that great identity and then walk in the guidance of God's Word and God's Spirit?

Accepting our identity in relation to God, and in relation to the community of faith, is incredibly important as our character is put on trial. There is no other way to victory. When we fail the test, our response must be to bring our poverty to God in mourning and meekness. We must learn to be quick to confess our sin and failure, our mistakes and our shortcomings. In our community of faith, we need to regularly confess our sin to God—and to each other. If we confess our sin, God forgives us and cleanses us from all unrighteousness. If we say we have no sin, we are lying to God and to ourselves. With confession comes forgiveness and reconciliation. We must practice this before God individually and collectively.

In a well-known passage, Paul wrote to the Ephesian church:

> Take up the whole armor of God, so that you may be able to withstand on that evil day, and having done everything, to stand firm. Stand therefore, and fasten the belt of truth around your waist, and put on the breastplate of righteousness. As shoes for your feet put on whatever will make you ready to proclaim the gospel of peace. With all of these, take the shield of faith. . . . Take the helmet of salvation, and the sword of the Spirit, which is the word of God. Pray in the Spirit at all times in every prayer and supplication. (Eph 6:13-18)

Character formation for biblical people and their communities is not merely an exercise in therapy or a philosophical quest. It is sometimes like a war. When the trial of our combat ends in failure, we have lost a battle but not the war. We confess our sins and receive forgiveness. Then, as Paul puts it, we stand up again and re-arm ourselves with truth, faith, righteousness and peace. We do not give up or abandon the goodness of God.

Peter Kreeft has said that there are three reasons why we should practice virtue, why we should seek to develop our character and community in conformity with the goodness of God: "one heavenly and two earthly. The highest and heavenly reason is to please God, out of love for God, who is love. The second reason is to be human, to have a healthy human soul. Virtue is soul-health. The third reason is to survive. In the nuclear age we must love one another or die. But the third reason will not work without the other two. For it fails to answer the crucial question, for what earthly or heavenly end?"[11]

Building good character glorifies God. It makes for a healthy self, and it contributes to the healing rather than the destruction of the

---

[11]Peter Kreeft, *Back to Virtue* (San Francisco: Ignatius, 1986), p. 192

world. We do not need nuclear war for our civilization to return to the dust or the jungle. Many other forces and threats are moving us to the same fate. Good character and good community, by their very existence, are the salt and light that God can use to retard the decay and promote the life of our world. Good characters and communities do not just *exist*, however; they also *act* in the face of the troubling dilemmas of our time. Good character and community enable us to "do the right," to discern the principles and carry out the practices that exhibit God's righteousness and make for his peace.

We have a job to do, an adventure to carry out. God calls us to see and hear his magnificent grace and love for us. He calls us to accept these gifts and join the community of those becoming faithful, holy disciples, humble servants, righteous leaders, loving peacemakers, and hopeful, joyful ambassadors in this hurting, troubled world. We do not regard these descriptions as costumes to be worn on rare occasions. We seek these characteristics as habits, inclinations, capacities and skills, as ongoing traits and virtues, during "all the days of our lives." We believe that if we do, surely goodness and mercy shall follow us all the days of our lives, and we will dwell in the house of the Lord forever (Ps 23:6).

For Reflection or Discussion

1. Do you agree that "accommodated conformists," "arrogant know-it-alls," "apathetic do-nothings," "divisive antagonists" and "selfish escapists" are likely to appear more and more if we do not actively cultivate their virtuous character opposites? Is Gill going overboard here in worrying about this?
2. Which of the seven deadly sins and the works of the flesh are the most common problems among Christians today? Which are the most serious? Why?
3. How do you feel about the threats to our character from the world, the flesh and the devil? What is your view of Satan?
4. Of the three temptations Jesus and we face, which is the greatest challenge to faithful Christian character and community in today's world?
5. How can we better survive the trial of our character and community now and in the future? What specific steps can we take in our personal lives? in our communities?

Index of Names